110 Experiences
for Multicultural
Learning

110 Experiences *for* Multicultural Learning

Paul B. Pedersen

AMERICAN PSYCHOLOGICAL ASSOCIATION

WASHINGTON, DC

Second Printing, September 2007
Published by
American Psychological Association
750 First Street, NE
Washington, DC 20002
www.apa.org

To order
APA Order Department
P.O. Box 92984
Washington, DC 20090-2984
Tel: (800) 374-2721; Direct: (202) 336-5510
Fax: (202) 336-5502; TDD/TTY: (202) 336-6123
Online: www.apa.org/books/
E-mail: order@apa.org

In the U.K., Europe, Africa, and the Middle East, copies may be ordered from
American Psychological Association
3 Henrietta Street
Covent Garden, London
WC2E 8LU England

Typeset in Trump Medieval by World Composition Services, Inc., Sterling, VA

Printer: Victor Graphics, Baltimore, MD
Cover Designer: Michael Hentges Design, Alexandria, VA
Technical/Production Editors: Kristen S. Boye and Tiffany Klaff

The opinions and statements published are the responsibility of the authors, and such opinions and statements do not necessarily represent the policies of the American Psychological Association.

Library of Congress Cataloging-in-Publication Data

Pedersen, Paul, 1936-
    110 experiences for multicultural learning / Paul B. Pedersen.—1st ed.
        p. cm.
Includes bibliographical references and index.
    ISBN 1-59147-082-X (alk. paper)
    1. Multicultural education—Activity programs—United States.
2. Multicultural education—United States—Psychological aspects.
I. Title: One hundred and ten experiences for multicultural learning.
II. Title.

LC1099.3.P53 2004
370.117—dc22   2003020360

British Library Cataloguing-in-Publication Data
A CIP record is available from the British Library.

Printed in the United States of America
First Edition

This book is dedicated to Anthony ("Tony") Marsella and Raymond ("Ray") Corsini, who have mentored me in ways that I am just beginning to understand and appreciate.

■ CONTENTS ■

Foreword: The Importance of Coursework on Multicultural Issues xi

Preface xv

Chapter One. Favorable Conditions for Multicultural Experiences 3

Chapter Two. Brief 30-Minute Warm-Up Experiences 11
    1. World Picture Test 13
    2. Capturing Cultural Bias 15
    3. Perception Versus Reality 17
    4. What Other People Say, Feel, and Mean 19
    5. Outside Experts 21
    6. Role-Playing Cultural Stories 23
    7. Drawing a House 25
    8. Cultural Bingo 27
    9. Learning to Grow Old 28
  10. Finding Common Ground in an Argument 30
  11. Gift Giving 32
  12. Checkers and Chess 34
  13. Inventing a Multicultural Retrospective 36
  14. Western and Non-Western Perspectives 38
  15. Coalitions and Trust Formation 40
  16. Fantasy Walk in the Woods 42
  17. Seeing Ourselves as Others See Us 44
  18. The Hidden Agenda 46
  19. Interpreting Policy in a Cultural Context 48
  20. Cultural Impact Storytelling 50
  21. Culture Shock Ratings and Symptom Checklist 52
  22. How to Sabotage Multicultural Groups 54
  23. Describing Cultural Identity 56
  24. Interpreting a Projective Picture 58
  25. Drawing Symbols of Your Culture 60
  26. Geometric Symbols of Cultural Values 62
  27. A Free Drawing Test 64
  28. Dialogue Within Ourselves 66
  29. Predicting the Decisions of a Resource Person 68

30. Capturing Cultural Metaphors and Similes 70
31. Multicultural Group Process Recall 72
32. Testing the Underlying "Truth" 74
33. Inference–Observation Test 76
34. The Test of Reasonable Opposites 79

Chapter Three. Longer One-Hour Experiences **81**
35. Talking About Multiculturalism in Primary Grades 82
36. Happy Hell or Lonely Heaven: The Brain Drain Problem 84
37. A Classroom Debate 88
38. Two Cultural Perspectives of Education 90
39. Two Levels of Communication in the Military Culture 92
40. The Plural Versus the Singular Cultural Perspective 94
41. The Importance of Key Words in a Transcript 95
42. Public and Private Self 96
43. The Johari Window 99
44. A Self-Assessment of Multicultural Awareness, Knowledge, and Skill 101
45. High- and Low-Context Cultures in Conflict 105
46. A Values Auction 107
47. Interviewing Local Resource People 109
48. Double-Loop Thinking 111
49. Stereotypes of Different Groups I 113
50. Stereotypes of Different Groups II 115
51. Cultural Value Systems With Conflicting Points of View 117
52. Describing the Feelings of a Resource Person 119
53. Fighting Fair 121
54. Making History Live 123
55. Prisoners' Dilemma 124
56. Four Contrasting Ethical Orientations 126
57. Finding Common Ground With Your Best Friend 129
58. Being "Abnormal" 131
59. Nominal Group Process 133
60. Separating Expectations From Behavior in 10 Synthetic Cultures 135
61. Gift Giving Across Cultures 139
62. Role-Playing a Hypothetical Problem in a Group 141
63. Role-Playing a Newspaper Incident 143
64. Listening to the Voices 145
65. Cultural Perspective Taking 147
66. Getting Feedback From Other Group Members 149
67. Cultural Value Systems in a Counseling Relationship 151
68. The Triad Training Model 153
69. Culture-Centered Genogram 156

Chapter Four. Two-Hour Laboratory Experiences **159**
70. Orientation for a Cross-Cultural Experience 160
71. Michigan International Student Problem Inventory 163
72. Critical Incidents in Airline Travel 166
73. Potluck Dinner 172
74. Evaluating a Workshop With a Pretest and a Posttest 174
75. Scripts for Trigger Videotapes 176
76. Intercultural Communication Skills for Help Providers in the Military 179

77. Rehearsal Demonstration Model 183
78. Role-Playing a Transcript 185
79. A Synthetic Culture Training Laboratory 187
80. Critical Incidents in Multicultural Ethics 196
81. American and Contrast-American Values 198
82. Decreasing Cultural Barriers 203
83. American Auction 205
84. Hearing the Sounds of a Cultural Context 207
85. Critical Incidents Involving Ethnic Minorities 209
86. Critical Incidents With International Students 218
87. Critical Incidents in Tourist Groups 221
88. Hearing the Devils and the Angels 224
89. Action Project 226
90. Lump Sum: A Budget Simulation 228
91. Culturally Learned Parent Roles for Immigrants and Refugees 232
92. Finding Common Ground in Sports and Athletics 235
93. Unanswered Questions and Knowledge Gaps 237

Chapter Five. Homework **239**
94. A Personal Cultural History 240
95. Applications of Critical Incidents 242
96. Analyzing a Transcript 244
97. A Culture-Centered Interview Guide 246
98. The Cross-Cultural Tradeoff 252
99. Adapting to the Culture of a University 259
100. No Questions Asked 264
101. Partners: A Sex-Role Training Experience 266
102. The Interpersonal, Intercultural, Psychopathological (IIP) Questionnaire 274
103. Developing Cultural Life Skills 279
104. International Student Survey of Strong Feelings 282
105. Shopping in an Unfamiliar Culture 288
106. A Simulation Designing Experience Called "Multipoly" 290
107. Lifestyles and Our Social Values 293
108. Locating Power Networks in Organizations 296
109. Writing an Ethnography 298
110. The Interpersonal Cultural Grid 300

Chapter Six. Conclusion: Staying Out of Trouble **303**

References **307**
Index **311**
About the Author **317**

■ FOREWORD: THE IMPORTANCE OF COURSEWORK ON MULTICULTURAL ISSUES ■

Richard W. Brislin

Psychologists have many opportunities to teach courses that deal with cultural issues and that can help students interact effectively in a multicultural world. Those with appointments in psychology may offer courses in cross-cultural psychology, multicultural counseling, ethnic relations, and the psychology of gender. For psychologists with appointments in speech or communication, courses may include intercultural communication and cross-cultural training. Psychologists working in business schools (my current affiliation) can teach international organizational behavior, international marketing, and cross-cultural consumer behavior. Those working in schools of education may teach courses on culture and education and the multicultural classroom and may provide practicum courses to support teachers taking assignments in school districts with students from many different cultural backgrounds. Furthermore, psychologists are increasingly involved in college-wide courses on culture and diversity that students must take as a mandatory part of their school's general education requirement. Psychologists also are involved in orientation programs for international students, and in some schools these extend over a semester and students receive course credit for successful completion.

THE CHALLENGES OF TEACHING MULTICULTURAL COURSES

Opportunities for teaching are many, but so are the challenges. Courses dealing with culture and cultural differences are very often difficult to teach. First, many students have not had extensive interactions with people from other cultural backgrounds. White American students, for example, may have gone to high school with African Americans and Hispanic Americans, but the relations among the groups may well have been casual and superficial. Many students have few opportunities to get to know culturally different people as individuals rather than as members of categories. Even if opportunities exist to share personal feelings and ambitions, well-trained facilitators who can encourage productive discussions that might challenge preexisting stereotypes are often unavailable.

A second reason for the difficulty in teaching courses dealing with culture, diversity, and behavior is that so many concepts are totally new to students. Few students have experience with the concepts likely to be introduced in class. Students who participated in an international exchange program during their high school years or who have recently returned from a semester abroad at a university in another culture are great assets to these courses, but such students are a distinct minority (Ward & Rana-Deuba, 2000).

The work of Hofstede (2001) has been extremely influential in cross-cultural psychology and international organizational behavior, and his work has been extended to multicultural counseling (see experiences 60 and 79 on synthetic cultures). One of his best-known concepts is the distinction between individualism and collectivism. In individualistic cultures, such as that of the United States, people are socialized to place importance on personal goals and to emphasize the skills, personality traits, and attitudes necessary for goal attainment. In collectivist cultures, such as many cultures in Asia and Latin America, people are socialized to integrate their goals with those of an important group such as the extended family. To achieve their goals, people place value on cooperation, harmony, and sensitivity to social norms. In my own teaching, students find this material both interesting and important. Eventually, they can think of examples of socialization in their own lives, but it takes many hours to encourage this level of understanding. This time needed for understanding contrasts with that of other courses I have taught, such as social psychology, in which it takes far less time to introduce central topics (e.g., groups, interpersonal attraction, friendship formation, pressures to conform, altruism) because students have had experience with them and can quickly add examples to class discussions.

A third reason for difficulties is that much material in multicultural coursework can cause students to be uncomfortable and anxious. If material on stereotypes and prejudice is introduced, many students will examine their own pasts and wonder if they have discriminated against someone. If material on different cultural guidelines about everyday behaviors is introduced (e.g., respect for elders, interactions between men and women), students may remember past interactions and wonder if they were culturally insensitive. If professors are blessed with students from different cultural backgrounds who are taking the same class, it is quite reasonable to encourage discussions about cultural values and norms. However, disagreements can become intense, and people from different cultures develop very different norms about how and when to disagree (Kowner, 2002). People from one culture may value disagreements as clearing the air and adding ideas to the mix, whereas people from other cultures may view disagreements as personal attacks and as threats to their worth as human beings.

SOME CONCLUSIONS

Today's college students will live in a multicultural world. They will interact with people who learned different behaviors as part of their socialization into another culture to achieve their life goals. These different people, who understand each other vaguely and imperfectly, will be thrust into frequent contact. Today's workplace is increasingly diverse; neighborhoods and schools continue to integrate; increasing numbers of immigrants are bringing their new ideas and skills; international travel during vacations is on the rise; and markets and joint business ventures are increasingly international (Brislin, 2000). Furthermore, people are becoming more aware that political activities in one country can have major impacts in other parts of the world.

Traditionally, psychologists and colleagues in related areas have contributed to students' education by emphasizing the cognitive aspects of education. They have investigated concepts, theories, and the results of research studies. These efforts should continue. Today, however, the affective component of extensive intercultural interaction is increasingly important, and experiences such as those presented in this volume can help professors begin to prepare students for this aspect of their futures. The challenges are great, and professors will have to develop new skills so that they can use the exercises wisely. But the rewards of guiding students toward more effective intercultural interactions will make these extra efforts a good investment of time, talents, and energy.

■ PREFACE ■

The fabled global community is now upon us. Psychology can assist in addressing and resolving these problems, especially if it is willing to reconsider some of its fundamental premises, methods, and practices that are rooted within Western cultural traditions and to expand its appreciation and use of other psychologies. (Marsella, 1998, p. 1282)

110 Experiences for Multicultural Learning combines simulations, exercises, and structured role-playing activities that have been used successfully in psychology classrooms to demonstrate the relevance of cultural diversity to psychological topics. Psychology instructors will find that these are more than just simulations, exercises, and structured role-playing activities; rather, these "experiences" aim to increase interactive learning both among culturally different people in the classroom and between students and the multicultural community context outside the classroom.

Overall, the objective of this book is to stimulate awareness, knowledge, and skills for managing the psychological dynamics of diverse cultural contexts in practical ways. Although these experiences can be used with a variety of students and classroom settings, most of the experiences are suited for teaching students in counseling programs. Instructors will do their students a great service by incorporating the experiences into the classroom, thereby blurring the boundaries between the classroom and multicultural community resources and helping students learn ways to use these experiences in their future practice of psychology.

MAKING
MULTICULTURAL
EXPERIENCES REAL

My own area of study is multicultural counseling and counselor education. I have used each of the experiences described in this book in my classroom teaching and community training workshops. Rather than talk about psychological constructs as abstractions, students and instructors can use these experiences to make the psychological constructs more realistic through interactive encounters that demonstrate the practical value of each construct. With the increased attention to multiculturalism throughout the field of psychology, classroom curricula must become more culture-centered. Likewise, with the increased attention to community issues in the practice of psychology, the inclusion of community resource people in the classroom, as structured in many of these experiences, is becoming more accepted. And with measures of quality in psychology education more frequently depending on classroom experiences that involve students interactively in the teaching–learning process, these experiences provide proactive opportunities. By defining culture broadly to include ethnographic, demographic, status, and affiliation variables, these experiences demonstrate that every classroom is multicultural and that every psychology student can expect to work in multicultural contexts.

USING THIS BOOK   There are many ways these experiences can be used. The experiences can be modified for collecting data that can be discussed in class and analyzed. Such data might result in a classroom project or even a publication. These experiences may be carried out in class or even with a population outside the classroom.

The experiences are organized into categories according to the time required, ranging from 30-minute brief experiences to longer laboratories and workshops to homework, depending on the needs of the instructor. Within each category, experiences are classified as low, moderate, or high risk; more highly structured and less ambiguous experiences are low risk, moderately structured experiences are considered moderate risk, and more unstructured experiences are designated as high risk. The high-risk experiences may be more suitable for instructors with some experience teaching about multiculturalism; however, it is unlikely that any of these experiences will get the instructor into difficulty. The instructor can reduce the risk of any activity by limiting the time spent on the experience or by structuring the categories of the students' responses more narrowly.

Each experience is described with the same format. The overall *objective* is summarized first. The *time required* and *risk level* (low, moderate, or high) follow, then the number of *participants needed* to teach the experience. Next, the *procedure* section identifies the step-by-step details for running the experience, followed by a *debriefing* section, in which instructors will find key questions to discuss, caveats to the experiences, background material, and any other information required to present the experience. Finally, an *insight*, or brief take-home message for the student, is identified; it describes the essence of the exercise.

A CLOSING CAVEAT
A CLOSING CAVEAT   Some of the most important skills can be learned but cannot be taught directly. Each of the following experiences provides a context in which learning will occur both directly from the instructor and indirectly from peers. These experiences will help students discover the culturally learned assumptions that control decision making and interviewing. The real lesson for students is to learn to guide themselves toward more accurate assessments, more meaningful understanding, and more appropriate interventions in each cultural context.

ACKNOWLEDGMENTS   The experiences in chapters 2 through 5 were gathered from a variety of published, unpublished, and anonymous sources. Many of the experiences are based on my own work, and they either are unpublished or were modified for this book with the permission of the publishers. Again, I would like to thank the publishers for granting permission to modify experiences for use in this book.

110 Experiences *for* Multicultural Learning

■ CHAPTER ONE ■

FAVORABLE CONDITIONS FOR MULTICULTURAL EXPERIENCES

People no longer assume that every individual within a group belongs to a single culture.[1] Current conceptualizations of globalization have demonstrated that every individual belongs to many different cultures at the same time. In broad definitions of culture, the unimodal perspective of a culture is out, and the multimodal perspective is in. Every group is multicultural to the extent that its members follow different patterns of assumptions to interpret the same situations. In groups in which these differences are most obvious, as in multinational or multiethnic groups, people are more likely to be aware that members may experience the same situation differently and thus will be more willing to accommodate different assumptions. However, in groups of people similar in, for example, gender role, socioeconomic status, lifestyle, age, or some other affiliation, we are perhaps more likely to overlook cultural differences and to assume that all members share the same values. In groups that share a characteristic, subtle cultural differences are frequently overlooked and, to that extent, are perhaps more likely to affect the outcome of an interaction than when cultural differences are more obvious.

---

[1]*Culture* in this book broadly includes ethnographic (nationality, ethnicity, race), demographic (age, gender, place of residence), status (economic, social, educational), and affiliation (formal—to family or organization—and informal—to an idea or belief) categories. Cultural differences should not be confused with individual differences.

Psychological theories have increasingly included multiculturalism as an important factor in defining behavior, personality, and development. This shift is due largely to pressure from the civil rights and the feminist movements, globalization, and various special interest groups who have been undervalued and marginalized to the extent that they deviated from White, middle-class, urban, male measures of normal behavior. Multiculturalism is emerging as a "fourth force" in psychology to supplement and ideally to strengthen the three historical orientations of humanism, behaviorism, and psychodynamism (Pedersen, 1999). Because all behaviors are learned and displayed in a cultural context, it is important not to ignore that multicultural context. Accurate assessment, meaningful understanding, and appropriate intervention require attention to the multicultural context, regardless of the theoretical orientation of the service provider.

Multiculturalism as a fourth force combines the alternatives of universalism and relativism by explaining behaviors by people from different cultures as simultaneously both similar and different. People are similar in being driven by positive expectations for truth, respect, success, harmony, and positive outcomes that provide the universal values shared across cultures. People are different to the extent that each culture teaches different behaviors to express those universal expectations. The melting pot metaphor made the mistake of overemphasizing the common-ground generalizations to the neglect of culturally unique perspectives. On the other hand, the phenomena of racism, sexism, ageism, and other exclusionary perspectives overemphasize culturally unique perspectives while neglecting the common-ground positive expectations that are shared across cultures. An inclusive, multicultural, fourth force perspective recognizes that similarities and differences coexist.

If all behaviors occur in a cultural context, then all theories of human behavior are fundamentally, but usually implicitly, cultural theories. Multiculturalism gives meaning to psychodynamic, humanistic, and behavioral interpretations, much as the fourth dimension of time gives meaning to three-dimensional space. The culture-centered perspective is not intended to displace or compete with other psychological perspectives, but rather to complement them by framing them in the multicultural contexts in which all psychological interpretation occurs. Cultural psychology presumes that every sociocultural environment depends on the way humans give each behavior meaning and in turn changes in response to that meaningful behavior. Cultural psychology studies the ways cultural traditions and social practices regulate, express, and transform people to fit multicultural patterns:

> Cultural psychology is the study of the ways subject and object, self and other, psyche and culture, person and context, figure and ground, practitioner and practice live together, require each other, and dynamically dialectically and jointly make each other up. (Shweder, 1990, p. 73)

The multicultural context provides the basis for a psychodynamic theory by revealing the unconscious dynamic of culturally learned beliefs as they influence a person's behavior. The multicultural context likewise provides the basis for understanding humanism by describing each person comprehensively in a person-centered perspective. The multicultural context also provides the basis for understanding behaviorism by linking each behavior to culturally learned rewards and reinforcing contingencies. The multicultural experiences in this book can be interpreted from a variety of theoretical perspectives, depending on the orientation of the instructor, as long as culture is central and not marginal to that interpretation.

Before people are born, cultural patterns of thought and action are already prepared to guide their ideas, influence their decisions, and help them take control of their lives. They inherit these cultural patterns from their parents and "culture-teachers," who teach them the rules of the game of life. Only later do they learn that their culture is only one of the many possible patterns of thinking and acting from which they can choose. By that time, however, they have already come to believe that their own culture is the best of all possible worlds. Even if they recognize that conventional values are false or inadequate when challenged by the stress of radical social change, it is not always possible to replace the worn-out habits with new alternatives.

Multicultural training also is no longer a one-time event, but an ongoing process that recognizes the complex and dynamic interaction of cultures across times and places. These changes have influenced training methods as well to move away from the goal of "dissonance reduction" and toward "tolerance of ambiguity" as the appropriate outcome measure. Research literature on contact hypotheses has demonstrated that favorable outcomes of cross-cultural contact can happen only under favorable conditions and that most spontaneous cross-cultural contact happens under unfavorable conditions. The primary goal of training is to construct those favorable conditions necessary for positive outcomes.

Gudykunst, Guzley, and Hammer (1996) classified multicultural training approaches according to two dimensions. The first dimension concerns whether the training method is experiential or didactic. Experiential approaches assume that learning occurs best when students have direct encounters with real or simulated experiences from which to learn cultural patterns. Didactic approaches assume that people need to understand the cultural patterns they can potentially encounter before engaging in real or simulated experiences.

The second dimension concerns whether the training method is generalized across cultures or is specific to a particular cultural context. Culture-general approaches assume that people can learn a repertoire of approaches that they can reconfigure to meet their needs in the context of any particular culture they might encounter. Culture-specific approaches assume that it is essential to first gain information about specific cultures before the student can generalize what he or she has learned about each group to the broader context. The structured experiences in this book focus primarily on culture-general and experiential activities.

IMPORTANT
INSIGHTS

Before getting to the structured experiences in this book, a review of the arguments both for and against their use in teaching and training is in order. Arguments for the use of multicultural experiences include the following:

- Research supports the conclusion that multicultural exercises and experiential learning will result in favorable outcomes through training.
- Structured experiences can extend the capability of multicultural groups to develop their own skills as they learn from multicultural interactions.
- Structured experiences can start a new group actively learning more rapidly and with less time required for warm-up than uninterrupted lectures and didactic methods.
- Structured experiences require less preparation time, especially when they can be borrowed or applied from collections of already prepared materials.

- Structured multicultural experiences are less ambiguous and can focus on an aspect of the particular curriculum, topic, or social problem.
- Structured experiences can contribute to research on social change through a controlled laboratory environment of the classroom.
- Structured experiences with unambiguous roles are less threatening than real-world situations to the extent that they provide clearly stated expectations, involve clearly defined behaviors, and present opportunities to rehearse responses.
- Structured multicultural experiences may match desired outcomes or changes in the participant's behavior later in the real world.
- Structured experiences force participants to clarify their objectives in understanding an otherwise ambiguous real world in a multicultural context.

Not everyone favors the use of structured experiences for multicultural training. There are numerous arguments against the use of structured multicultural experiences, such as the following:

- Structured experiences are culture bound, favoring those cultures in which role-playing, games, and direct or open communication are desirable. Participants from cultures unfamiliar with structured activities may find these experiences offensive, artificial, or embarrassing.
- There is an assumption in Western cultures that openness, required by many structured experiences, contributes to understanding and has an unquestioned positive value. However, many non-Western cultures value hiding one's feelings and not revealing one's thoughts as having a higher value than openness. Confrontation or open opposition would be difficult for a representative of a self-effacing culture. In addition, some Asian students may feel "forced" into game playing because refusing to participate would be impolite.
- Many structured experiences require direct rather than indirect communication of meaning and impose the rules of direct communication on participants without regard for their preferences. Many cultures rely more on silence and nonverbal cues and prefer to refrain from speaking rather than discussing an issue.
- Participants from hierarchical societies in which status is important might have difficulty in structured experiences in which everyone is treated equally.
- Some structured experiences present a simplistic view of other cultural groups, leading participants toward superficial stereotypes of one another's culture.

Although there are arguments for and against the use of structured exercises and experiences, the use of structured experiential exercises to supplement other didactic methods has become an established educational process. There is an extensive literature supporting the use of experiential methods in multicultural training.

HOW TO LEARN FROM MULTICULTURAL EXPERIENCES

Experiential exercises and structured experiences are widely used in the classroom and have demonstrated their importance in the literature (Brislin, 1997; Crookall & Arai, 1995; Kagan, 1999; Pedersen, 1995a, 2000b). However, the usefulness of these experiences depends a great deal on how they are used. The debriefing of each experience links that experience to the specific teaching–learning objectives of the classroom. Perhaps more important, instructors must set up a safe context for exploring potentially uncomfortable issues so that participants feel protected during these experiences, particularly when they highlight sensitive multicultural values. By sharpening the focus on specific cultural aspects and specific microskills, the experiences in this book help instructors avoid the ambiguity that might lead to misunderstanding in experiential activities. If participants do not feel that the multicultural experiences are safe, they will not take risks. If they do not take risks, they will not learn much from the experiences. Creating a safe place for the multicultural experiences is therefore essential. There are several ways that an instructor can make these multicultural experiences a safe way to learn.

Participants

The instructor should know each participant's motivations, special needs, and attitudes toward participating in the multicultural experience. A formal or informal needs assessment is one way to assess the appropriateness of a multicultural experience for a particular group. For favorable conditions to occur, the participants will need to be matched with the experience.

Preparation

The instructor needs to prepare the participants for the longer multicultural experiences by giving them the opportunity to think about their role in the experience ahead of time. When possible, it is a good idea to distribute the guidelines for the longer multicultural experiences for students to read and discuss ahead of time. In many cases, the shorter multicultural experiences might be part of an orientation to a longer course or event. It is useful for participants to know the instructor's expectations for them and to clarify their own expectations about the experience. Students who prefer not to participate in a multicultural experience should not be forced to participate.

Confidentiality

The instructor needs to remind the participants that their privacy will be protected and that if a person chooses to share private or sensitive information during the experience, this information will remain confidential. Participants need to be reminded of their ethical responsibility to keep confidential whatever information about one another they learn through the multicultural experience; otherwise they will be unlikely to want to self-disclose. When the participants are below the age of legal consent, many states require that the instructor obtain permission from their parents or guardians before participation. This is especially true if audio or video recordings of the multicultural experience are made.

Neutrality and Dual Relationships

It is important that the instructor refrain from imposing personal values on the other participants. As the group leader, the instructor is in a position of power from which it would be easy to impose guidelines on participants' behavior. The instructor must guide the discussion with extreme sensitivity, especially when the best interests of the group, as best they can be determined, are in conflict with the preferred behavior of any one or more participants. The instructor has the responsibility to guide and lead participants through the multicultural experience in a way that will positively increase their multicultural awareness.

The problem of dual relationships is also an issue. The instructor must refrain from participating as a group member. In cases in which the instructor has dual or multiple relationships with group participants that cannot be eliminated, the problems presented by dual relationships cannot be completely avoided. By examining this issue ahead of time, however, the instructor will be more likely to find a way to manage the dual relationships constructively.

Superficial Interpretations and Threatening Situations

Multicultural experiences are linked to techniques and strategies that lend themselves to superficial interpretations. There is no quick and easy way to achieve multicultural awareness. It is important for the instructor to discourage participants from drawing conclusions too quickly and easily and to recognize the limitations of brief multicultural experiences. It is ironic that multicultural experiences may lead participants to form stereotypes about a particular cultural group unless a skilled instructor prevents that misinterpretation.

It may be necessary to terminate the multicultural experience prematurely if the welfare of one or more participants is threatened. Role-playing always has the potential to drift from playacting to realistic responses during an interaction. The instructor has a responsibility to stop the multicultural experience as quickly as possible once the actions of one or more participants threaten other participants' feeling of safety. The instructor has to make a difficult decision about when to stop the interaction, balancing the need for realism with the need for safety in the group.

Debriefing

Debriefing is always an important part of the successful multicultural experience. The multicultural experiences in this book include guidelines for debriefing the experience. The instructor can focus the debriefing to fit with the rest of the course or curriculum focus.

In debriefing the experience, there are several objectives: (a) to find out whether the participants increased their multicultural awareness of themselves and of others; (b) to find out whether the participants gathered any new knowledge, information, or questions for future reference; and (c) to find out whether the participants developed any new skills. The instructor begins the process by asking if anyone learned anything. Those who raise their hands are asked to say what they learned to begin the discussion. The instructor then proceeds through the debriefing objectives, repeating the experience insight as needed.

Evaluation and Follow-Up

It is important to evaluate the multicultural experience, whether in a formal or an informal way. The evaluation may ask for responses to a list of learning goals and objectives, or the evaluation may be open-ended. The evaluation can be completed immediately after the experience or at some later point in time to examine long-term effects. The evaluation may focus on affective, cognitive, or behavioral changes as a result of the experience. A good evaluation will provide data so that the instructor will become better able to focus future multicultural experiences on the needs of the students.

There may well be a need to follow up the multicultural experience with further interaction with individual members or with the group as a whole. In some cases, students may be referred to other resources either to remediate an inadequacy or to follow up some exciting learning opportunity. The group as a whole may have new questions they want to follow up on in their class or curricula. If the experience was successful, the group may well want to try additional multicultural experiences. In any case, the multicultural experiences can be designed to build toward long-term educational goals and outcomes so that each experience builds on the previous experiences in an intentional progression of culture-centered skill.

ADDITIONAL RESOURCES

The structured experiences described in this book may form the basis of a course or training curriculum. In addition, the considerable literature and resources for teaching multicultural exercises and structured experiences may also be helpful. Following are some examples:

Teaching About Culture, Ethnicity, and Diversity (Singelis, 1998) is designed for use by "teachers who function outside the traditional classroom, but are no less concerned about issues involving culture, ethnicity and diversity" (p. ix).

The excellent resource book *Cross-Cultural Explorations: Activities in Culture and Psychology* (S. Goldstein, 2000) is "designed to contribute to the inclusion of cultural perspectives in the psychology curriculum by providing students with hands-on experiences that facilitate the understanding and application of major concepts and principles in the study of culture and psychology" (p. vi).

Intercultural Sourcebook: Cross-Cultural Training Methods (Fowler & Mumford, 1999) is a sourcebook for cross-cultural training methods in two volumes that includes traditional training and new inventories, videotapes, visual imagery, dialogues, cultural self-awareness practice, and other innovative training methods.

Exploring Culture: Exercises, Stories, and Synthetic Cultures (Hofstede, Pedersen, & Hofstede, 2002) focuses on the use of "synthetic cultures" in training, based on Gert Hofstede's 55-country database. This book is valuable for those using the Synthetic Culture Laboratory.

Kohls's (1996) *Survival Kit for Overseas Living: For Americans Planning to Live and Work Abroad* is an excellent book of training materials.

Brislin and Yoshida's (1994a) "The Content of Cross-Cultural Training: An Introduction" and Cushner and Brislin's (1997) *Improving Intercultural Interactions: Vol. 2. Modules for Cross-Cultural Training Programs* are two matched volumes of multicultural training modules used in training programs at the East West Center and elsewhere for improving intercultural interactions. Each chapter provides a separate module with its own self-assessment measure and conceptual background materials.

Intercultural Interactions: A Practical Guide (Brislin, Cushner, Cherrie, & Yong, 1986) provides one of the most extensive recent resources on the use of critical incidents modeled after the culture assimilator model for multicultural training. The authors collected stories from a variety of multicultural settings and organized them around culture-general patterns.

Critical Incidents in School Counseling (Tyson & Pedersen, 2000) is a collection of critical incidents provided by counselors working in schools. Each incident description is accompanied by the responses of two different reactors who describe their own reactions to each incident.

The Five Stages of Culture Shock: Critical Incidents Around the World (Pedersen, 1995a) is a collection of 350 critical incidents reported by students in three classes taught on the University of Pittsburgh "Semester at Sea" Spring 1992 voyage. These incidents are organized to illustrate the five stages of culture shock.

Decisional Dialogues in a Cultural Context: Structured Exercises (Pedersen & Hernandez, 1997) includes 40 multicultural activities that focus on the interviewing skills of decision makers, counselors, and human service providers.

Instructor's Manual for Intentional Group Counseling: A Microskills Approach (Pedersen, Ivey, Ivey, & Kuo, 2001) reviews an assortment of multicultural training activities for training group leaders.

CONCLUSION   This chapter has focused on preparing the instructor to use multicultural experiences by constructing favorable conditions that enhance positive outcomes from each multicultural experience. Although there are important precautions to consider, the literature supporting experiential activities is very persuasive.

The multicultural experiences described in this book may seem misleadingly simple, and some books about multicultural experiences, structured exercises, and simulations resemble a cookbook of shortcut activities to learn about human behavior. This simplistic approach to using multicultural experiences minimalizes the educational potential that each experience provides. At the same time, it is important to recognize that participation in these multicultural experiences can be a fun activity for the participants and for the instructor as well. My graduate school advisor described education as "something that happens by accident when you are trying to do something else." The way students know that they have learned something new is that they have a sense of surprise. At that point they have two choices. First, they can enjoy the warm feelings of the event without self-examination, in which case the pleasant feeling will quickly vanish. Alternatively, they can focus on what they learned to capture the insights and make them explicit. It is my hope that these experiences surprise both students and instructors and that the learning will be theirs forever.

■ CHAPTER TWO ■

BRIEF 30-MINUTE
WARM-UP EXPERIENCES

The multicultural experiences described in this chapter are designed to warm up the class—that is, to enable them to better know one another and to become more comfortable working together. The focus of the experiences is on demonstrating both cultural similarities and cultural differences within the group. The brief experiences are intended to stimulate interest, raise questions, and motivate the students to take a more culture-centered perspective toward interpreting the behaviors of themselves and others. Instructors can modify the experiences to complement the content being studied in the class and to personalize the experience between and among the students. These brief experiences are particularly helpful for classes where the students do not yet know one another, providing a structure for them to interact.

Some of these experiences are more projective and ambiguous than others (and are rated high risk). As a general rule, the more ambiguous the experience, the more skill will be required for the instructor to interpret student responses. Instructors with less experience teaching about multiculturalism might feel more comfortable with the more highly structured experiences (rated low risk), which require less interpretation. As instructors become more comfortable with teaching about multiculturalism, the more ambiguous and projective experiences might become more appropriate.

In any case, there is a greater danger in overinterpretation than in underinterpretation. Instructors should resist imposing their interpretation of students' responses, except perhaps as questions that students might want to ask themselves and to think about. Students will inevitably ask the instructor, "Yes, but what does it mean?" Students are generally in a better position to discover the "meaning" of their responses, perhaps with help from the instructor, than the instructor is to explain it.

One function of training is to create a certain amount of dissonance between the students' realization of what is real and what is ideal. Thus, these experiences will raise more questions for students than they answer. With proper guidance, students will learn most about themselves and others if they are discouraged from accepting easy answers to complex questions. Helping students ask the right questions is at least as important as helping them find answers to those questions.

1 WORLD PICTURE TEST

> *Objective:* To clarify students' understanding of various countries and cultures through their knowledge of world geography.

TIME REQUIRED   15–20 minutes

RISK LEVEL   Low

PARTICIPANTS NEEDED   Any number of participants might do this experience

PROCEDURE   Please take the following steps:

1. Give each participant a sheet of paper and a pen.
2. Ask the students to draw a map of the world as best they can within 5 minutes.
3. Have students name as many of the countries as they can.
4. Ask students to place a check mark on any country they have visited for a week or longer.
5. Direct students to exchange papers with another member of the group.
6. Ask students to identify differences between their own and their partners' maps.

DEBRIEFING   When students have completed discussing their world maps with their partners, they can discuss the following points:

1. Does a person's awareness of the shape of a country reveal that person's awareness of the shape of the culture?
2. When a person leaves out a country, what does this mean?
3. When a person leaves out a continent, what does this mean?

Note. From *Decisional Dialogues in a Cultural Context: Structured Exercises* (p. 9), by P. B. Pedersen and D. Hernandez, 1997, Thousand Oaks, CA: Sage. Copyright 1997 by Sage. Adapted with permission.

4. What country did the person place in the center of the map, and what does that mean?
5. When a person draws a country out of place in relation to other countries, what does this mean?
6. Were students better acquainted with the countries they drew accurately?
7. When a person objects violently to doing the drawing, what does that mean?
8. How well did students draw the home countries of other group members?
9. What do students plan to do as a result of what they learned in this experience?

INSIGHT   The more familiar one is with a country, the more accurate one is likely to be in drawing a picture of that country.

2 CAPTURING CULTURAL BIAS

Objective: To become aware of one's own cultural behaviors and biases.

TIME REQUIRED 30 minutes or less

RISK LEVEL Low

PARTICIPANTS NEEDED Any size class or discussion group, plus one group facilitator

PROCEDURE Please take the following steps:

1. Explain that people are limited to understanding all other people from their own cultural point of view and are trapped by a limited and rigid set of culturally learned rules regarding behaviors they like and those they do not like.
2. Hand out copies of Exhibit 2.1 to members of the group.
3. Ask each participant to circle five adjectives describing people they like to be around and to underline five adjectives describing people they do not like to be around. Participants may add adjectives of their own.
4. Discuss the results as a class or in smaller groups if necessary.

DEBRIEFING Encourage participants to examine why they like some behaviors and do not like others. Questions for discussion may include the following:

1. Why did you not like some behaviors?
2. Why did you like other behaviors?
3. Where did you learn to like and dislike those behaviors?
4. Who were the significant culture teachers in your life who taught you about these behaviors?
5. Is it possible to change your preference for some behaviors over others?

INSIGHT Each person has his or her own cultural biases linking behaviors they like or do not like with particular cultural groups.

Exhibit 2.1   *Adjectives Describing Culturally Learned Behaviors*

adventurous	helpful	shy
affectionate	independent	soft on subordinates
ambitious	indifferent to others	stern
appreciative	intolerant	submissive
argumentative	jealous	successful
competitive	kind	sympathetic
complaining	loud	tactful
considerate of others	neat	talkative
discourteous	needing of much praise	teasing
distant	obedient	thorough
dominating	optimistic	thoughtful
easily angered	orderly	touchy, cannot be kidded
easily discouraged	readily giving of praise	trusting
easily influenced	rebellious	uncommunicative
efficient	responsible	understanding
enthusiastic	sarcastic	varied interests
false	self-centered	very dependent on others
forgiving	self-respecting	warm
fun loving	self-satisfied	well-mannered
good listener	shrewd, devious	willing worker

3 PERCEPTION VERSUS REALITY

> *Objective:* To understand how culturally learned perceptions control descriptions of reality.

TIME REQUIRED   30 minutes or less

RISK LEVEL   Low

PARTICIPANTS NEEDED   Any size group, plus one facilitator

PROCEDURE   Please take the following steps:

1. Ask group members to describe what is taking place in a picture of a group. The picture may be taken from a magazine advertisement; a picture of a group of people or even a collection of stick figures drawn spontaneously on the blackboard or flip chart will also work.
2. For small groups (five to eight people), ask each member to give his or her interpretation of the picture or drawing in turn. If the group is larger, divide it into smaller groups.
3. After every member has given his or her interpretation, begin a group discussion of the similarities and differences in their interpretations.

DEBRIEFING   The discussion will focus on similarities and differences in the interpretations students project onto the picture of the group. Discussion questions might include the following:

1. Why was your interpretation different from the interpretations of others in the group?

Note. From *Decisional Dialogues in a Cultural Context: Structured Exercises* (p. 79), by P. B. Pedersen and D. Hernandez, 1997, Thousand Oaks, CA: Sage. Copyright 1997 by Sage. Adapted with permission.

2. Why was your interpretation similar to those of others in the group?
3. Where did you learn to interpret this picture in that particular way?
4. Who were the significant culture teachers in your life?
5. Can you change your perception of these pictures if you want to?

INSIGHT We project meaning onto what we see based on our learned cultural patterns.

4 | WHAT OTHER PEOPLE SAY, FEEL, AND MEAN

Objective: To recognize the difficulty in listening to and retelling another person's feelings and meaning about his or her culture without projecting one's own interpretations onto the description.

TIME REQUIRED   30 minutes or less

RISK LEVEL   Low

PARTICIPANTS NEEDED   Any number of students, plus one facilitator

PROCEDURE   Please take the following steps:

1. Divide the members into two-person groups.
2. Have one person be the speaker and the other the listener. The speaker will talk about his or her culture for 1 minute, without interruption, while the listener listens carefully without taking notes.
3. When the first minute is up, the instructor will ask the listener to repeat back everything the speaker said, felt, and meant about his or her culture without interruption for 1 minute.
4. When the second minute is up, both speaker and listener discuss for 1 minute how accurate and complete the listener was in repeating back what he or she heard.
5. When the third minute is up, the speaker and the listener exchange roles and repeat the experience in the new roles. It is possible to use three people in the experience with the third person as observer to report back what the speaker said, felt, and meant.

Note. From *A Handbook for Developing Multicultural Awareness* (3rd ed., p. 141), by P. B. Pedersen, 2000, Alexandria, VA: American Counseling Association. Copyright 2000 by the American Counseling Association. Adapted with permission. No further reproduction authorized without written permission of the American Counseling Association.

DEBRIEFING   In the debriefing, the instructor can discuss how people define culture broadly to include ethnographic (ethnicity, nationality), demographic (age, gender, place of residence), status (social, educational, economic), and affiliation (formal, informal) characteristics. The instructor might also point out how difficult it is to really listen and repeat back what others said, felt, and meant. Some discussion questions might include the following:

1. Were you able to hear accurately what your partner said about his or her culture?
2. If you were to do the experience over, would you emphasize the same aspects of your culture?
3. In describing your culture, did you include demographic, status, and affiliation variables?
4. Were you able to describe your culture in a way that your partner could remember?
5. If you were to repeat the experience, could you improve your ability to listen?

INSIGHT   What we hear and what the other person says may be different.

5 OUTSIDE EXPERTS

Objective: To recognize the importance of cultural patterns in communication.

TIME REQUIRED   30 minutes or less

RISK LEVEL   Low

PARTICIPANTS NEEDED   At least 10 students are needed, plus one facilitator

PROCEDURE   Please take the following steps:

1. Send three or four volunteer group members out of the room. They will be labeled "outside experts." The rest of the members are organized into members of a "culture group."
2. When the outside experts have left the room, instruct the culture group to follow three rules:
   a. Members can respond only yes or no, and this rule will be disclosed to the experts when they return to help them work.
   b. Men may not talk with women experts, and women may not talk with men experts, because it would be embarrassing and impolite. This rule will not be disclosed to the outside experts.
   c. As appropriate responses to all serious questions, if the outside expert is smiling, the member will respond "yes," because that is the response the expert seems to want; likewise, if the outside expert is not smiling, the member will respond "no." This rule will not be disclosed to the outside experts.

Note. From *A Handbook for Developing Multicultural Awareness* (3rd ed., p. 59), by P. B. Pedersen, 2000, Alexandria, VA: American Counseling Association. Copyright 2000 by the American Counseling Association. Adapted with permission. No further reproduction authorized without written permission of the American Counseling Association.

3. Have the outside experts return, and instruct them to ask yes-or-no questions of each of the group members to gather data on who the group is, what they need and want, how they feel about the outside experts, where they live, and any other relevant information.
4. At the end of 5 or 6 minutes, ask the outside experts to report back individually on what they have learned about this group.
5. After reporting back to the group, have the outside experts take their seats, and lead a round of applause for their work.

DEBRIEFING

In the debriefing, the instructor should point out that nonverbal cues (e.g., gender, smiling) are very important, that "yes" may not always mean yes as group members understand it, that people tend to evaluate groups quickly as "good" or "bad," and that apparent inconsistency in information about the culture may be an artifact of the expert (e.g., smiling or not smiling) rather than of the host culture group. Patterns characteristic of any group are typically much more complicated than in this three-rule cultural group. Discussion questions may include the following:

1. Have you ever worked in a culture whose rules you did not understand?
2. Did you project your own self-reference criterion, rather than the host culture's perspective, in your evaluation of the group?
3. How would you prevent such misunderstandings in your future contacts with other cultures?
4. How do you think members of the culture group would have described the outside experts when talking about them later?
5. How can you avoid imposing your own cultural rules on others when your rules might not be appropriate?

INSIGHT

Many cultural misunderstandings are unintentional when we interpret behaviors out of context.

6 ROLE-PLAYING CULTURAL STORIES

Objective: To recognize cultural stories and points of view from the perspective of the storyteller.

TIME REQUIRED   30 minutes or less

RISK LEVEL   Low

PARTICIPANTS NEEDED   Any number of participants, plus one facilitator

PROCEDURE   Please take the following steps:

1. Identify a volunteer to tell a culturally significant story to the group. A resource person from outside the group might also be brought in to tell a culturally significant story.
2. After the story, select group members to take on the roles of people in the story to interact with the storyteller. Begin the story again with the role-players acting as characters in the story. Role-players are free to interpret their roles as they see appropriate.
3. As the story continues, add role-players until most or all of the class is involved in the story.
4. Have the original storyteller become a coach to shape the interaction of the other role-players without taking the primary role himself or herself. As the instructor, it is important to keep the situation safe and to stop the interaction if members take too big a risk too early in the group experience.
5. Discuss what group members have learned when the story has reached its conclusion.

DEBRIEFING   The students will role-play the original story presented by the storyteller, but the participants will also have the opportunity to change or "re-story" the events as culturally appropriate. The role-played story might be quite different from the story-teller's presentation. Some of the discussion questions might include the following:

1. How authentic were the students role-playing the original story?
2. How and why did the role-players change the story?
3. Were the changes in the story realistic?
4. Did role-players feel empowered when they re-storied the events?
5. What was the most important aspect of this story?

INSIGHT   Every story can have many different endings.

7 DRAWING A HOUSE

Objective: To examine culturally learned behavior patterns that focus on leader–follower and task–relationship orientations.

TIME REQUIRED   30 minutes or less

RISK LEVEL   Low

PARTICIPANTS NEEDED   Any number of participants, plus one facilitator

PROCEDURE   Please take the following steps:

1. Ask each group member to choose a partner.
2. Give each team of two people a single pen and a single piece of paper.
3. Instruct each team to hold on to the same pen and draw a house on the piece of paper, without talking during the experience.
4. After the participants have worked about 3 or 4 minutes drawing the house, ask the teams to stop and to hold up their picture for others around them to see.

DEBRIEFING   The debriefing will focus on two culturally learned patterns: (a) leader versus follower and (b) task versus relationship. The instructor should point out that "whose pen it was" and "who had control of the bottom of the pen" significantly influenced the experience. It is also useful to talk about how task-oriented people have a difficult time in cultures that emphasize relationship and vice versa. Some discussion questions might include the following:

1. Did your preferred pattern as leader or follower in this experience reflect your real-life cultural pattern in your daily activities?

Note. From *A Handbook for Developing Multicultural Awareness* (3rd ed., p. 194), by P. B. Pedersen, 2000, Alexandria, VA: American Counseling Association. Copyright 2000 by the American Counseling Association. Adapted with permission. No further reproduction authorized without written permission of the American Counseling Association.

2. Did your preferred pattern emphasizing relationship or task in this experience reflect your real-life cultural pattern in your daily activities?
3. Did similarities or differences in age, gender, or status with your partner influence what you did?
4. Might this experience be useful in marriage counseling or in preparing partners to work together?
5. Were you able to communicate with your partner without talking?

INSIGHT   Each of a person's behaviors symbolizes his or her culturally learned beliefs.

8 Cultural Bingo

Objective: To share special information about cultural background in a multicultural group.

Time Required   30 minutes or less

Risk Level   Low

Participants Needed   Any number of participants, plus one facilitator

Procedure   Please take the following steps:

1. Collect one example of generally unknown information about each group member before the experience, and print this information on a grid resembling a bingo sheet.
2. Distribute the bingo sheets, and instruct group members to circulate among one another to match participants with their "secrets."
3. Continue until a participant is able to match all secrets with the correct participant.

Debriefing   In the debriefing, the instructor will point out how relatively little people know about one another, even when they are good friends. The largest part of people is private and secret. Discussion questions may include the following:

1. Were you surprised by the secrets of the other participants?
2. Did you tend to underestimate the resources represented by other participants?
3. Do you feel closer to other participants now that you know their secrets?
4. Were you embarrassed to disclose your secret?
5. Were you surprised by any of the secrets?

Insight   As we get to know one another, we learn special and unique information about them.

9 LEARNING TO GROW OLD

Objective: To understand the constraints faced by the culture of people who are elderly.

TIME REQUIRED	30 minutes or less
RISK LEVEL	Low
PARTICIPANTS NEEDED	Any number of participants, plus one facilitator
PROCEDURE	Please take the following steps:

1. Give the group members Exhibit 2.2, a list of 25 life priorities, and ask them to identify their own top 10 priorities from this list.
2. Instruct group members to pick those priorities most essential to their quality of life.
3. When everyone has identified their 10 priorities, tell the group that 10 years have passed, and they will have to give up three of these priorities due to aging.
4. When they have crossed off three of their top priorities, tell them that 20 years have passed, and they will have to give up three more priorities.
5. When they have crossed three more priorities off the list, tell them that 30 years have passed, and they will have to cross off three more priorities. This leaves them with only one of the 10 priorities left.
6. Discuss the implications of dwindling priorities.

DEBRIEFING In debriefing this experience, the instructor may want to compare the similarities and differences among group members regarding the one remaining priority. The instructor

---

Note. From *Culture-Centered Counseling Interventions: Striving for Accuracy* (pp. 291–292), by P. B. Pedersen, 1997, Thousand Oaks, CA: Sage. Copyright 1997 by Sage. Adapted with permission.

Exhibit 2.2   *Twenty-Five Life Priorities*

1. Helping others and community involvement	14. Love and the opportunity to love
2. Exercise	15. Family and relationships with relatives
3. Self-respect	16. Sex and intimate relationships
4. Health	17. Friends and relationships with friends
5. Happiness and inner peace	18. Work and gainful activity
6. Mobility	19. Humor
7. Pets	20. Travel
8. Independence	21. Creativity and self-expression
9. Hobbies	22. Finances and financial security
10. Sports	23. Freedom and choices
11. Safety and security	24. Wisdom and intellectual development
12. Music and the arts	25. Shopping
13. Faith, religion, spiritual development	

will also want to have the members tell how they felt about giving up their quality of life priorities. What were the consequences of having to give up these priorities, which were so meaningful? The debriefing discussion will compare and contrast the students' responses. Some questions for discussion might include the following:

1. Were you surprised by the one remaining priority in your short list?
2. Why do you suppose that you ended up choosing that particular priority?
3. If you were to go through the experience again, would you have different results? Why?
4. Were you surprised by the top priority chosen by others in your group?
5. What do the priorities you choose tell you about your values?

INSIGHT   Growing old is a process of narrowing your priorities.

10 FINDING COMMON GROUND IN AN ARGUMENT

> *Objective:* To identify shared values or expectations, even though behaviors may be dissonant, in an argument across cultures.

TIME REQUIRED   30 minutes or less

RISK LEVEL   Low

PARTICIPANTS NEEDED   Any number of participants, plus one facilitator

PROCEDURE   Please take the following steps:

1. Ask for two volunteers from the group, one man and one woman, to role-play a husband and a wife wanting to get a divorce. (A variation of this would be an employer in conflict with an employee or even any two people who are in conflict, defining culture broadly to include work roles.)
2. Have each describe for a minute or two (no longer) why they want the divorce or how they have been badly treated by the other.
3. At the end of these two brief, uninterrupted monologues, ask the rest of the group members to act as marriage counselors (or conflict managers) and ask questions of one or the other person, who remain in role. The other group members may work individually or build on one another's comments, but ideally everyone will have a chance to contribute.
4. Interrupt the group member "marriage counselors" from time to time, reminding them to avoid interpreting the behavior out of context.
5. At the end of the role-play, have both people comment on what advice was most useful.

DEBRIEFING   In debriefing the leader asks each of the two role-players to tell how they felt during the interaction and to recall which comments seemed most helpful and why. As long as the marriage counselors' comments focus on the "bad" *behaviors* of one or the other person, the conflict will be seen to escalate (and it is very hard not to focus on the behaviors). However, if the group members address the topic of positive shared *expectations* (e.g., "Tell me about when the two of you met and fell in love") without discussing behaviors until both parties in the conflict can clearly see that they share the common ground of wanting respect, fairness, trust, safety, or some other positive expectation, the conflict can be contained, even though their behaviors for expressing or getting that expectation might be different.

Discussion questions might include the following:

1. Was it difficult to avoid focusing on the behaviors of the people in conflict?
2. Were you surprised by the comments identified as "most helpful"?
3. Why is it important to establish common ground in managing conflict constructively?
4. Can conflict ever be managed constructively without first finding common ground?
5. Why does the argument escalate when you focus on behaviors?
6. How does this strategy fit with your natural method of managing conflict?

INSIGHT   The same behaviors can have different meanings, and different behaviors can have similar meanings across cultures.

11 GIFT GIVING

> *Objective:* To reward culturally different group members for their special and unique contribution to the group.

TIME REQUIRED 30 minutes or less

RISK LEVEL Low

PARTICIPANTS NEEDED Any number of participants, plus one facilitator

PROCEDURE Please take the following steps:

1. Announce this experience at least 1 week in advance to give participants time to think of an appropriate gift to give to another individual in the group.
2. Ask students to present a gift to another member of the group who has made a special and unique contribution to the group or who may be culturally different from them.
3. Ask each student in turn to describe the gift they received and the gift they are giving back. If it would make members uncomfortable to share their gift in public, a less formal presentation can be made where individuals seek out one another.
4. Follow the gift giving by a general discussion of the cultural role of gift giving.

DEBRIEFING The "gifts" that are given may be a comment, observation, or insight that was meaningful to the receiver who wants to thank the giver. In debriefing this experience, the instructor needs to be sensitive to the possibility that some individuals in the group may not be singled out for thanks and that this might be embarrassing to those

---

Note. From *Instructor's Manual for Intentional Group Counseling: A Microskills Approach* (p. 136), by P. B. Pedersen, A. E. Ivey, M. B. Ivey, and Y. Y. Kuo, 2001, Belmont, CA: Brooks/ Cole. Copyright 2001 by Brooks/Cole. Adapted with permission of Wadsworth, a division of Thomas Learning.

individuals. To some extent this is a "natural consequence" of their contribution to the group. However, the leader might be able to do a Positive Asset Search and discover some example for these individuals so that they will not feel left out. Questions for discussion might include the following:

1. Do you normally give gifts to people who have helped you?
2. Are all gifts symbolic, and if so, what do they symbolize?
3. Why would some cultures encourage gift giving more than others?
4. How can gift giving become offensive?
5. What is the social function of gift giving?

INSIGHT   Recognizing the gifts given by others is especially important across cultures.

12 CHECKERS AND CHESS

Objective: To experience competition with a partner using different rules as a metaphor for societies in which different groups or individuals interact according to different culturally learned rules.

TIME REQUIRED   30 minutes or less

RISK LEVEL   Low

PARTICIPANTS NEEDED   Any number of participants working in two-person teams, plus a facilitator

PROCEDURE   Please take the following steps:

1. Organize the class in dyad groups.
2. Give one person checker game pieces and the other person chess game pieces and a game board appropriate to both chess and checkers.
3. Instruct the dyads to play: one using chess pieces and rules and the other using checker pieces and rules.
4. Have the groups play the games until all the game pieces of one partner have been captured.

DEBRIEFING   Although the interaction will be frustrating to both players and may at first involve some confusion, the metaphor provides a powerful analogy to multicultural interactions in society. Discussion questions might include the following:

1. Can you think of an example in society where two people or groups interact even though their culturally learned rules are different?
2. Give an example of an event that might have positive consequences for one group but negative consequences for the other group.
3. Without changing the rules for either group, how would you make their working together easier?

4. Can you identify an individual from a different group who interacts with you according to different rules than yours?
5. If you change the criteria of winning, how would that change the interaction?
6. Is it possible for both sides to win?

INSIGHT   We are all playing the same game but sometimes use different rules.

13 INVENTING A MULTICULTURAL RETROSPECTIVE

Objective: To look at one's multiple cultural identities in retrospect and to judge the choices made that are likely to work best.

TIME REQUIRED   30 minutes or less

RISK LEVEL   Low

PARTICIPANTS NEEDED   30 or more participants, plus a facilitator

PROCEDURE   Please take the following steps:

1. Ask each member of a multicultural group to select a partner from a different culture.
2. Have the partners carry on a conversation with one another for 5 minutes about what was happening in the group as if this were the next day and the group had already happened. Each member will have an opportunity to rehearse telling others about the group experience as if it were already over, identifying strengths and weaknesses, insights, and opportunities.
3. Next, ask each dyad to describe their retrospective account to the entire group.

DEBRIEFING   In debriefing it is important for the instructor to recognize that no one knows what will happen in the future and that these speculations are only good guesses. Some discussion questions might include the following:

1. Are your future behaviors predictable?
2. Did imagining you were in the future give you insights?
3. Was it difficult for you to put yourself into the future?

4. Which cultures are most ready to do an experience such as this one?
5. Are some people better than others at imagining themselves in the future?

INSIGHT   Getting a different time perspective will help to clarify the immediate multicultural group dynamics.

14 WESTERN AND NON-WESTERN PERSPECTIVES

Objective: To assess one's affiliations to Western and non-Western identities and to determine what is most relevant to one individually.

TIME REQUIRED	30 minutes or less
RISK LEVEL	Low
PARTICIPANTS NEEDED	Any number of participants, plus one facilitator
PROCEDURE	Please take the following steps:

1. Distribute the scale in Exhibit 2.3 to the participants; each person receives one scale.
2. Ask participants to circle the number between 1 and 7 that indicates their own perspective, with a higher number indicating a non-Western preference and a lower number a Western perspective.
3. Ask the students to add up the numbers they circled and report their score.
4. As students report their scores, draw a graph on the board or flip chart illustrating which perspective was more popular.

DEBRIEFING   Although there are no right or wrong answers to this test of perspectives, participants may be surprised or even offended by their scores relative to the scores of others in the class. Some questions for discussion include the following:

1. Define the Western perspective.
2. Define the non-Western perspective.

Note. From *Culture-Centered Counseling Interventions: Striving for Accuracy* (pp. 96–97), by P. B. Pedersen, 1997, Thousand Oaks, CA: Sage. Copyright 1997 by Sage. Adapted with permission.

Exhibit 2.3 *Western and Non-Western Perspectives*

Circle the number indicating your preference toward a Western or non-Western perspective.

Western perspective	Rate yourself	Non-Western perspective
Life before death	1 2 3 4 5 6 7	Life after death
Individualized self	1 2 3 4 5 6 7	Spiritualized self
Self-centered	1 2 3 4 5 6 7	Social centered
Independence as healthy	1 2 3 4 5 6 7	Dependence as healthy
Child is free	1 2 3 4 5 6 7	Child is interdependent
No obligation to parents	1 2 3 4 5 6 7	Big obligation to parents
Child–parent interdependence	1 2 3 4 5 6 7	Child–parent dependence
Individualism	1 2 3 4 5 6 7	Collectivism
Truth is clear authority	1 2 3 4 5 6 7	Truth is paradoxical
Authority inhibits growth	1 2 3 4 5 6 7	Growth requires authority
Logic oriented	1 2 3 4 5 6 7	Experience oriented
One-directional norms	1 2 3 4 5 6 7	Two-directional balance
Personality is not contextual	1 2 3 4 5 6 7	Personality is contextual

Note. From *Culture-Centered Counseling Interventions: Striving for Accuracy* (pp. 96–97), by P. B. Pedersen, 1997, Thousand Oaks, CA: Sage. Copyright 1997 by Sage. Adapted with permission.

3. Can you name countries likely to be more Western or non-Western?
4. What problems occur when the Western perspective dominates a society?
5. What problems occur when non-Western perspectives dominate a society?

INSIGHT   The term *Western* describes a perspective that may characterize people living in non-Western societies, and the term *non-Western* may characterize people living in Western societies.

15 COALITIONS AND TRUST FORMATION

Objective: To examine the importance of trust in the creation of lasting coalitions for a mixed group.

TIME REQUIRED   30 minutes or less

RISK LEVEL   Low

PARTICIPANTS NEEDED   Any number of participants, plus one facilitator

PROCEDURE   Please take the following steps:

1. Recruit three volunteers representing different cultural groups, broadly defined, for a 5-minute experiment.
2. Seat all three people around a table, with the other participants seated or standing so they can hear what is happening.
3. Lay four quarters (25-cent coins) in front of the three people and tell them that the distribution of the total sum of money will depend on majority rule by the three parties in this experiment.
4. Explain that the amount of money cannot be divided into smaller units such as dimes and nickels. Typically, the three people will divide the money as equally as possible and declare the experience over.
5. At that point, remind them that the experience is to last a full 5 minutes, and sit quietly and wait.
6. Carefully monitor the experience, but do not interfere. Typically, within a minute or two one of the players will suggest a two-way split of the money, and the other person will agree. Then, within another minute, the third person will agree to a 75:25 split rather than lose everything, and that coalition will last, cutting out the first person who suggested a 50:50 split.
7. Discuss the outcome of this experience.

The facilitator may want to explore the logic behind whatever distribution of the four quarters occurred during the 5 minutes and why. Some discussion questions include the following:

1. Why was the first person to suggest a 50:50 split cut out of the lasting coalition?
2. What strategy would you use to end up with the most money?
3. Would the same dynamics occur in all cultures?
4. If the negotiation was not about money, would the outcome be different?
5. What feelings did participants have during the experience?

INSIGHT Lasting coalitions across different cultures and individuals depend on each party trusting the other party or parties.

16 FANTASY WALK IN THE WOODS

Objective: To examine the symbolic meanings of fantasy experiences as a way of exploring attitudes and values.

TIME REQUIRED   30 minutes or less

RISK LEVEL   Low

PARTICIPANTS NEEDED   Any number of participants, plus one facilitator

PROCEDURE   Please take the following steps:

1. Ask the participants to close their eyes and imagine walking through a dark wood on a dimly lighted path. They walk and walk for a long time on the path, until suddenly they emerge into a meadow with bright sunlight, long soft grass, butterflies and birds, and gentle breezes.
2. Ask participants to imagine themselves as they move out of the dark woods into the meadow and to imagine what they would do next.
3. Pause a few moments, and then ask the participants to imagine that they are now on the other side of the meadow, continuing on the trail through the dark woods for a long, long time, until suddenly they turn a corner and meet a large bear standing on its hind legs, as surprised as they are.
4. Again, have the participants imagine what they would do in this circumstance.
5. Pause a few moments, and then ask the participants to imagine that the bear is now gone and that they are continuing on the path again for a long, long time, until they reach the bottom of a tall cliff that rises straight up in front of them into the clouds. There is no obvious path to the right or left; the path seems to just end at the bottom of this cliff.
6. Again, have the participants imagine what they would do in this circumstance.
7. Pause a few moments, and then inform the participants that the path symbolizes life's journey, the meadow represents sexuality, the bear represents life's problems, and the cliff represents death.

8. Ask the participants to disclose only as much of their responses as they choose and to make their own interpretations of what those responses might mean.

DEBRIEFING   The facilitator will need to be careful that participants not self-disclose to the point of being uncomfortable. The group may want to explore how life problems, sexuality, and death are experienced differently in different cultures, broadly defined. Some discussion questions include the following:

1. Did the interpretation make sense to you?
2. Would the same symbols have the same meanings across cultures?
3. Knowing what the symbols represent, would you change your responses?
4. What feelings did you experience during the fantasy?
5. Were you surprised at any point by your own thoughts?

INSIGHT   Each culture provides different interpretations of normal life experiences.

17 SEEING OURSELVES AS OTHERS SEE US

Objective: To show how we often attach labels to people and behave toward them as though those labels were true.

TIME REQUIRED	20–30 minutes
RISK LEVEL	Moderate
PARTICIPANTS NEEDED	Any size class or discussion group of 10 to 30 students, plus one facilitator
PROCEDURE	Please take the following steps:

1. Prepare a set of typed labels that each list a positive adjective such as *friendly, helpful, smart, generous, loving,* and so forth. A more risky alternative is to generate a list of less positive labels, such as the following:
   - Tell me I'm right.
   - Flatter me.
   - Ignore me.
   - Criticize me.
   - Treat me as a sex object.
   - Tell me I'm smart.
   - Interrupt me.
   - Tell me I'm wrong.
   - Treat me as a helpless person with nothing worthwhile to say.
2. Arbitrarily assign these labels to participants and attach a label to each person's back so that they will not know what their own label says.
3. Instruct the participants not to tell others what their labels say.

Note. From *Decisional Dialogues in a Cultural Context: Structured Exercises* (pp. 3–4), by P. B. Pedersen and D. Hernandez, 1997, Thousand Oaks, CA: Sage. Copyright 1997 by Sage. Adapted with permission.

4. Divide participants into groups of six to eight participants.
5. Engage the groups in a discussion for 10 minutes, and ask all participants to treat the others in the group as though the labels were true.
6. At the end of 10 minutes, have each participant guess what his or her label says.
7. After they have guessed, have the participants peel off their labels and read them.
8. When each participant has had a chance to see his or her label, return to a large group for discussion. Encourage participants to convey to the group how they felt about how the others were acting toward them.

DEBRIEFING   The attachment of invisible labels might apply to situations one experiences in real life. Examples of questions to discuss include the following:

1. Did you feel helpless to change how others perceived you?
2. Did the other group members seem simplistic in their judgments?
3. Did you find it uncomfortable to treat others according to the label?
4. Were you able to accurately interpret how others acted toward you?
5. Do you think you are really wearing a label that you cannot yourself see?

INSIGHT   The labels others attach to us influence their behavior toward us.

18 THE HIDDEN AGENDA

> *Objective:* To understand the process of how different cultures manage group situations and pressures by assigning a "hidden agenda."

TIME REQUIRED   20–30 minutes

RISK LEVEL   Moderate

PARTICIPANTS NEEDED   A group or groups of about six to eight students each, plus one facilitator

PROCEDURE   Please take the following steps:

1. Design a list of role tasks that reflect cultural stereotypes relating to patterns of behavior. These are referred to in this experience as "hidden agendas." Examples of such role tasks are to always answer in the negative or always in the positive, to befriend one other person, to get into an argument with one other person, or to talk a great deal of the time or not to talk at all.
2. Give each member of the group a slip of paper with one hidden agenda role task written on it.
3. Divide the group into "committees" and charge them with making a decision on an assigned topic.
4. Ask the group to discuss the topic for 10 minutes while each member performs the role task described in his or her hidden agenda. No member will be informed of what role task was assigned to the other members of the group, and each member will be instructed to keep others from finding out his or her role task.

DEBRIEFING   After the 10-minute discussion is completed, the group members can discuss what they thought the other members' hidden agenda may have been, how the task influ-

Note. From *A Manual of Structured Experiences for Cross-Cultural Learning* (p. 45), by W. H. Weeks, P. B. Pedersen, and R. W. Brislin, 1977, Yarmouth, ME: Intercultural Press. Copyright 1977 by Intercultural Press. Adapted with permission.

enced their perception of the person, and how performance of those role tasks affected the committee's productivity. Some discussion questions might include the following:

1. Were you able to accomplish your hidden agenda without being discovered?
2. Were other group members accepting of your hidden agenda?
3. How did you feel about imposing your hidden agenda on the group?
4. If you were to do the experience again, would you become more skillful in manipulating the group?
5. How could you prevent any group member from imposing the hidden agenda of their special interests on others?

INSIGHT   Culturally defined hidden agendas influence the process and content of our role in groups through patterns of culturally learned behavior.

19 INTERPRETING POLICY IN A CULTURAL CONTEXT

Objective: To identify culture-specific patterns of common and variant interpretations as expressed in words added or left out of policy statements.

TIME REQUIRED 30 minutes or less

RISK LEVEL Moderate

PARTICIPANTS NEEDED Any size class or discussion group, plus one facilitator

PROCEDURE Please take the following steps:

1. Select one or more paragraphs from a document describing the policies of an organization.
2. Delete at least 10 or 15 key words, keeping the space where these words were extracted blank for the participants to write in their own words as they consider appropriate.
3. Give participants a copy of the paragraph and a pencil and ask them to fill in the blanks to give the paragraph meaning.
4. After filling in the blanks, read the original paragraph.
5. Have the participants compare their interpretations and discuss them according to culture-specific variables.

DEBRIEFING As students compare how they filled in the blanks to complete the policy statement, some discussion questions to consider include the following:

1. Does the way you filled in the blanks reflect your own cultural values?
2. How does your completed paragraph compare with the original paragraph?

Note. From *A Manual of Structured Experiences for Cross-Cultural Learning* (p. 28), by W. H. Weeks, P. B. Pedersen, and R. W. Brislin, 1977, Yarmouth, ME: Intercultural Press. Copyright 1977 by Intercultural Press. Adapted with permission.

3. Would you be willing to defend the policy statement in your completed paragraph?
4. Has this experience given you any new insights about the original policy statement?
5. What special interests are represented in the original policy statement?

INSIGHT   Cultural patterns are expressed through the words we choose to use or leave out in our writing.

20 CULTURAL IMPACT STORYTELLING

> *Objective:* To understand cultural learned patterns in the context of storytelling.

TIME REQUIRED 30 minutes or less

RISK LEVEL Moderate

PARTICIPANTS NEEDED Any number of participants, plus at least one facilitator

PROCEDURE Please take the following steps:

1. Distribute large sheets of paper and crayons and ask students to draw stick-figure sketches to represent the events, the joys, the sorrows, the people, and the decisions that have had an effect on their unique cultural development. As students perform the experience, have them think specifically of those people or events that significantly affected them from a cultural perspective.
2. As they look over their picture stories, ask the students to place a plus (+) sign by the events they consider to have been highly positive experiences.
3. Next, ask participants to place a minus (–) sign by the events they believe were extremely negative experiences.
4. Ask the students to hang the graphic drawing where all can see and to tell their stories to their small group, describing in detail their positive and negative experiences.
5. Analyze the variables that were most important to the stories and their positive or negative impact.

Note. From *Decisional Dialogues in a Cultural Context: Structured Exercises* (pp. 15–16), by P. B. Pedersen and D. Hernandez, 1997, Thousand Oaks, CA: Sage. Copyright 1997 by Sage. Adapted with permission.

DEBRIEFING   In attempting to understand the psychological dynamics of the positive and negative events in their lives, people focus on how these events can be explained by the cultural context. Discussion questions for the group may include the following:

1. If you were to redraw the picture, would you focus on the same events?
2. Did you know at the time of the event how important it would be to your identity?
3. Do you know what it was about each event that was such a powerful learning experience?
4. Would you change your story if you could?
5. What new insights did you learn from the stories told by others in your group?

INSIGHT   Much of our evaluative thinking process is guided by culturally learned stories.

21 CULTURE SHOCK RATINGS AND SYMPTOM CHECKLIST

Objective: To help students measure the presence or absence of symptoms of culture shock and life changes in their own lives.

TIME REQUIRED   30 minutes or less

RISK LEVEL   Moderate

PARTICIPANTS NEEDED   Any size class or discussion group, plus one facilitator

PROCEDURE   Please take the following steps:

1. Ask the students to indicate where they feel they stand personally, all things considered, at the present time in their various cultural roles. They can use a scale where 0 represents life at its worst and 10 represents life at its best as the student views it.
2. Observe as the students score themselves in the same way on their different cultural roles, including their ethnographic, demographic, status, and affiliation variables.
3. Distribute Exhibit 2.4 and have the students ask themselves, "How often in the past two weeks or so have I experienced the following reactions or feelings?"
4. Have the students circle their responses for each item on the checklist and link their reactions or feelings to their roles. Discuss the connections students make.

DEBRIEFING   Students will come to understand that they are going through some degree of culture shock all the time and that change requires some degree of culture shock. Discussion questions might include the following:

Note. From *Decisional Dialogues in a Cultural Context: Structured Exercises* (p. 77), by P. B. Pedersen and D. Hernandez, 1997, Thousand Oaks, CA: Sage. Copyright 1997 by Sage. Adapted with permission.

Exhibit 2.4 *Culture Shock Feelings and Reactions*

Feeling or reaction	Not at all	Rarely	Occasionally	Frequently	Almost always
Anxiety (worry or fear about something)	0	1	2	3	4
Depression (unhappiness, moodiness)	0	1	2	3	4
Sleep problems	0	1	2	3	4
Digestion, elimination problems	0	1	2	3	4
Tiredness, fatigue	0	1	2	3	4
Anger, irritability, impatience	0	1	2	3	4
Loneliness	0	1	2	3	4
Forgetfulness	0	1	2	3	4
Difficulty concentrating	0	1	2	3	4
Feelings of being "different," not fitting in or belonging	0	1	2	3	4
Nostalgia for remembered pleasures	0	1	2	3	4

Note. From *Decisional Dialogues in a Cultural Context: Structured Exercises* (p. 77), by P. B. Pedersen and D. Hernandez, 1997, Thousand Oaks, CA: Sage. Copyright 1997 by Sage. Adapted with permission.

1. Which one of your cultural roles involves the most culture shock, and why?
2. Which one of your cultural roles involves less culture shock, and why?
3. How can going through culture shock become a positive learning experience?
4. How can you prepare to go through culture shock?
5. Who would be most vulnerable to culture shock?

INSIGHT   A person may be experiencing more culture shock than he or she imagines.

PEDERSEN, P.B. (2004). 110 Experiences for multicultural learning. Washington, D.C: American Psychological Association.

22 HOW TO SABOTAGE MULTICULTURAL GROUPS

Objective: To identify behaviors that prevent multicultural groups from succeeding and thriving.

TIME REQUIRED 30 minutes or less

RISK LEVEL Moderate

PARTICIPANTS NEEDED Any number of participants, plus one facilitator

PROCEDURE Please take the following steps:

1. Distribute the list of 13 strategies for sabotaging a multicultural group in Exhibit 2.5 to the participants.
2. Read each of these strategies out loud to the group of participants.
3. As you read off each strategy, ask the students to provide examples they have observed or experienced of that particular strategy at work. Students may choose to work in small groups to discuss these strategies and how to best cope with them in groups.

DEBRIEFING In debriefing this experience, the leader may want to be careful in case one or another of these strategies has frequently been used by one or more group member in the past. Questions for discussion might include the following:

1. Do you think the strategies will work?
2. Can you think of a situation where you might use one or more of these strategies?

Note. From "How to Become a More Sophisticated Saboteur in Groups," by B. Gertz, 1969, in C. R. Mill (Ed.), *Selections From Human Relations Training News* (pp. 87–88), Washington, DC: NTL Institute. Copyright 1969 by NTL Institute. Adapted with permission.

Exhibit 2.5 *Saboteur Skills*

Listed below are typical tactics of a saboteur in group dynamics:

1. Find a scapegoat to blame, or ultimately blame the "social order."
2. Declare that you do not have "the" answer, which gets you out of having any answer at all.
3. For every proposal made, come up with an opposite so that the middle ground (no proposal at all) appears to be the wisest choice.
4. Argue that the group must not move too rapidly, which avoids the necessity of getting started.
5. Point out how any attempt to reach a conclusion is a "futile quest for certainty" and that doubt promotes growth so that, if challenged, you say something that nobody in the group can understand.
6. Look slightly embarrassed when the problem is brought up, hinting that it is in bad taste or too simplistic to discuss.
7. Point out that no problem can be separated from any other problem, so no problem can be solved until all problems have been solved.
8. Suggest that the problem is simply a projection by unhappy group members of their personal problems onto the group.
9. Ask what is meant by the question, which will consume the discussion until time runs out.
10. Point out all sides of every issue to hide your own indecisiveness behind the illusion of objectivity.
11. Insist that the group wait until an expert can be consulted.
12. Retreat into general objectives on which everybody agrees but that are so general that they do not suggest a course of action.
13. Give heartfelt thanks to the person raising the problem and praise the profound discussion the problem has stimulated before declaring the meeting closed.

Note. From "How to Become a More Sophisticated Saboteur in Groups" (pp. 87–88), by B. Gertz, 1969, in C. R. Mill (Ed.), *Selections From Human Relations Training News,* Washington, DC: NTL Institute. Copyright 1969 by NTL Institute. Adapted with permission.

3. Can you identify examples where you have seen these strategies at work?
4. Are there strategies for making groups work better as well?
5. Do some cultures use these strategies more than others?

INSIGHT   Multicultural groups are vulnerable to intentional and unintentional saboteurs.

23 DESCRIBING CULTURAL IDENTITY

Objectives: To identify the complex culturally learned roles and perspectives that contribute to an individual's identity and to become more aware of one's multiple memberships in different cultural groups.

TIME REQUIRED   30 minutes or less

RISK LEVEL   Moderate

PARTICIPANTS NEEDED   Any number of participants, plus one facilitator

PROCEDURE   Please take the following steps:

1. Ask participants to write answers to the simple question "Who are you?" They should give as many answers as they can think of.
2. Write the answers (a format is suggested in Exhibit 2.6) in the order that participants suggest them.
3. Go along fairly quickly. Allow participants 7 minutes.

DEBRIEFING   Think about the following questions:

1. If you had the time, would you be able to list a larger number of identities for yourself?
2. Which identities are most important to you?
3. How can these multiple identities be helpful to you?
4. Are all these identities equally strong for you?
5. Is there a maximum number of identities for an individual?

Note. From *Culture-Centered Counseling Interventions: Striving for Accuracy* (pp. 25–26), by P. B. Pedersen, 1997, Thousand Oaks, CA: Sage. Copyright 1997 by Sage. Adapted with permission.

Exhibit 2.6   *Cultural Identities and Group Membership*

Complete the list indicating your cultural roles.

I am _____

I am _____

I am _____

I am _____

I am _____

I am _____

I am _____

I am _____

I am _____

I am _____

Note. From *Culture-Centered Counseling Interventions: Striving for Accuracy* (pp. 25–26), by P. B. Pedersen, 1997, Thousand Oaks, CA: Sage. Copyright 1997 by Sage. Adapted with permission.

INSIGHT   Each of us belongs to many different potentially salient cultural identities at the same time.

24 INTERPRETING A PROJECTIVE PICTURE

Objective: To help multicultural group members identify similarities and differences in their perception of an ambiguous picture.

TIME REQUIRED	30 minutes or less
RISK LEVEL	Moderate
PARTICIPANTS NEEDED	Any number of participants may be involved, plus one facilitator
PROCEDURE	Please take the following steps:

1. Show the picture in Figure 2.1 to members of a multicultural group, and ask the group members to shout out what they see happening in this ambiguous drawing in as much detail as possible.
2. Ask the following questions:
   a. Who are these people?
   b. What is each person doing?
   c. What objects are shown in the drawing?
   d. What are the clues that helped you identify what is happening?

DEBRIEFING The facilitator can lead a discussion on the meaning of similarities and differences in the participants' descriptions. Some discussion questions might include the following:

1. Were you able to see several different possible interpretations of the drawing?
2. Did smaller details of the drawing take on symbolic meaning for you?
3. How would you score people's different responses to this drawing?
4. Would this experience work equally well in all cultures?
5. What did you learn about yourself from your responses to the drawing?

INSIGHT Perception is more important than reality in our decision-making processes.

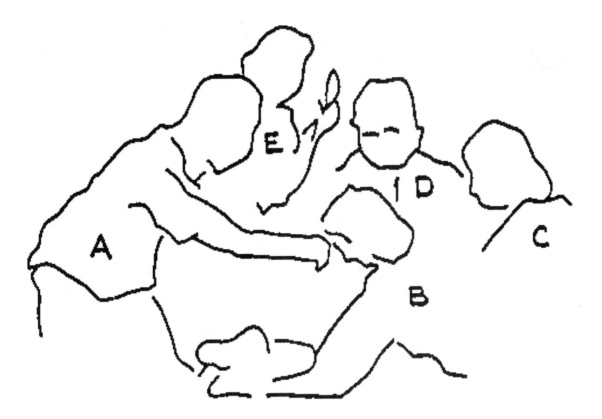

Figure 2.1. An unspecified group of people doing an unspecified activity.

25 DRAWING SYMBOLS OF YOUR CULTURE

Objective: To describe nonverbally the events and symbols of your culture as a means to understand other people's cultures.

TIME REQUIRED   30 minutes or less

RISK LEVEL   Moderate

PARTICIPANTS NEEDED   Any number of participants, plus one facilitator

PROCEDURE   Please take the following steps:

1. Have every group member spend 5 minutes drawing symbols (designs, figures, stick-figures, scribbles, and anything else, *but no words*) that demonstrate how that member has been influenced through participation in the group thus far. Alternative topics could be "your culture" or "your cultural identity."
2. When everyone has finished or when a time limit of about 10 minutes is up, have members of the group (or subgroups if the group is larger than five people) describe and explain their drawings of the symbolic ways they have been influenced and maybe have influenced others through their interaction in the group.

DEBRIEFING   The leader might want to point out that the drawings indicate both similarities and differences among individual members. By avoiding the use of words, the experience is focused on the emotional and nonverbal aspects of the member's influence, and typically the discussion becomes much less abstract or intellectualized as a result. Some discussion questions include the following:

Note. From *A Handbook for Developing Multicultural Awareness* (3rd ed., p. 81), by P. B. Pedersen, 2000, Alexandria, VA: American Counseling Association. Copyright 2000 by the American Counseling Association. Adapted with permission. No further reproduction authorized without written permission of the American Counseling Association.

1. Which symbols were shared across all or most students as common ground?
2. Which symbols were more unique?
3. What did you learn about yourself and others from this experience?
4. Do symbols work better than words in describing the meaning of your culture?
5. Which symbols were most important for you?

INSIGHT   Symbols may be more descriptive than words in talking about culture.

26 GEOMETRIC SYMBOLS OF CULTURAL VALUES

Objective: To use geometric shapes as symbolic metaphors for describing cultural values.

TIME REQUIRED   30 minutes or less

RISK LEVEL   Moderate

PARTICIPANTS NEEDED   Any number of participants, plus one facilitator

PROCEDURE   Please take the following steps:

1. Ask participants to close their eyes and imagine a perfectly shaped circle, square, triangle, and scribble (formless tangle of lines).
2. Have participants identify which geometric symbol they like first, second, third, and fourth, in their own preference, for whatever reason.
3. Next, ask them to write down the order of their preference for each symbolic form.
4. When all participants have written down their preferences, provide the following interpretation.
   a. The rounded form of a circle is often found in sensual or sexual images and might indicate sexuality as a valued preference.
   b. The right angles of a square indicate rationality and intelligence as a valued preference or cultural value.
   c. The triangle is present in many religious symbols, art, architecture, and other forms and indicates stability.
   d. The scribble indicates creativity as a valued preference.

DEBRIEFING   Participants may agree or disagree with the hierarchy of value preferences indicated by these symbolic geometric forms. The interpretations of these symbols just described is not based on empirical psychological data and should not be taken too seriously by the participants or the facilitator. Rather, they serve to demonstrate the presence of cultural similarities and differences among students. Some discussion questions include the following:

1. To what extent did you agree with the interpretation of your choices?
2. What are other significant differences and similarities in your group?
3. Which cultures do you associate with these conventional interpretations?
4. Would you change your worldview if you could?
5. What are the dangers of simplistic tests such as this one?

INSIGHT   Symbols may provide valuable indirect insights about our valued preferences.

27 A FREE DRAWING TEST

Objective: To discover subconscious responses to culture-loaded concepts.

TIME REQUIRED   30 minutes

RISK LEVEL   High

PARTICIPANTS NEEDED   Any number of participants, plus one facilitator

PROCEDURE   Please take the following steps:

1. Select a number of word concepts (e.g., nouns, verbs) that seem to participants to be clearly related to their respective cultures.
2. Ask each person to draw an X in the middle of a blank sheet of paper.
3. Ask each person to place his or her pencil on the center of the X and begin drawing when the facilitator mentions one of the previously selected concepts. The participants should not be given any guidance on what to draw but merely instructed to form one continuous line in any direction or shape as they are motivated by the announced concept, without lifting their pen or pencil from the paper.
4. Advise the participants to use a new page for each concept.
5. Apply a scoring method to compare the drawings, assigning a score according to whether the drawing is open, closed, large, small, complex, simple, angular, or rounded; whether it required more time or less time to complete; how many directional changes or reversals there are; and whether any recognizable picture begins or ends with an upstroke or downstroke. The group may suggest other

---

Note. From *A Manual of Structured Experiences for Cross-Cultural Learning* (p. 77), by W. H. Weeks, P. B. Pedersen, and R. W. Brislin, 1977, Yarmouth, ME: Intercultural Press. Copyright 1977 by Intercultural Press. Adapted with permission.

criteria to compare the drawings growing out of apparent similarities and differences.

Discuss whether similarities and differences in the drawings seem to coincide with cultural differences in the group in terms of the covert effects culture has on behavior. Questions for discussion may include the following:

1. What are the similarities and differences in your drawings as you let the pen respond to the word?
2. Were you able to interpret your drawings as they related to culturally connected words?
3. Were you surprised by any of the drawings?
4. If you were to repeat the drawing for culturally connected words, would the drawings be similar?
5. How would others interpret your drawings, and why?

We are not consciously aware of all our culturally learned patterns.

28 DIALOGUE WITHIN OURSELVES

Objective: To hear the multitude of voices in one's self-talk to demonstrate how cultural roles influence one's thinking.

TIME REQUIRED   30 minutes or less

RISK LEVEL   High

PARTICIPANTS NEEDED   Any number of participants, plus one facilitator

PROCEDURE   Please take the following steps:

1. Select a cross-cultural subject that produces ambivalent or controversial thoughts and feelings within the students.
2. Ask the students to tune in to their ambivalent thoughts and listen to the several sides of their internal dialogue, according to their different cultural roles.
3. Instruct students to write down, as a script of a play or transcript of a conversation, the dialogue between their several internal voices.
4. Have students identify the evidence of cultural bias and self-reference in their scripts or transcripts.

DEBRIEFING   Internal dialogue is more chaotic and inconsistent than verbal dialogue, so it will be difficult to focus on an imaginary conversation between two contrasting identities or "selves" in one's own mind. We don't think in complete sentences and often ramble in discontinuous ways, interrupted by other competing thoughts that may be entirely irrelevant to the topic under discussion. The student needs to take control of the dialogue and impose some rules just as might be needed when moderating a group of

---

Note. From *A Manual of Structured Experiences for Cross-Cultural Learning* (p. 77), by W. H. Weeks, P. B. Pedersen, and R. W. Brislin, 1977, Yarmouth, ME: Intercultural Press. Copyright 1977 by Intercultural Press. Adapted with permission.

people discussing a controversial issue. It will help if the student can assign a name to each participant in the imaginary discussion, guided by their contrasting agenda and needs. Some questions for discussion might include:

1. How did you decide which "imaginary voices" to allow into the dialogue?
2. Were you surprised by any of the things one or the other person mentioned during this imaginary dialogue?
3. What examples of cultural bias were demonstrated during the dialogue?
4. What strategies did the positive or negative voice use in this imaginary dialogue?
5. How did this experience help you better understand the thinking process?

INSIGHT   Our internal dialogue is a discussion between the positive and negative voices of our culturally defined roles.

29 PREDICTING THE DECISIONS OF A RESOURCE PERSON

Objective: To learn how people from other cultures make decisions.

TIME REQUIRED 30 minutes or less

RISK LEVEL High

PARTICIPANTS NEEDED Any number of participants, plus one facilitator and one culturally different community resource person

PROCEDURE Please take the following steps:

1. Select an articulate and authentic resource person from the community, and bring that resource person into the classroom.
2. Ask the resource person to describe the events leading up to a decision, but do not disclose the decision he or she made.
3. Ask each student to guess what the resource person decided and why.
4. When all students have guessed what the resource person decided, the resource person explains what decision he or she made and why.

DEBRIEFING It is a good idea for the instructor to have worked with the resource person ahead of time and coached that person to help teach the concepts of logical consequences or reflection of meaning, as they are different in each cultural context. In debriefing this exercise, the instructor should allow participants to ask questions directly of the resource person and back off as a leader as much as possible. Questions for discussion include the following:

1. Did you agree with the resource person's decision, and if so, why?
2. Did you disagree with the resource person's decision, and if so, why?
3. Did the resource person represent the perspective of others from that same group in the community?

4. Was the resource person able to change your mind about an appropriate response to the decision?
5. What would have been the consequences of your working with this resource person before understanding how that person made decisions?

INSIGHT   The self-reference criterion that reflects our own view may not apply to others.

30 CAPTURING CULTURAL METAPHORS AND SIMILES

Objective: To describe objects in the room using metaphors and similes as a means to explain characteristics of oneself that may be difficult to express directly.

TIME REQUIRED   30 minutes or less

RISK LEVEL   High

PARTICIPANTS NEEDED   Any number of participants, plus one facilitator

PROCEDURE   Please take the following steps:

1. Instruct group members to look around the room and find one object that is like them in some way and that represents one or more cultural value from their background. You may model this task by selecting a piece of chalk "that gives of itself until it is finally used up completely" and by describing how you are like that object.
2. Have the participants describe how they are like one or another item in the room in turn. If they have difficulty finding an object in the room, the facilitator can assign them an item; for example, "How are you like that light bulb above us?"
3. Then discuss cultural value similarities and differences among members.

DEBRIEFING   Projecting characteristics of themselves through metaphor and simile helps students express characteristics of their culture, especially if their first language is not English. Some discussion questions include the following:

1. Do you see this experience as giving you any new insights into your identity?
2. Would people from other cultures find this experience helpful or offensive?

3. Which item in the room best represents an important value of yours?
4. Did you learn anything new about others in the group through this experience?
5. Did you learn anything new about yourself through this experience?

INSIGHT   Metaphors and similes are useful for describing cultural values indirectly.

31 MULTICULTURAL GROUP PROCESS RECALL

> *Objective:* To debrief an audiotape or videotape of a multicultural group as a method to find insight into one's internal dialogue during a particular event.

TIME REQUIRED 30 minutes or less

RISK LEVEL High

PARTICIPANTS NEEDED Any number of students, plus one facilitator

PROCEDURE Please take the following steps:

1. Make an audiotape or videotape of a multicultural group for about 30 minutes as the group discusses a topic or does a task of their choice.
2. Play the audiotape or videotape back to the group.
3. Ask group members to stop the recording when they recall feeling or thinking something but not sharing it at that particular time. Examples of comments participants might make at this time include the following:
   a. "What did you mean when you said that?"
   b. "I didn't ask you then, but I would like to ask you now."
   c. "I was feeling . . ."
   d. "Why didn't you talk more?"

DEBRIEFING The facilitator will direct the discussion toward improving the group members' insights into the multicultural group process. Some discussion questions include the following:

1. Were you surprised by anything in the group recording?
2. Were some patterns easier to perceive by listening to or watching the recording?
3. Would this experience work equally well in all cultures?
4. Did the recording change the dynamics of the group in any way?

5. What will you do differently in the future as a result of listening to or viewing this recording?

INSIGHT   Reviewing a recording of the group will help members understand group process dynamics.

32 TESTING THE UNDERLYING "TRUTH"

> *Objective:* To see how people from different cultures experience a different "truth" from the perspective of their cultural values.

TIME REQUIRED   30 minutes or less

RISK LEVEL   High

PARTICIPANTS NEEDED   Any number of participants, plus one facilitator

PROCEDURE   Please take the following steps:

1. Ask each participant to write down a statement he or she believes to be true.
2. As an alternative, the whole group might identify a statement that all members believe to be true.
3. Ask members to write a sentence explaining why the statement is true.
4. Next, ask members to write a second statement explaining why their first explanation is true.
5. Next, ask members to write a third statement explaining why their second explanation is true.
6. You may go on to ask members to write a fourth, fifth, and more statements, but usually by this time the class has become hostile and refuses to continue the experience, perhaps saying, "I don't know or care *why* it's true! It's *just true!*"
7. Ask the participants to present their chain of linked explanations leading back to the statement of truth, and look for similarities and differences among participants' chains of explanations.

DEBRIEFING   When we are pushed back to the reasons behind the reasons of how we define truth (as in arguments on religion or politics or emotional topics), we typically become upset and anxious. Some discussion questions may include:

1. What do we mean by "truth"?
2. Can two contrasting or contradictory ideas both be true?

3. Why do we ignore basic underlying assumptions in our discussions with others?
4. What does "relativism" mean?
5. Has your idea of what is true changed over time?

Insight   People from different cultural backgrounds may believe in similar truths for different reasons or different truths for similar reasons.

33 INFERENCE–OBSERVATION TEST

> *Objective:* To demonstrate the difference between fact and inference to illustrate how often one may assume or infer something to be factual when there is no evidence.

TIME REQUIRED   30 minutes or less

RISK LEVEL   High

PARTICIPANTS NEEDED   Any number of participants, plus one facilitator

PROCEDURE   Please take the following steps:

1. Before distributing the story in Exhibit 2.7, read the following directions to the students: "Assume that all information is accurate. Read carefully. You can refer to the story whenever you wish." You may wish to read the story out loud rather than distribute it in written form.
2. Next, instruct participants to read the statements about the story and to indicate whether each item is true, false, or uncertain. If a participant doubts any part of the statement, he or she should check "uncertain."
3. Direct participants to answer each statement in turn and not to go back and change any answer later. In addition, participants should not reread any statement after they have answered. This will distort their score.

DEBRIEFING   The facilitator needs to be sensitive to the defensiveness of participants whose answers were wrong. Students may be frustrated by the number of wrong answers they have on this test. The challenge to separate fact from inference is difficult. Some discussion questions include the following:

Note. From *Uncritical Inference Test,* by W. V. Haney, 1979. Copyright 1979 by William V. Haney. Adapted with permission. The full-length test is available from International Society for General Semantics, P.O. Box 2469, San Francisco, CA 94126.

Exhibit 2.7   *Inference Test*

The Story

A businessman had just turned off the lights in the store when a man appeared and demanded money. The owner opened a cash register. The contents of the cash register were scooped up, and the man sped away. A member of the police force was notified promptly.

Statements About the Story

Statement	True	False	Uncertain
1. A man appeared after the owner had turned off his store lights.			
2. The robber was a man.			
3. The man who appeared did not demand money.			
4. The man who opened the cash register was the owner.			
5. Someone opened a cash register.			
6. After the man who demanded the money scooped up the contents of the cash register, he ran away.			
7. The cash register contained money, but the story does not state how much.			
8. The robber demanded money of the owner.			
9. It was broad daylight when the man appeared.			
10. No one demanded money.			
11. The story concerns a series of events in which only three persons are referred to: the owner of the store, a man who demanded money, and a member of the police force.			
12. The following events occurred: Someone demanded money, a cash register was opened, its contents were scooped up, and a man dashed out of the store.			

(continued)

1. Distinguish what you mean by fact from what you mean by inference.
2. To what extent can we be sure we are not presenting our inferences as fact?
3. Why is this distinction especially important in discussing other cultures?
4. Do different cultures have different notions of what is factual?
5. What constitutes evidence to prove something to be factual?

INSIGHT   Sometimes, particularly in multicultural settings, we confuse inference with fact.

Exhibit 2.7   *Inference Test (Continued)*

Inference–Observation Answers

Statement number	Correct answer	Explanation
1.	Uncertain	Do you know that the "businessman" and the "owner" are one and the same?
2.	Uncertain	Was there necessarily a robbery involved here? Perhaps the man was the rent collector or the owner's son—they sometimes demand money.
3.	False	An easy one, to keep up the test taker's morale.
4.	Uncertain	Was the owner a man?
5.	True	The story says that the owner opened the cash register.
6.	Uncertain	We don't know who scooped up the contents of the cash register or that the man necessarily ran away.
7.	Uncertain	The sentence is unclear—the cash register may or may not have contained money.
8.	Uncertain	Again, a robber?
9.	Uncertain	Stores generally keep lights on during the day.
10.	False	The story says that the man who appeared demanded money.
11.	Uncertain	Are the businessman and the owner one and the same, or two different people? The same goes for the owner and the man who appeared.
12.	Uncertain	"Dashed"? Could he not have "sped away" on roller skates or in a car? And do we know that he actually left the store? We don't even know that he entered it.

Note. From *Uncritical Inference Test,* by W. V. Haney, 1979. Copyright 1979 by William V. Haney. Adapted with permission. The full-length test is available from International Society for General Semantics, P.O. Box 2469, San Francisco, CA 94126.

34 THE TEST OF REASONABLE OPPOSITES

Objective: To challenge one's prevailing culturally learned assumptions about a topic or issue and to evaluate the opposite view as possibly rational.

TIME REQUIRED   30 minutes or less

RISK LEVEL   High

PARTICIPANTS NEEDED   Any number of participants, plus one facilitator

PROCEDURE   Please take the following steps:

1. Identify a culturally learned assumption that you have assumed to be true.
2. Identify an alternative position that would reverse that assumption and constitute an opposite position.
3. Compare the two statements to see which alternative is more reasonable.
4. Some examples of opposite positions include the following:
   a. Differences are important. Similarities are important.
   b. Counseling decreases pain. Counseling increases pain.
   c. Clients should come to counseling. Counseling should come to clients.

DEBRIEFING   Assumptions are usually so fuzzy that it is hard to find an opposite to what you assume. Once an opposite position has been generated, it is often as reasonable as the original statement. The test of reasonable opposites forces one to generate new and creative alternatives that one would never have considered. Some discussion questions include the following:

1. Were you able to find a reasonable opposite to something you always believed to be true?
2. What makes an idea reasonable?
3. What are the implications of two opposite positions both being reasonable?

4. Is our thinking nonrational?
5. Might two people from different countries disagree without either one being wrong?

INSIGHT   We need to escape from our own self-reference criteria to see other cultural perspectives.

■ CHAPTER THREE ■

LONGER ONE-HOUR EXPERIENCES

The experiences described in this chapter require more time than the brief warm-up experiences in chapter 2. These experiences will fit into a 50-minute class period without difficulty and can be extended by providing a more comprehensive debriefing. It will be useful to prepare the students in the class meeting before the experience takes place and to debrief students on what they learned during the class meeting after the experience has taken place.

Most, if not all, of the guidelines provided in chapter 2 on brief experiences also apply to these longer experiences, the main difference being that more time is allowed for the latter. The additional time allows the instructor to help the class recover from any misunderstandings or mistakes that might arise during the experience. These longer experiences are sometimes safer than the brief experiences, where there is time to get into trouble but no time to recover.

The instructor using the experiences in this chapter needs to monitor events carefully. For this reason it is recommended that the instructor not participate as a member, but rather observe from the outside so that he or she can prevent any potentially embarrassing or unnecessarily stressful situation and, if necessary, stop the experience prematurely.

35 TALKING ABOUT MULTICULTURALISM IN PRIMARY GRADES

> *Objective:* To teach young children that they are both the same as and different from others.

TIME REQUIRED   About an hour

RISK LEVEL   Low

PARTICIPANTS NEEDED   Any number of multiethnic primary or intermediate school children, plus one facilitator

PROCEDURE   Please take the following steps:

1. Assemble the students in a large group in the center of the floor. Tables and chairs should be moved to one side or to a corner of the room.
2. Give the children directions for separating into groups, such as "All those wearing red move to the right side of the room, and all those not wearing red move to the left side of the room." The "team" that assembles first "wins" that set. A list of neutral characteristics that would be likely to divide the group should be decided on beforehand. Other appropriate divisions could be by shoe color (e.g., black, brown, and other-colored shoes), clothes patterns (e.g., those wearing stripes and those not wearing stripes), and other similarly neutral categories.
3. Continue to provide directions to create other ways to divide the group in a series of sets.
4. After the group has become familiar with the experience, use more personal group divisions such as hair color, eye color, height, or other characteristics of

---

Note. From *Decisional Dialogues in a Cultural Context: Structured Exercises* (p. 21), by P. B. Pedersen and D. Hernandez, 1997, Thousand Oaks, CA: Sage. Copyright 1997 by Sage. Adapted with permission.

the individuals. The more obviously cultural differences such as sex, national background, race, and so forth should be saved for the end.

DEBRIEFING   The experience should follow a lecture or class discussion about prejudice, discrimination, or problems people from some cultures have experienced as a result of being different.

After the experience the discussion could center around racial and cultural differences being just one of the significant components of our individuality that define us but that should not be used to evaluate our worth. (The experience may be somewhat noisy and chaotic, so other classes in the area should be warned of the possible noise.)

Additionally, the discussion might focus on the role of competition both in the experience, where the students were on different teams for each set, and in real life, where people who are different struggle against one another. The students might be encouraged to share incidents of how they have experienced differentness in themselves and in others. Some discussion questions include the following:

1. Can you identify similarities between yourself and others in the group?
2. Can you identify differences between yourself and others in the group?
3. Can you see how someone very different from you might share your ideas at the same time?
4. Can you see how someone very similar to you in some ways might also be different from you in other ways?
5. Why is it important to look at both similarities and differences at the same time?

INSIGHT   The shifting dynamics of salience similarity are balanced with differences across cultures.

36 HAPPY HELL OR LONELY HEAVEN: THE BRAIN DRAIN PROBLEM

> *Objective:* To personalize the dilemma facing international students trying to decide whether or not to return home after studying abroad.

TIME REQUIRED   At least an hour

RISK LEVEL   Low

PARTICIPANTS NEEDED   A group where at least half the members are international students, plus one facilitator

PROCEDURE   Please take the following steps:

1. Distribute the case examples in Exhibit 3.1 describing problems experienced by international students who have returned home after study abroad.
2. Ask the participants to identify a case example they could role-play effectively.
3. Ask each participant in turn to study the case example and then stand before the other participants role-playing the returnee in that particular case. The other participants will provide advice and suggestions to the person role-playing the returnee for about 10 minutes.
4. After 10 minutes in role, have the returnee go out of role and give feedback about the suggestions and advice he or she was given.

Note. From "Happy Hell or Lonely Heaven: The Brain Drain Problem," by P. B. Pedersen and K. S. Lee, 2000, *The Asian Journal of Counseling,* 7(2), pp. 61–84. Copyright 2000 by The Hong Kong Professional Counselling Association and The Chinese University of Hong Kong. Adapted with permission from the Hong Kong Institute of Educational Research, The Chinese University of Hong Kong, Sha Tin, New Territories, Hong Kong.

Exhibit 3.1 *International Student Case Studies*

Case Study 1: Research Facilities

The returnee is an associate professor in engineering. He finished his PhD in the United States, took a temporary teaching job there for several years, and is now back in Taiwan. Although his home university department has been supportive of his research and very encouraging, he is frustrated by the lack of research equipment. The promised computer facilities have not yet been installed, and there are not enough books and research materials in the library on recent developments. Also, there is no support or facilities for organizing an international research conference he would like to do. This situation makes it very difficult for him to do even basic research in his specialized field. He has been thinking about returning to the United States. His wife has a sister in New York and would like to live in the United States permanently. He is thinking of applying for a position to teach in the United States. After graduation his academic advisor had suggested that he remain and they work on a research grant together. He is certain that this opportunity is still available. However, he likes living in Taiwan, enjoys being with his friends and family, and feels that the interpersonal relationships in Taiwan are closer and more satisfying than in the United States. Also, he feels loyal to his home university and does not want to leave so soon after starting his new job.

Case Study 2: Promotion

The returnee is a manager in a small company in Taiwan. Although he enjoys his work and gets along well with the other engineers on his team, he feels that the system of promotion and salary allocation is unfair. The pay scale is based solely on seniority and does not consider the employee's ability. This seems especially unfair to the returning students who have been abroad and are highly trained. The returnee has little chance of promotion, because so many of his colleagues have worked there longer than he has. These policies seem like a waste of human resources, and he wonders what can be done about it. The other managers do not seem to mind, but they have all been there longer than the returnee and have not been abroad for their studies.

Case Study 3: Work Relationships

The returnee has just returned from a U.S. university to Taiwan, where he is now an industrial engineer in the import–export field. In his new position, he finds that some of his colleagues are uncomfortable around him. Some of them seem to distrust him and envy him because he studied abroad. It was especially difficult at first, because his boss respected his opinion a great deal, and some of his colleagues resented this. Although they respect his training and his advanced degree, they have difficulty relating to him. His boss is planning to promote him to an administrative position that has nothing to do with his area of training, and he is frustrated at not being able to use his skills and training.

(continued)

DEBRIEFING

In debriefing this experience, the instructor will need to make sure that the other participants know that this is a role-play and not a self-disclosure by the role-playing volunteer. Discussion questions may include the following:

1. Why should an international student return home after graduation?
2. Why should an international student remain in the United States after graduation?
3. Was it difficult to role-play the returnee?
4. Which suggestions by the other participants seemed most helpful?
5. What would you expect the returnee to do in the future, and why?

INSIGHT

The reentry decision is a difficult choice for international student graduates, and the final choice may not always be what others from the home or host culture expect.

Exhibit 3.1   *International Student Case Studies (Continued)*

Case Study 4: Government

The returnee has been in Taiwan for several months after spending 5 years in graduate school in the United States. Although he was happy to return to Taiwan, he wishes that the political environment were a bit more liberal. He feels that the Taiwan government lacks flexibility. The Taiwan government does not respect the opinions of the people, in his opinion. He feels that the government should become more liberal so that people have the right to discuss their positions and argue for their viewpoints. Although he realizes that it is difficult to change a political system, he wishes there were more tolerance for individual viewpoints and individual rights. He believes that Taiwan would be a stronger country if this were the case. The returnee does not want to appear dissatisfied, so he does not express his opinions about this matter to others. It would be easier to leave than to try and change things.

Case Study 5: Family

The graduate returned to Taiwan recently after spending 5 years at a U.S. graduate school. When she first arrived in the United States, it was difficult to take care of herself because she was used to sharing responsibilities with her family. Soon she came to like and even prefer taking care of herself as an individual. When she returned to Taiwan, she was reminded that, as an individual, she is not very important. What is important is her responsibility to the family. In her extended family, she is an only child and lives with her parents. She realizes that it will take some time to readjust to her family system, but sometimes she feels torn between family responsibility and her own individual plans for the future.

Case Study 6: Professional Competence

The graduate returned to Taiwan 3 months ago after studying in the United States. She considered remaining in the United States because she had been offered a postdoctoral position to stay on and continue her research. However, she felt she should return home out of duty. She is now an assistant professor in Taiwan and is finding it difficult to continue her research. Her teaching load is demanding, and it is taking a lot of time just to get used to her new job. Also, she spends a lot of time training new research assistants. There is a high turnover of assistants because their pay is very low. She may eventually have the opportunity to go abroad again to do research through a university exchange program, but this probably won't be possible for at least 5 years. She is worried about falling behind in her field and not staying competitive. She would like to return to the United States and take a postdoctoral position that is still available.

Case Study 7: Inconvenience

The graduate returned to Taiwan after living in the United States for 8 years. She is now living in Taiwan and is surprised to find that there are aspects of living there that seem inconvenient. It seems that the traffic jams, the noise, the crowding, and especially the pollution have all gotten much worse than they were before she left. It also bothers her that people do not seem to care about the environment. There is no administrative or government incentive to change things. People seem very selfish in establishing new laws for their own profit that damage the environment. They do not consider the possible consequences to the whole society. The problems of bureaucracy seem overwhelming. She feels that the Taiwan she left behind to study abroad is gone forever.

Case Study 8: Education

The graduate returned to Taiwan after receiving a doctorate with honors in the United States. He has been teaching at a university in Taiwan and thinks that there are some problems with the educational system in Taiwan. There seems to be a great deal of pressure on students to achieve. The best students, therefore, seem to leave Taiwan to study abroad and often do not return, leaving the universities and corporations with a shortage of human resources and administrative instability. The returnee would like the educational system to be more like education in the United States, where the demands are more realistic, which would give incentives for students to stay in Taiwan rather than go abroad to study. None of the returnee's colleagues have been to the United States, and they are unacquainted with the U.S. educational system. They resent the returnee's criticism of education in Taiwan.

(continued)

Exhibit 3.1 *International Student Case Studies (Continued)*

Case Study 9: Job Satisfaction

The graduate returned to Taiwan after completing a PhD in computer science. When she returned she obtained a position as administrator in a public hospital. Although her work is related to computer science, it does not allow her to use her computer knowledge as much as she hoped it would. Her salary is less than it would be if she were working in a corporation, where her parents prefer that she work. She believes that she can make a better contribution in the public hospital, even though she is dissatisfied there. She enjoys the administrative aspects of her job, but she wishes that she could use more of her specialized training. She fears that she will fall behind in her profession if she has no opportunities to use her skills.

Case Study 10: Personal Matters

The returnee has been in Taiwan for several months after completing graduate work in the United States. He is discovering that he has difficulties sometimes with his family and friends. For one thing, they seem to ask him very personal questions about his private life and personal affairs. Also, his friends drop in to see him without calling first. This is particularly bothersome when he is trying to work at home. His friends seem extremely insensitive to his need for privacy. He realizes that since living in the United States, he has become used to having more privacy. He feels really inconvenienced now because he wants to establish his own style of living, independent of his family and others. He doesn't see how he can succeed in his profession unless he can live his own life as he chooses.

Case Study 11: Practical Training

The graduate is completing her practical training in a major public library in the United States. She received her master's degree in library science from a U.S. university as a sponsored student and has lived in the United States for almost 4 years. While she was applying for a practical training visa, her employer in her home country suggested that she return home or lose her old position in Taiwan. The graduate consulted her academic advisor, who encouraged her to expand her professional goals. She decided to stay in the United States and accept the new assignment. Her previous employer in Taiwan wrote her to say she must return home after completing her practical training for a new assignment in testing and measurement, where she will supervise a staff who have built that division in the past 5 years. She does not feel competent in the testing and measurement area. The returnee is confused and worried and feels helpless. She is 32 years old and single, which is no problem in the United States but a big problem back in Taiwan. She has learned to like suburban living, but back in Taiwan she will live in a city of more than six million people. She likes the freedom of having her own car, but in Taiwan she will have to live with relatives and use public transportation.

Case Study 12: Marriage

The graduate completed her master's degree in the United States as a sponsored student after 3 years of study. Last year she married an American student who is Catholic, which shocked her family back home. None of her family came for the wedding, and most of her close friends from Taiwan who were in the United States also did not attend the wedding. Her family is traditionally Confucian. Her 2-year scholarship has expired, and she supports herself as a graduate assistant. She is delaying the completion of her doctorate so that her husband can graduate first. He has applied for several positions in the United States and has been promised an internship at a major corporation with good pay but no benefits. The graduate just discovered she is pregnant. Her health insurance applies only as long as she is a student. Her employer back in Taiwan has called and asked her to complete her degree and return home as soon as possible to begin fulfilling the 2-year requirement to work in Taiwan after graduation. If she returns to Taiwan, she will lose medical benefits, and her husband will lose the internship.

Note. From "Happy Hell or Lonely Heaven: The Brain Drain Problem," by P. B. Pedersen and K. S. Lee, 2000, *The Asian Journal of Counseling, 7*(2), pp. 61–84. Copyright 2000 by The Hong Kong Professional Counselling Association and The Chinese University of Hong Kong. Adapted with permission from the Hong Kong Institute of Educational Research, The Chinese University of Hong Kong, Sha Tin, New Territories, Hong Kong.

37 A CLASSROOM DEBATE

> *Objective:* To use a debate format in giving people from several cultures the opportunity to express their different viewpoints.

TIME REQUIRED   A week of preparation and an hour in class

RISK LEVEL   Low

PARTICIPANTS NEEDED   Students for two debate teams, plus observers–scorers and one facilitator

PROCEDURE   Please take the following steps:

1. Select a debate topic and assign the two teams to debate the topic.
2. Ensure that the participants have time beforehand to prepare for the arguments and to collect supporting data to present during the debate.
3. Present the topic and format of the debate. An example topic of a debate might be the following:
   - Side 1: Cultural differences need more emphasis to define one's culture in specific terms that highlight the separate identity of each group.
   - Side 2: Cultural similarities need more emphasis to show how we are all working together toward shared goals and responsibilities irrespective of differences.

   An example format of the debate might be as follows:

   - Side 1 presents opening arguments, with three members each giving a 3-minute statement.
   - Side 2 presents opening arguments, with three members each giving a 3-minute statement.
   - Side 1 has 3 minutes for rebuttal.
   - Side 2 has 3 minutes for a rebuttal.
   - Side 1 has 3 minutes for a second rebuttal.

Exhibit 3.2 *Scorecard for Debate Experience*

Scoring criteria: Rate each team on each criterion from 1 = low to 10 = high.

Criterion	Team 1 score	Team 2 score
1. Analytical skill		
2. Clarity of argument and position		
3. Sophistication of argument		
4. Integration of theory and practice		
5. Relation of argument to reported research		
6. Relation of argument to current events		
7. Effective presentation skills		
8. General effort involved by the team		
9. Innovative and creative ideas		
10. Ability to work within the stated time limits		

- Side 2 has 3 minutes for a second rebuttal.
- Side 1 has 5 minutes for a conclusion.
- Side 2 has 5 minutes for a conclusion.

4. The rest of the class will score the debate using the scorecard in Exhibit 3.2.

DEBRIEFING Complicated cultural issues can be clarified by listening to the arguments by advocates for each side. Taking sides makes an otherwise abstract cultural issue more personal. Some questions for discussion are:

1. Did you believe in the point of view you were presenting?
2. Do you think those on the other side of this debate believed in the viewpoint they were presenting?
3. Did the debate help you balance the positive and negative aspects of both sides?
4. Is it possible for one side to be completely right?
5. What are the dangers of oversimplifying a viewpoint on a cultural issue?

INSIGHT There are at least two sides to every culturally defined issue.

38 TWO CULTURAL PERSPECTIVES OF EDUCATION

Objective: To identify different beliefs about education in a multicultural group.

TIME REQUIRED   About an hour

RISK LEVEL   Low

PARTICIPANTS NEEDED   Any number of participants, plus one facilitator

PROCEDURE   Please take the following steps:

1. Read the following directions to a group: "In multicultural education generally, it seems to me that we teacher-learners are in the middle of an argument. Our problem is to restate the argument in such a way that we can find a balance. This experience is about trying to understand what we know about cultural patterns for learning wherever they occur and to see what the implications are for classroom situations. An expression of the argument is through a sampling of the value conflicts it contains in two contrasting cultural perspectives of education."

2. Ask the students to circle the number in Exhibit 3.3 that reflects their level of commitment to their own basic focus on the role of education in society.

3. Ask the students to count up their scores. Higher scores indicate a preference for society-centered education, and lower scores indicate a preference for individual-centered education.

4. Divide the students into small groups to compare and discuss similarities and differences.

Note. From *Culture-Centered Counseling Interventions: Striving for Accuracy* (p. 11), by P. B. Pedersen, 1997, Thousand Oaks, CA: Sage. Copyright 1997 by Sage. Adapted with permission.

Exhibit 3.3   *Rating Scale for Contrasting Perspectives of Educational Emphasis*

Individual perspective								Society perspective
Child-centeredness	1	2	3	4	5	6	7	Subject-centeredness
Guidance	1	2	3	4	5	6	7	Instruction
Discussion	1	2	3	4	5	6	7	Lecture
Pupil planning	1	2	3	4	5	6	7	Teacher planning
Intrinsic motivation	1	2	3	4	5	6	7	Extrinsic motivation
Insight learning	1	2	3	4	5	6	7	Drill and practice
Growth	1	2	3	4	5	6	7	Achievement
Firsthand experience	1	2	3	4	5	6	7	Vicarious experience
Freedom	1	2	3	4	5	6	7	Dominance
Democratic view	1	2	3	4	5	6	7	Authoritarian view
Subjective world	1	2	3	4	5	6	7	Objective world
Spontaneity	1	2	3	4	5	6	7	Conformity

Note. From *Culture-Centered Counseling Interventions: Striving for Accuracy* (p. 11), by P. B. Pedersen, 1997, Thousand Oaks, CA: Sage. Copyright 1997 by Sage. Adapted with permission.

DEBRIEFING   Each culture defines its own unique preference for educational methods. These assumptions are typically implicit and are seldom examined directly. Here are some questions for discussion:

1. Were you surprised by similarities with responses by others? Why?
2. Were you surprised by differences from responses by others? Why?
3. Can you see the advantages and disadvantages of each extreme perspective?
4. Is there one best way to educate in all cultures?
5. How can you accommodate both perspectives in a multicultural classroom?

INSIGHT   There is more than one way to look at the ideal educational process.

39 TWO LEVELS OF COMMUNICATION IN THE MILITARY CULTURE

Objective: To rehearse ways of managing conflict by identifying unspoken messages in military contexts.

TIME REQUIRED   About an hour

RISK LEVEL   Low

PARTICIPANTS NEEDED   At least two role-players from different cultures in the military, with an "alter ego" for each, plus one facilitator

PROCEDURE   Role-players will read the following scripts and continue spontaneously in a conversation, and the alter ego will participate in the script and provide feedback after the script ends.

Commander

Commander:	Our unit has the best racial climate on the base, and I'm sure you'll agree.
Alter Ego:	This should stop any further questions.
Second Lieutenant (SL):	That depends on how you look at it.
Alter Ego:	Personally, I think it's the worst on base.

Supervisor

Supervisor:	I talk things over with my people before I act.
Alter Ego:	These people know nothing about management.
SL:	That's a good procedure to follow.
Alter Ego:	Then why am I here with a complaint in my hand?

Client

Client: This supervisor I work for is always on my back about something, like my work or my "looks."

Alter Ego: I know this guy is going to get me out of this.

SL: Why do you think he's always after you?

Alter Ego: OK, now tell me what you've done.

Two Social Actions Personnel (Captain and Master Sergeant [MSgt])

Captain: This Staff Assistance Visit will probably be a touchy situation. The Commander wants an in-depth report. Do you think you can handle it, or should I take it?

Alter Ego: I sure don't want this thing screwed up.

MSgt: Yes, I can handle it about as well as anyone else.

Alter Ego: The heck with it, you think I'm going to screw it up anyway.

DEBRIEFING   Some discussion questions may include the following:

1. Do you believe rank and service branch function like cultures?
2. How does reframing military communication into cultural categories facilitate interviews?
3. How accurate were the alter ego role-plays to the internal dialogue?
4. How will you use what you learned in this experience?
5. What are the possible negative consequences of this experience?

INSIGHT   Multilevel communication is particularly important in contact with people from other cultures.

40 THE PLURAL VERSUS THE SINGULAR CULTURAL PERSPECTIVE

Objective: To contrast the cultural focus on the individual self versus the focus on the group by understanding that the words we use make a great deal of difference in how we are understood.

TIME REQUIRED   About an hour

RISK LEVEL   Low

PARTICIPANTS NEEDED   Any number of students, plus one facilitator

PROCEDURE   Please take the following steps:

1. Suggest that the group reflect on or discuss their experiences in the classroom thus far in two brief (5- to 8-minute) episodes.
2. In the first episode, everyone will use an individualistic perspective exclusively and speak *only* in the first person singular (i.e., I, me, my) and *not* in the plural.
3. In the second episode everyone will use *only* a collectivistic perspective (i.e., we, our) and avoid using the singular.

DEBRIEFING   The content of the discussion will be influenced by the individualistic and the collectivistic perspective. Some discussion questions include the following:

1. Was the plural or the singular easier for you to use?
2. How did the plural or singular change the content of your discussion?
3. Which cultures are more likely to use the plural voice?
4. Which cultures are more likely to use the singular voice?
5. Can you learn to intentionally change from plural to singular and back again when appropriate?

INSIGHT   The words we use influence and are influenced by who we are.

41 THE IMPORTANCE OF KEY WORDS IN A TRANSCRIPT

> *Objective:* To identify key words in a transcript and understand their importance to demonstrate how some words are more important than others, particularly in communication across cultures.

TIME REQUIRED   About an hour

RISK LEVEL   Low

PARTICIPANTS NEEDED   Any number of participants, plus a facilitator

PROCEDURE   Please take the following steps:

1. Organize the class into two- or three-person groups.
2. Provide each group with a transcript of two or more people from different cultures interacting.
3. Have the group members identify a limited number of key words in the transcript. Each group reports back to the larger group on which key words they chose and why.
4. Ask the group to discuss the similarities and differences in the key words chosen.

DEBRIEFING   In debriefing this experience, it will be useful to have newsprint and colored markers handy to record the key words for class discussion of why some words were more important or frequently used than others. Some discussion questions may include the following:

1. What is a key word, and how do you find it?
2. Do different cultures favor different key words?
3. Why is it important to identify key words in a transcript?
4. What are some key words that you use frequently?
5. How do key words contribute to understanding feeling and meaning?

INSIGHT   Not all words are created equal.

42 PUBLIC AND PRIVATE SELF

Objective: To demonstrate individual and cultural differences in one's level of privacy.

TIME REQUIRED   About an hour

RISK LEVEL   Low

PARTICIPANTS   Any number of participants, plus one facilitator
NEEDED

PROCEDURE   Please take the following steps:

1. Prepare a copy of the self-disclosure checklist in Exhibit 3.4.
2. Read all of the items from a master list, rather than handing the list out to participants.
3. Read each item slowly and clearly at least twice while participants decide if that item is private or public to them. Ask participants to keep track of how many items they consider private.
4. When finished reading the list, ask students to count up the number of items they considered private.
5. Go through the six categories of items and ask how many items within each category students considered private.
6. Discuss whether students scored more or fewer items as private relative to the other group members.

Note. From *A Handbook for Developing Multicultural Awareness* (3rd ed., p. 157), by P. B. Pedersen, 2000, Alexandria, VA: American Counseling Association. Copyright 2000 by the American Counseling Association, where it was published with permission from Dr. Dean Barnlund, San Francisco State University. Adapted with permission. No further reproduction authorized without written permission of the American Counseling Association.

Exhibit 3.4   *Privacy Checklist*

Read the following list and indicate whether you consider each item to be public or private.

Attitudes and Opinions

1. What I think and feel about my religion
2. My views on communism
3. My views on racial integration
4. My views on sexual morality
5. The things I regard as desirable for a person to be

Tastes and Interests

6. My favorite and least favorite foods
7. My likes and dislikes in music
8. My favorite reading matter
9. The kinds of movies and TV programs I like best
10. The kind of party or social gathering I like best

Work or Studies

11. What I feel are my shortcomings
12. What I feel are my strong points
13. My goals and ambitions
14. How I feel about my career
15. How I really feel about the people I work for or with

Money

16. How much money I make
17. Whether I owe money
18. My total financial worth
19. My most pressing need for money right now
20. How I budget my money

Personality

21. Aspects of my personality I dislike
22. Feelings I have trouble expressing or controlling
23. Facts of my present sex life
24. Things I feel ashamed or guilty about
25. Things that make me feel proud

Body

26. My feelings about my face
27. How I wished I looked
28. My feelings about parts of my body
29. My past illnesses and treatments
30. Feelings about my sexual adequacy

Note. From *A Handbook for Developing Multicultural Awareness* (3rd ed., p. 157), by P. B. Pedersen, 2000, Alexandria, VA: American Counseling Association. Copyright 2000 by the American Counseling Association. Adapted with permission. No further reproduction authorized without written permission of the American Counseling Association.

DEBRIEFING   In debriefing this experience, the leader may want to have members report their total combined scores in five point categories to prevent putting anyone on the spot. It is also important to point out that being public or private is not bad or good, but merely a personal choice. The privacy scores will probably be distributed in a bell-shaped curve. You can discuss the effect of respecting or not respecting one another's sense of privacy in a group. Some discussion questions may include the following:

1. Were you more private than you expected? Why?
2. Were you less private than you expected? Why?
3. Which areas were most likely to be private, and why?
4. Would different cultures have different levels of privacy? Give examples.
5. Would similar cultures have similar areas of privacy? Give examples.

INSIGHT   Even groups that consider themselves culturally homogenous have significant differences regarding privacy.

43 THE JOHARI WINDOW

Objective: To understand what we do and do not know about ourselves.

TIME REQUIRED   About an hour

RISK LEVEL   Low

PARTICIPANTS   Any number of participants, plus one facilitator
NEEDED

PROCEDURE   Please take the following steps:

1. Divide the class into two- or three-person teams.
2. Have each team create a Johari Window as described in Exhibit 3.5 and attempt to identify data from all four quadrants for each team member. For example: (1) you know what your shoes look like and so does everyone else around you; (2) you know what you are thinking but other people don't; (3) other people know what "people say" about you but you generally don't; and (4) nobody knows what will happen tomorrow.
3. When all team members have identified data in all four quadrants, ask the teams to report to the large group what they learned.
4. Organize the team members into a large group for discussion.

DEBRIEFING   In debriefing the leader might have a large diagram on the board or overhead of the Johari Window's four quadrants to help the group visualize the model. As two people

---

Note. From *Instructor's Manual for Intentional Group Counseling: A Microskills Approach* (p. 124), by P. B. Pedersen, A. E. Ivey, M. B. Ivey, and Y. Y. Kuo, 2001, Belmont, CA: Brooks/Cole. Copyright 2001 by Brooks/Cole. Adapted with permission of Wadsworth, a division of Thomas Learning. For more information see "The Johari Window," by J. Luft, 1969, in C. R. Mill (Ed.), *Selections From Human Relations Training News* (pp. 74–76), Washington, DC: NTL Institute.

Exhibit 3.5   *The Johari Window*

The Johari Window is used to examine one's own behavior and perception of that behavior in relation to others. This has had heuristic value for speculating about human behavior in groups. The Johari Window has four quadrants:

- In quadrant 1 the behavior and motivation are known both to self and to others.
- In quadrant 2 others can see things about us that we are unaware of.
- In quadrant 3 we can see things about ourselves that others do not know about.
- In quadrant 4 there are things about us that neither we nor others are yet aware of but may learn about in the future.

Note. From *Instructor's Manual for Intentional Group Counseling: A Microskills Approach* (p. 124), by P. B. Pedersen, A. E. Ivey, M. B. Ivey, and Y. Y. Kuo, 2001, Belmont, CA: Brooks/Cole. Copyright 2001 by Brooks/Cole. Adapted with permission of Wadsworth, a division of Thomas Learning. For more information see "The Johari Window," by J. Luft, 1969, in C. R. Mill (Ed.), *Selections From Human Relations Training News* (pp. 74–76), Washington, DC: NTL Institute.

become better acquainted, they are likely to move into quadrant 1, and fewer entries will be left in the other three quadrants. The leader might want to discuss the consequences for a group of any one quadrant being larger or smaller than the others. Discussion questions may include the following:

1. What have you learned about yourself and your culture?
2. What have you learned about others in the group?
3. Is it desirable for more data to be in quadrant 1? Why?
4. Are some cultures likely to prefer less data in quadrant 1? Why?
5. How will you use what you learned in this experience?

INSIGHT   It is useful to see ourselves as others see us.

44

A Self-Assessment of Multicultural Awareness, Knowledge, and Skill

---

Objective: To audit your own abilities to demonstrate multicultural awareness, knowledge, and skill.

TIME REQUIRED   About an hour

RISK LEVEL   Low

PARTICIPANTS NEEDED   Any number of participants, plus one facilitator

PROCEDURE   Please take the following steps:

1. Ask each student to read the self-test in Exhibit 3.6 and to indicate how well they think they would be able to answer the questions (using their own criteria) if they were to write out an answer.
2. Tell students to grade their ability to answer the questions as follows: If they think they could provide an excellent answer, they should give themselves an A; for a generally good answer, a B, and for an acceptable but not as good an answer, a C. If they feel unable to answer the question, then they should give themselves an F.
3. At the end of this self-assessment, have the students compute a "grade point average" by first adding up the points (an A is worth 3 points, a B 2 points, a C 1 point, and an F 0 points) and then dividing the number of points by the number of items.

Note. For more information see "Multicultural Counseling Competencies and Standards: A Call to the Profession" by D. W. Sue, P. Arredondo, and R. J. McDavis, 1992, *Journal of Counseling and Development, 70,* pp. 477–486. Also see "Position Paper: Cross-Cultural Counseling Competencies" by D. W. Sue, Y. Bernier, A. Durran, L. Feinberg, P. B. Pedersen, E. J. Smith, and E. Vasquez-Nuttal, 1982, *Counseling Psychologist, 19*(2), 10, pp. 45–52.

Awareness Questions

1. Can you construct a genogram of your family for the last three generations on your mother's and father's side?
2. What is your "cultural heritage"?
3. How well do you value, respect, and model cultural differences in your life?
4. Who are the significant people in your life who have influenced your attitudes, values, and biases?
5. Which are the cultures you least understand, and why?
6. What do you do to recruit clients who are different from you in race, ethnicity, culture, and beliefs?
7. What culturally learned assumptions do you have that are different from those of other counselors?
8. In what ways do issues of oppression, racism, discrimination, and stereotyping influence how you do counseling?
9. To what extent would you consider yourself as having racist attitudes, beliefs, and feelings?
10. Have you had any social impact in your career as a counselor?
11. Can you do counseling in a variety of different communication styles?
12. Do you know how your culturally different clients feel about your natural communication style?
13. In what specific ways have you trained yourself to work with culturally different clients?
14. In what specific ways do you evaluate your counseling work with culturally different clients?
15. When do you refer your culturally different clients to others better trained to work with them?
16. When have you sought consultation from more qualified resource persons when working with culturally different clients?
17. How well do you understand yourself and your own cultural identity?
18. How well are you able to present a nonracist identity as a counselor to culturally different clients?
19. Do you have a plan for increasing your multicultural awareness in the future?
20. Do you consider yourself to have achieved multicultural awareness?

Knowledge

1. Can you describe the social, political, and economic history of negative emotional reactions toward specific racial and ethnic groups?
2. How well can you do counseling with clients whose beliefs and attitudes are profoundly different from your own?
3. Can you be nonjudgmental toward clients whose beliefs are profoundly different from your own?
4. Are you aware of stereotypes and preconceived notions in your counseling practice?
5. Do you provide counseling to clients without knowing about their cultural attitudes, values, and backgrounds?
6. Are you aware of the life experiences, cultural heritages, and historical backgrounds of your culturally different clients?
7. Are you aware of the similarities and differences between yourself and your clients?
8. Are you able to explain how your client's cultural background affects
   a. personality formation?
   b. vocational choices?
   c. manifestation of psychological disorders?
   d. help-seeking behavior?
   e. appropriate counseling approaches?
9. Can you intelligently discuss sociopolitical issues that influence the quality of life of your clients?
10. Can you discuss the following immigration issues that influence the quality of life of your clients?
    a. poverty
    b. racism
    c. stereotyping
    d. powerlessness

(continued)

Knowledge *(continued)*

11. In the last month, have you read books or articles regarding the culture and mental health issues of clients within your client population?
12. In the last month, have you participated in training to increase your knowledge and understanding of cultural contexts where counseling occurs?
13. In the last month, have you been actively involved in any of the following ways with cultural minority groups outside your role as a counselor?
    a. community events
    b. social functions
    c. political functions
    d. celebrations
    e. friendships
    f. neighborhood gatherings

Skills

1. Do you refer in counseling to your client's religious and spiritual beliefs and values?
   a. to their attributions?
   b. to their taboos?
   c. to their worldviews?
2. Do you understand how these beliefs and attitudes affect psychosocial functioning and expressions of distress?
3. Can you talk with your clients about their indigenous helping practices and respect indigenous help-giving networks?
4. Are you able to defend the positive value of bilingualism or multilingualism?
5. Do you understand the generic characteristics of counseling and therapy?
   a. the culture-bound features of counseling and therapy?
   b. the class-bound features of counseling and therapy?
   c. the linguistic features of counseling and therapy?
6. Can you explain why clients from a minority group might be reluctant to seek out counseling?
7. Can you identify ways that your own cultural background might cause conflict with your clients from a different background?
8. Do you compensate for the cultural bias in tests developed in and for one cultural context when those tests are used with a culturally different population?
9. Do you interpret your assessment data differently to culturally different clients who come from significantly different backgrounds?
10. Do you incorporate information about the following aspects of your client's indigenous family structure into your counseling interviews?
    a. hierarchies
    b. values
    c. beliefs
    d. community resources
11. Are you able to change relevant discriminatory practices in the community that affect the psychological welfare of your clients?
12. Do you have a large repertory of verbal and nonverbal skills to match with the cultural contexts of your different clients?
13. Is the verbal message your client receives the same as the message you send and intend?
14. Is the nonverbal message your client receives the same as the message you send and intend?
15. Are you skilled in a variety of different helping roles, methods, or approaches?
16. When your helping style is limited or inappropriate, will you know enough to change?
17. Are you able to intervene with and change the social institutions in your client's cultural context?
18. Are you able to tell when a client's problem relates to cultural bias by others versus when the problem might be personal to the client?

(continued)

Skills *(continued)*

19. Do you consult with the following resources from your client's cultural context?
    a. traditional healers
    b. religious leaders
    c. spiritual leaders
    d. other practitioners
20. Are you fluent in the first language of your clients?
21. Do you use a translator when working with clients whose language you do not understand?
22. Do you incorporate traditional assessment and testing instruments from your clients' cultural contexts into your counseling with them?
23. Do you always have the necessary technical skills in the tests or measures you use with your culturally different clients?
24. Do you work actively to eliminate biases, prejudices, and discriminatory practices in your community?
25. Do you take responsibility for educating your clients about your own culturally learned orientation to psychological intervention, outcome goals, expectations, and legal rights?

Note. For more information see "Multicultural Counseling Competencies and Standards: A Call to the Profession" by D. W. Sue, P. Arredondo, and R. J. McDavis, 1992, *Journal of Counseling and Development, 70,* pp. 477–486. Also see "Position Paper: Cross-Cultural Counseling Competencies" by D. W. Sue, Y. Bernier, A. Durran, L. Feinberg, P. B. Pedersen, E. J. Smith, and E. Vasquez-Nuttal, 1982, *Counseling Psychologist, 19*(2), 10, pp. 45–52.

DEBRIEFING

Some cultures put more emphasis on culture than others. After students have calculated a grade point average from their self-assessments of their own multicultural competencies, lead a general group discussion. Some discussion questions include the following:

1. Is it possible to earn an A grade in the multicultural awareness, knowledge, and skill competencies?
2. Did you underestimate your level of competence before taking this test?
3. Did you overestimate your level of competence before taking this test?
4. What are the consequences of not having multicultural competence?
5. How do you plan to increase your level of multicultural competence?

INSIGHT

Most of us have a long way to go in developing multicultural awareness, knowledge, and skill competencies.

45 HIGH- AND LOW-CONTEXT CULTURES IN CONFLICT

Objective: To help participants assess their own attitudes and approaches to conflict and mediation and to understand the role of context.

TIME REQUIRED   About an hour

RISK LEVEL   Low

PARTICIPANTS NEEDED   Any number of participants, plus one facilitator

PROCEDURE   Please take the following steps:

1. Copy and distribute the rating sheet in Exhibit 3.7 to student participants.
2. Ask students to indicate agreement or disagreement with each statement as honestly as possible by circling one of the responses.
3. Once students have responded to all 15 items, have them score their answer sheets and report their final scores.
4. Present the distribution of scores describing the extent to which the group of students favored high or low context in their conflict management strategies.

DEBRIEFING   Students should not be made to feel that either high- or low-context thinking is preferred. The emphasis should be on the consequences of high- and low-context thinking in conflict management. Some discussion questions include the following:

1. Which cultures do you think are more high context in their thinking?
2. Which cultures do you think are more low context in their thinking?

Note. From "Conflict and Mediation Across Cultures," by T. Singelis and P. B. Pedersen, 1997, in K. Cushner and R. W. Brislin (Eds.), *Improving Intercultural Interactions: Vol. 2. Modules for Cross-Cultural Training Programs* (pp. 185–187), Thousand Oaks, CA: Sage. Copyright 1997 by Sage. Adapted with permission.

Exhibit 3.7   *Conflict Resolution Rating Sheet*

Rate each of the statements using the following scale: 1 = strongly disagree, 2 = disagree, 3 = disagree somewhat, 4 = don't agree or disagree, 5 = agree somewhat, 6 = agree, 7 = strongly agree.

1. In resolving conflicts, personalities are more important than facts.	1 2 3 4 5 6 7
2. A fair outcome requires a neutral mediator.	1 2 3 4 5 6 7
3. In resolving conflicts, the status of the parties is an important consideration.	1 2 3 4 5 6 7
4. It is normally possible to resolve conflicts if the people involved are honest and direct.	1 2 3 4 5 6 7
5. The best mediator is one who knows the parties well.	1 2 3 4 5 6 7
6. The first step to resolving a conflict is to get the parties to admit the conflict face to face.	1 2 3 4 5 6 7
7. If I were asked to help resolve a conflict, the first thing I'd want to know is some history of the people involved.	1 2 3 4 5 6 7
8. It is not right to apologize if you are not at fault in a conflict.	1 2 3 4 5 6 7
9. It is often wise to depend on someone else to work out your conflict for you.	1 2 3 4 5 6 7
10. Formal rituals are necessary to successfully resolve declared conflicts.	1 2 3 4 5 6 7
11. A mediator unknown to both parties is best, because this assures neutrality and anonymity.	1 2 3 4 5 6 7
12. Sometimes the best way to deal with conflict is to keep silent.	1 2 3 4 5 6 7
13. Conflict represents a challenge and an opportunity for change.	1 2 3 4 5 6 7
14. To ensure fairness in mediation, communication rules must be applied in the same way in all settings.	1 2 3 4 5 6 7
15. One should look to the future and not the past when finding solutions to conflicts.	1 2 3 4 5 6 7

Self-Assessment

High context: Higher scores on statements 1, 3, 5, 7, 9, 10, and 12 indicate a tendency to view conflict and mediation from a high-context perspective.

Low context: Higher scores on statements 2, 4, 6, 8, 11, 14, and 15 indicate a tendency to view conflict and mediation from a low-context perspective.

Note. From "Conflict and Mediation Across Cultures," by T. Singelis and P. B. Pedersen, 1997, in K. Cushner and R. W. Brislin (Eds.), *Improving Intercultural Interactions: Vol. 2. Modules for Cross-Cultural Training Programs* (pp. 185–187), Thousand Oaks, CA: Sage. Copyright 1997 by Sage. Adapted with permission.

3. Can you see the advantages and disadvantages of both high- and low-context thinking as a strategy for managing conflict?
4. Were you surprised by your score on this rating sheet?
5. Were you surprised by the scores of others in your group?

INSIGHT   It is important to manage conflict according to the high- or low-context orientation of the people in conflict.

46 A VALUES AUCTION

> *Objective:* To identify the individual and collective priorities of a group.

TIME REQUIRED   About an hour

RISK LEVEL   Low

PARTICIPANTS NEEDED   Any number of participants, plus an "auctioneer" and one facilitator

PROCEDURE   Please take the following steps:

1. Distribute $10,000 in play money to each participant in $100 and $500 bills. (The amount may be $100,000 allocated in $1,000 and $5,000 bills if desired.) Each participant should be given the same amount of play money.
2. Distribute a values auction worksheet that lists the items to be auctioned. An example is provided in Exhibit 3.8.
3. Ask the participants to construct a budget of how much of their $10,000 they are willing to allocate for purchasing each item. This budget will serve as a guideline for each participant once the bidding starts, although participants are not required to stay with their item budgets.
4. When each item is sold, have participants record on their worksheets the highest amount they bid on the item and the amount for which the item finally sold.

DEBRIEFING   Priorities are indicated by the amount of each individual's limited resources that are allocated to a particular goal compared with the amount others in the group are willing to allocate in the final purchase of that goal. When the auction has been completed, the instructor can lead the group in a discussion of those items for which the bids were high and those for which the bids were low. Some discussion questions include the following:

1. Did everyone want the same items, or did they have different wants?
2. If you were to do the experience over, would you act differently, and if so, how?

Exhibit 3.8 *Values Auction Worksheet*

Items for sale	Budget	Bid	Final bid
A satisfying marriage			
Freedom to do what you want			
A chance to direct national destiny			
The love and admiration of friends			
Travel and tickets to any cultural or athletic event			
Complete self-confidence with a positive outlook on life			
A happy family relationship			
Recognition as the most attractive person in the world			
A long life free of illness			
A complete library for your private use			
A satisfying religious faith			
A month's vacation with nothing to do but enjoy yourself			
Lifetime financial security			
A lovely home in a beautiful setting			
A world without prejudice			
The elimination of sickness and poverty			
International fame and popularity			
An understanding of the meaning of life			
A world without graft, lying, or cheating			
Freedom within your work setting			
A really good love relationship			
Success in your chosen profession			

3. Were you surprised at the similarities or differences between your priorities and the priorities of others in the class?
4. Does the choice of these priorities indicate important cultural values in your life?
5. Are your implicit or "hidden" values more important than the explicit values you talk about?

INSIGHT   The values people say they believe in may be different from the values toward which they allocate their resources.

47 INTERVIEWING LOCAL RESOURCE PEOPLE

Objective: To show the importance of including resource people from a cultural group.

TIME REQUIRED   About an hour

RISK LEVEL   Moderate

PARTICIPANTS NEEDED   Any number of students, a facilitator, and one or more community resource person

PROCEDURE   This experience has two parts to help participants tap into the resource person's expertise in training situations. It is important to find resource people who are both articulate and authentic to a particular cultural group.

1. Ask each person in the group to make one statement about the culture represented by the resource person based on the group member's previous experience. Then have each person ask the resource person a question about the local culture.
2. After all members of the group have had a chance to reveal their own experiences with the local culture and ask a question, have the resource person describe the attitudes of the group and what the members could do to increase the accuracy of their intercultural perception.
3. Next, have the resource person stand in front of the group and carry on a conversation with one of the group members.
4. Assign another person to stand behind each of the speakers and say aloud what he or she believes the person is thinking, but not saying, as the two people carry out their conversation. The observing classroom group then has a picture of both the spoken and unspoken levels of communication in the exchange. The exchange and side comments may be videotaped and the videotape played back to the class later for analysis and discussion.

DEBRIEFING Resource people bring the real world into the classroom, perhaps more vividly than abstract ideas about the real world contained in textbooks. The facilitator and students need to be sensitive to the feelings of the resource person, who is their guest, so that they are gracious hosts. The resource person should not feel used or manipulated by the group, and the perspective of the resource person should be respected even if students disagree with that perspective. Some questions for discussion include the following:

1. What new information did you learn from the resource person?
2. How typical do you think that resource person is of her or his cultural group?
3. Will you maintain continuing contact with the resource person?
4. Will you be able to incorporate learning from other community people as a resource for your own continued education?

INSIGHT Not all cultural similarities and differences are obvious.

48 DOUBLE-LOOP THINKING

Objective: To analyze a cross-cultural situation from two perspectives.

TIME REQUIRED About an hour

RISK LEVEL Moderate

PARTICIPANTS NEEDED Ten or more students to form two teams, plus one facilitator

PROCEDURE Please take the following steps:

1. Select one of the critical incidents from other experiences in this book. Critical incidents involving conflict between two individuals work best for this experience.
2. Assign the critical incident to one or more participants, asking them to discuss the incident from the perspective of one individual in the incident.
3. Ask one or more other participants to discuss the same incident from the contrasting perspective of another individual in the incident.
4. Ask each participant to describe the perspective assigned to them according to the behaviors displayed, the expectations the individual had for consequences of the behavior, and the value reflected in the behavior and expectation.
5. After the two groups of participants have discussed their contrasting perspectives for 10 minutes, have a spokesperson from each group report the behaviors, expectations, and values of the perspective assigned to them.
6. Next, ask the two groups of participants to switch sides and repeat the process, describing the behaviors, expectations, and values of the perspective of the contrasting individual in the critical incident.
7. As an additional experiment, take a newspaper article about an "enemy" group presumed to be hostile toward "us." Wherever the article uses the word *they*, substitute the word *we*, and see how that perspective changes the meaning of the article toward inclusiveness.

DEBRIEFING   In debriefing this experience, discuss the following questions:

1. Is there an area of common ground between the two parties?
2. Can a skilled individual see the same incident from different, contrasting perspectives?
3. What is the advantage of being able to see both perspectives?
4. What is the disadvantage of being able to see both perspectives?
5. What cultures or special interest groups are most likely to be able to see both perspectives?

INSIGHT   It is possible to hold two opposing positions in one's mind at the same time.

49   STEREOTYPES OF DIFFERENT GROUPS I

> *Objective:* To create awareness of stereotypic attitudes held toward different groups of people.

TIME REQUIRED   About an hour

RISK LEVEL   Moderate

PARTICIPANTS NEEDED   Any number of students, plus a facilitator

PROCEDURE   Please take the following steps:

1. Select five cultural or special interest groups.
2. Prepare a chart with the five groups at the top and the list of statements along one side. An example of such a chart is provided in Exhibit 3.9.
3. Distribute the chart to students and ask them to rank order the frequency with which "most people" would apply the characteristic to the groups. The group the characteristic most applies to would be rank ordered 1, and decreasing rank would reflect decreasing frequency of application.
4. Ask the students to meet in small groups to discuss the similarities and differences in their responses.
5. Ask the students to compare their rank orderings of the characteristics by each group.

DEBRIEFING   Students may resist matching any particular statement with a particular group as disregarding of within-group differences. The instructor might explain that this experience looks at stereotypes and that students do not have to personally agree with the stereotypes. Some questions for discussion include the following:

1. Why does stereotyping persist?
2. Is stereotyping in any way useful?

Exhibit 3.9 *Groups and Their Characteristics*

Group 1	Group 2	Group 3	Group 4	Group 5	Characteristic
					Are not at all aggressive
					Are conceited about appearance
					Are very ambitious
					Almost always act as leader
					Do not hide emotions
					Are very independent
					Are sneaky
					Cry easily
					Are very active
					Are very logical
					Are not at all competitive
					Have easily hurt feelings
					Are not at all emotional
					Have a very strong need for security
					Are easily influenced
					Are very objective
					Have difficulty making decisions
					Are dependent
					Like math and science very much
					Are very passive
					Are very direct
					Know the way of the world
					Are excitable in a minor crisis
					Are very adventurous
					Are very submissive
					Are hardworking
					Are industrious
					Are not comfortable about being assertive

3. Is stereotyping in any way harmful?
4. What kind of situations tend to promote the stereotyping of people?

INSIGHT   Stereotypes control our thinking, with or without our permission.

50 STEREOTYPES OF DIFFERENT GROUPS II

Objective: To identify where stereotypes are found and how they are reinforced and to examine how beliefs about others influence one's behavior.

TIME REQUIRED   An hour

RISK LEVEL   Moderate

PARTICIPANTS NEEDED   Any size class or discussion group of 10 or more students, plus one instructor and four or five student volunteers as group monitors and discussion leaders

PROCEDURE   Please take the following steps:

1. Ask the group to respond to the statements in Exhibit 3.10 on paper. Each response should be recorded on a separate piece of paper. Encourage group members to record their own personal opinions or statements according to what they think or to what "everyone knows" about a particular group mentioned. Collect the papers.
2. Reread the first statement. Then read its corresponding responses while the group monitors make observations (and record reactions) to the responses.

Exhibit 3.10   *Stereotype Statements*

---

1. Intelligent, educated, assertive American women today are _____.

2. Consistent personal characteristics of people over age 65 include _____.

3. Black people raised in the ghetto are _____.

4. Problems with Asian Americans are _____.

5. True or false: Almost everyone belonging to a minority group would agree that most middle-class White people are racist.

---

3. Continue with each statement. Each monitor will take notes on one group's responses and will lead the subsequent group discussion.
4. Student monitors start the discussion by first rereading the statement, then reading the responses. They will follow this same procedure for each statement and response grouping.
5. As needed, guide the discussion by focusing on key words in each statement and responses. Help students understand what influenced the development and maintenance of that stereotype.
6. Ask the group to identify where stereotypes are found and how they are reinforced. Remind the group that stereotypes are defined by generalizations and can be based on some fact, attributes, or categories of description.

DEBRIEFING   Instructors need to be sensitive to any negative stereotypes expressed by group members and work to help the group avoid embarrassment and unnecessary stress, which will interfere with the experience. At the same time, instructors should encourage students to self-disclose. Some discussion questions might include the following:

1. Why do certain assumptions exist for American women? Do these assumptions exist for all American women? for women from other countries as well?
2. What is meant by "consistent" personal characteristics? Do older people begin to act in certain ways because we expect them to?
3. Where does the word *ghetto* come from? What do we mean by *ghetto*? How many people are familiar enough with a ghetto to have an idea what life is like there? How do the media influence our expectations that Black people and ghettos go hand-in-hand?
4. How do we define Asian Americans? What are some of the problems that Asian Americans themselves identify as being part of a minority in the United States? Who has this problem?
5. What is a middle-class White person? How do we define the word "racist"?

INSIGHT   Stereotypes can guide our thinking when we don't think about them openly.

51 CULTURAL VALUE SYSTEMS WITH CONFLICTING POINTS OF VIEW

> *Objective:* To demonstrate contrasting and conflicting aspects of interactions between people who do not share the same basic assumptions by discussing value conflicts.

TIME REQUIRED   About an hour

RISK LEVEL   Moderate

PARTICIPANTS NEEDED   Any number of participants sufficient for two teams, plus one facilitator

PROCEDURE   Please take the following steps:

1. Divide the participants into two or more individual or group units.
2. Generate alternative value systems from the members' own backgrounds (e.g., a system that is property- or rule-oriented and one that is person oriented).
3. Assign each value system to one of the individual or group units.
4. Discuss a topic in which those value systems are likely to contrast or conflict with one another.
5. Require each individual or group unit to maintain a position consistent with the assigned value system.
6. Assign one or more observers to take notes and referee.
7. Evaluate the units according to the criteria of (a) whether they maintained a position consistent with their assigned value system and (b) whether they were skillful in developing a powerful argument for their position based on these borrowed values.

Note. From *A Manual of Structured Experiences for Cross-Cultural Learning* (p. 39), by W. H. Weeks, P. B. Pedersen, and R. W. Brislin, 1977, Yarmouth, ME: Intercultural Press. Copyright 1977 by Intercultural Press. Adapted with permission.

DEBRIEFING The instructor should be careful in the evaluation process that the students' role-plays are evaluated fairly. The discussion should focus on whether this experience gave new insight into the local issue. Some discussion questions might include the following:

1. What did you learn from the experience about the local issue or problem?
2. Did participation in this experience change your opinion about the issue or problem?
3. Was there any point of special importance in the role-play?
4. Did any participants have particularly strong feelings about the problem?
5. Did you really believe what you said, or were you pretending?

INSIGHT Cultures are not always in agreement on important issues.

52 DESCRIBING THE FEELINGS OF A RESOURCE PERSON

Objective: To compare predictions about the feelings of a culturally different resource person.

TIME REQUIRED   About an hour

RISK LEVEL   Moderate

PARTICIPANTS NEEDED   Any number of students, at least one community resource person, and a facilitator

PROCEDURE   Please take the following steps:

1. Identify an appropriate community resource person who is authentic to a particular cultural group, preferably one different from that of students.
2. Distribute a previously prepared list of emotions, which may include, among others, love, happiness, fear, anger, contempt, mirth, surprise, determination, suffering, and disgust.
3. Ask the resource person to describe for 2 or 3 minutes an event that happened to him or her that gave rise to strong positive or negative feelings or both.
4. Ask all participants to rate from 1 (low) to 10 (high) how intensely the resource person felt each of the emotions on the list (a) at the time of the event and (b) as he or she was telling about the event.
5. Have the resource person give his or her own rating of all the emotions listed. The group members can then question the resource person about the emotions they rated incorrectly.

Note. From *A Handbook for Developing Multicultural Awareness* (3rd ed., p. 100), by P. B. Pedersen, 2000, Alexandria, VA: American Counseling Association. Copyright 2000 by the American Counseling Association. Adapted with permission. No further reproduction authorized without written permission of the American Counseling Association.

6. After they have done this two or three times, the group members may become much more accurate in reflecting the feelings of a resource person telling his or her story.

DEBRIEFING   In debriefing it is important to point out the natural tendency to project one's own "sympathetic" feelings onto others (How would I feel if it were me?). Such projection results in error, because each of us experiences feelings in different ways and to different degrees when faced with the same event. Some discussion questions may include the following:

1. Which feelings of the resource person did you score accurately, and why?
2. Which feelings of the resource person did you score inaccurately, and why?
3. Do you think you know better than the resource person how he or she should have scored his or her "real" feelings?
4. Did the explanations of the resource person surprise you?
5. Do different cultures show their feelings in different ways? Can you give examples?

INSIGHT   Others may feel differently than you would in the same circumstances.

53 FIGHTING FAIR

Objective: To learn how to disagree with someone from another culture.

TIME REQUIRED   About an hour

RISK LEVEL   Moderate

PARTICIPANTS NEEDED   Any even number of participants, plus a facilitator

PROCEDURE   Please take the following steps:

1. Divide the group into two-person culturally similar teams.
2. Match each team with one other team to role-play a conflict situation in which each team takes opposing sides.
3. Identify the topic of the disagreement.
4. Distribute the list of fighting rules to each team (see Exhibit 3.11).
5. One team will "fight clean" and the other team will "fight dirty" for 5 minutes.
6. Discuss what happened for 5 minutes.

DEBRIEFING   The leader can review the rules for fighting fair and fighting dirty to see how each approach influenced the debate or discussion. Some questions for discussion include the following:

1. Did fighting clean work better than fighting dirty?
2. Have you experienced a debate or discussion with another culture where one or both of you fought dirty?

Note. From *Instructor's Manual for Intentional Group Counseling: A Microskills Approach* (p. 111), by P. B. Pedersen, A. E. Ivey, M. B. Ivey, and Y. Y. Kuo, 2001, Belmont, CA: Brooks/Cole. Copyright 2001 by Brooks/Cole. Adapted with permission of Wadsworth, a division of Thomas Learning.

Exhibit 3.11   *Rules for Fighting Fair and Fighting Dirty*

Rules for Fighting Fair

1. Be respectful.
2. Be direct and honest.
3. Stay calm and in control of yourself.
4. Take responsibility for your part of the problem.
5. Focus on solutions and not blame. (Let go of making the other person wrong.)
6. Listen with an open mind. (The angrier you are, the harder this is.)
7. Stay in the present.
8. Acknowledge the other person's feelings and point of view (even if you don't agree).
9. Be flexible and willing to work with, instead of against, the other person.

Rules for Fighting Dirty

1. Be disrespectful (e.g., name call, laugh at, put down).
2. Don't take responsibility for your part of the problem.
3. Ignore the other person's concerns. (Who cares!)
4. Blame, judge, and criticize.
5. Bring up the past.
6. Interrupt and try to get in the last word.
7. Bump, shove, hit, or threaten to do so.
8. Generalize by saying, "you always . . ." or "you never . . . ."
9. Avoid or ignore the problem, and stuff the angry feelings deep inside.
10. Don't budge, and act as if winning is more important than the relationship.

3. Which approach would work better for short-term relationships?
4. Which approach would work better for long-term relationships?
5. Are some cultures more likely to fight clean than others?

INSIGHT   There are right ways and wrong ways to disagree across cultures.

54 MAKING HISTORY LIVE

Objective: To take on the role of historical figures from different cultural backgrounds and bring those figures to life.

TIME REQUIRED	About an hour
RISK LEVEL	Moderate
PARTICIPANTS NEEDED	Any number of participants, plus one facilitator
PROCEDURE	Please take the following steps:

1. Select four or five historical leaders from different cultures.
2. Match one student with each leader.
3. Allow the students a week to prepare to role-play that leader in class. These students will take on the identities of the leaders and participate in a discussion on which social theory is best.
4. Organize a role-played classroom discussion between the leaders for about 15 to 30 minutes.
5. Organize a large group discussion on what they discussed.

DEBRIEFING	The group leader will want to point out any inconsistencies of interpretation by the role-playing volunteers and perhaps alternative strategies the role-playing volunteers might have used but did not. Some discussion questions might include the following:

1. How well prepared were the role-players to represent the leaders?
2. Were you surprised by the interaction of the leaders?
3. What did you learn from the experience?
4. Which leader did you most agree with?
5. Which leader did you least agree with?

INSIGHT	Role-playing historical figures brings them to life.

55 PRISONERS' DILEMMA

Objective: To demonstrate the difficulty of compromise and cooperation across cultures.

TIME REQUIRED   About an hour

RISK LEVEL   Moderate

PARTICIPANTS NEEDED   At least 10 students, plus one facilitator

PROCEDURE   Please take the following steps:

1. Divide into four teams of five people each so that each team has one area of obvious similarity (e.g., gender, age, ethnicity).
2. Pair each team with one other team as opponents. The objective of the game is for each team to maximize its own score, regardless of how the other team does. The game has 10 rounds. The teams sit separately and are not allowed to communicate with one another unless otherwise instructed.
3. Give each team 3 minutes to choose X or Y after mentioning that X means cooperation and Y means refusal to cooperate.
4. After 3 minutes, ask the teams to present their decisions. If both teams independently select X—in other words, decide to cooperate—award each team three points each. If one team selects Y and the other selects X, the noncooperative team wins six points and the cooperators lose six points. If both teams defect by selecting Y, each team loses three points.
5. At the end of each round, inform each team of the other's decision so they can tell how their strategy is working.
6. Rounds 5, 8, and 10 are bonus rounds in which the points won and lost are doubled.
7. Allow the teams to negotiate in direct communication before rounds 5, 8, and 10 through a designated representative for 3 minutes to see if they want to change their strategy.

8. At the end of the game, tally up each team's accumulated points.
9. Discuss the choices each team made in the various rounds and how they obtained the score they did.

DEBRIEFING   The Prisoners' Dilemma experience is well-known in game theory and demonstrates the consequences of competition and cooperation in a group. This version of Prisoners' Dilemma has been modified to focus on multicultural issues of competition and cooperation. Although the game is not complicated, the insights gained from this experience are considerable. The game's structure imitates life, where there are both benefits and risks in choosing to cooperate. Some questions for discussion include the following:

1. Did you prefer to cooperate or compete?
2. Would you have been more cooperative if you felt you would not be taken advantage of?
3. Did the opportunity to speak face to face with someone from the other group result in more cooperation?
4. Which cultural groups might prefer to cooperate rather than compete?
5. Does our educational system promote competition or cooperation?

INSIGHT   It is difficult to develop trust across cultural boundaries.

56 FOUR CONTRASTING ETHICAL ORIENTATIONS

Objective: To better understand one's own culturally learned patterns of determining what is right and what is wrong.

TIME REQUIRED   About an hour

RISK LEVEL   Moderate

PARTICIPANTS NEEDED   Any number of participants, plus one facilitator

PROCEDURE   Please take the following steps:

1. Distribute the rating sheet in Exhibit 3.12 to each student in class and ask them to rate their reaction to each item as indicated.
2. When the students have completed their ratings, ask them to compute their scores as indicated.
3. Post all the scores to determine which ethical tradition is most popular and which is least popular among the students.

DEBRIEFING   The four classical positions of ethical thinking are "Consequentialists" who judge according to consequences, "Intentionalists" who judge according to the person's intention, "Absolutists" who judge according to a set of absolute standards, and "Relativists" who judge the person in context. Students may be surprised by their ethical position and may want to go back and examine the items themselves to make sure you have classified their scores correctly. They may want to discuss in dyads or small groups the similarities and differences in their ethical position compared to the ethical position of others. There are no right or wrong ethical positions among the four just indicated;

Note. From "Doing the Right Thing: A Question of Ethics," by P. B. Pedersen, 1997, in K. Cushner and R. W. Brislin (Eds.), *Improving Intercultural Interactions: Vol. 2. Modules for Cross-Cultural Training Programs* (pp. 149–164), Thousand Oaks, CA: Sage. Copyright 1997 by Sage. Adapted with permission.

Exhibit 3.12   *Classical Positions of Ethical Thinking*

The four classical positions of ethical thinking are consequentialism, or judgment according to consequences; intentionalism, or judgment according to the person's intention; absolutism, or judgment according to a set of absolute standards; and relativism, or judgment of the person in context. The following rating sheet will help you better understand the extent to which you follow one or another of these positions.

Respond to the following statements by indicating how much you agree or disagree or whether you are uncertain. Assign scores as follows:

1 = agree very much
2 = agree somewhat
3 = agree very little
4 = am uncertain
5 = disagree very little
6 = disagree somewhat
7 = disagree very much

1. Actions are judged according to their good or bad consequences.
2. There is an appropriate behavior for every situation.
3. Some decisions must be in the best interest of the group at the expense of the individual.
4. The consequences of rules and regulations will change from one situation to another.
5. Decisions are made by balancing the good and bad consequences.
6. Public leaders make decisions according to the consequences of their actions.
7. There are basic moral principles to guide us in all our decisions.
8. It is essential to know a person's good or bad intention in order to judge that person's behavior.
9. Individuals or groups acting in good faith are not responsible for the consequences of their actions.
10. Teaching the rules of morality will lead to higher levels of ethical behavior.
11. Moral decisions depend on encouraging people to be well intentioned.
12. Public actions are typically defended by the high moral intention of the promoters.
13. Biological factors are likely to determine a person's behavior.
14. Culture has a limited role in justifying variations in behavior.
15. Similarities are more important than differences across populations.
16. Cultural differences are not important.
17. It is possible to compare measured levels of moral development across cultures.
18. A good test will be valid in different cultural settings.
19. Variations in behavior are usually the result of cultural differences.
20. Apparent similarities across cultures are misleading.
21. Each culture influences its members to behave in unique ways.
22. Each culture must be understood from its own indigenous cultural perspective.
23. It is usually not possible to judge a person's behavior outside that person's cultural context.
24. Measures always need to be generated or modified to fit each cultural context.

Scoring

1. Derive a score for items 1 through 6 by adding up your scores for each item. A high score will demonstrate your affiliation with the consequentialist approach to ethical judgment.
2. Derive a score for items 7 through 12 by adding up your scores for each item. A high score will demonstrate your affiliation with a nonconsequentialist, intentionalist approach to ethical judgment.
3. Derive a score for items 13 through 18 by adding up your scores for each item. A high score will demonstrate your affiliation with an absolutist approach to ethical judgment.
4. Derive a score for items 19 through 24 by adding up your scores for each item. A high score will demonstrate your affiliation with a relativist approach to ethical judgment.

Note. From "Doing the Right Thing: A Question of Ethics," by P. B. Pedersen, 1997, in K. Cushner and R. W. Brislin (Eds.), *Improving Intercultural Interactions: Vol. 2. Modules for Cross-Cultural Training Programs* (pp. 149–164), Thousand Oaks, CA: Sage. Copyright 1997 by Sage. Adapted with permission.

however, it is important that students be intentional in deliberately defining their position if they expect to "do the right thing." Some discussion questions are as follows:

1. What are the good and bad consequences of following each of the four traditions?
2. Are you comfortable with your own preferred style of ethical thinking?
3. Are you able to work with others who may belong to a different tradition than yours?
4. Would you be able to change your own style of ethical thinking?
5. Which countries or cultures do you associate with each of these classical traditions?

INSIGHT   There is more than one way of deciding what is right and wrong across cultures.

57 FINDING COMMON GROUND WITH YOUR BEST FRIEND

Objective: To generalize the skill of finding common ground with best friends to finding common ground with people of other cultures.

TIME REQUIRED   About an hour

RISK LEVEL   Moderate

PARTICIPANTS NEEDED   Any number of participants, plus one facilitator

PROCEDURE   Please take the following steps:

1. Have students identify a best friend of theirs with whom they have recently had an argument or disagreement.
2. Prepare the following checklist and ask students to circle all categories that are approximately the same for both themselves and their best friends:
   - demographic: age, gender, neighborhood of residence
   - ethnographic: ethnicity, nationality, language, religion
   - status: social, economic, educational
   - affiliation: formal, nonformal, informal
3. Have students list examples of specific similarities and differences between themselves and their best friends.
4. Have students list the following three categories in their relationship with their best friend:
   - same behaviors, different behaviors
   - same positive expectations, different expectations
   - same values, different values
5. Lead a discussion on how students can accommodate differences with their best friends better than they can with strangers.

DEBRIEFING   In debriefing point out the way students find common ground with their best friend as a metaphor for finding common ground with others who are different as well.

Typically people's best friends do not look like them, dress like them, or talk like them and are often extremely different from them. However, the common ground implied by the term *best friend* is strong enough so that the many other differences actually enrich the friendship. With their best friend as an example, students can see that they already know how to find common ground. Now they only need to generalize that skill to other situations. Some discussion questions are as follows:

1. Do differences enhance the quality of your relationship with your best friend?
2. Might not differences also enhance other relationships with different people if you could find common ground with them?
3. How do you deal with conflicts with your best friend, and can you generalize the same method to other relationships?
4. What other kinds of common ground are there besides best friendship?
5. What prevents you from using the best friend analogy?

INSIGHT   Different behaviors may indicate similar positive expectations if there is a strong enough platform of common ground to stand on.

58 BEING "ABNORMAL"

Objective: To identify how each participant's uniqueness is perceived positively and negatively.

TIME REQUIRED   About an hour

RISK LEVEL   Moderate

PARTICIPANTS   Any number of participants, plus a facilitator
NEEDED

PROCEDURE   Please take the following steps:

1. Make copies of the worksheet in Exhibit 3.13. Additional reference group categories can be added to the list.
2. Ask students to work individually to indicate ways they are "abnormal," or different, according to the cultural rules of each reference group.
3. Ask the students to indicate positive as well as negative examples of how they are different.
4. When all students have completed filling out the worksheet, organize a general discussion. You may wish to organize the students into small three- to four-member groups to discuss their responses before the general discussion.

DEBRIEFING   When all participants have completed identifying positive and negative aspects of their being abnormal as members of their reference group, ask them to select a partner they know well and trust to compare and discuss each other's list of positive and negative consequences of their reference group membership. Some discussion questions include the following:

1. Are within-group differences important to the functioning of a group, and if so, how?
2. Which reference groups were most important to you?
3. Do these reference groups constitute "cultures"?

Exhibit 3.13 *"Abnormality" Worksheet*

In the space provided indicate (a) the way in which you are "abnormal," or different, for each of your reference groups, (b) the ways that your being different from most is a positive quality you want to keep, and (c) the ways that your being different from most is a negative quality that interferes with your life in some ways.

Reference group	Ways you are abnormal	Positive quality	Negative quality
Your ethnicity			
Your nationality			
Your religion			
Your language			
Your age			
Your gender			
Your place of residence			
Your social status			
Your educational level			
Your formal affiliations to groups			
Your informal affiliations to ideas			

4. Would you rather be more "normal" for your reference groups?
5. How do cultural groups enforce more typical behavior among members?

INSIGHT   Being different from others in your reference group has both positive and negative consequences.

59   NOMINAL GROUP PROCESS

Objective: To make sure that group participation is not dominated by members who are more articulate, assertive, and powerful in a multicultural group.

TIME REQUIRED   About an hour

RISK LEVEL   Moderate

PARTICIPANTS NEEDED   Any number of participants, plus one facilitator

PROCEDURE   Please take the following steps:

1. Have the participants arrange themselves in a circle.
2. Instruct the participants that each group member will have a turn to make one statement or express one idea, but not more than one idea, during each turn.
3. Begin the discussion on a particular topic.
4. Monitor this process, and prevent any group member from expressing more than one idea or statement during his or her turn. Each group member will, in turn, provide an insight, idea, question, or statement to the group. If a group member has nothing to say, he or she has the right to pass up the opportunity to speak.
5. Allow the discussion to proceed from one member to the next around the circle until all group members have had an opportunity to express their ideas, insights, questions, or statements to the rest of the group.

DEBRIEFING   One frequent problem in multicultural groups is that some members are more assertive and aggressive in expressing their viewpoints than others. Typically, these stronger group members dominate the discussion, and others in the group have no opportunity to express their own ideas. This procedure provides one way to balance the unequal distribution of power in a multicultural group. This process was developed by the Tavistock Institute in England (www.tavistockinstitute.org) and provides a level playing field for multicultural groups so that group members have an equal opportunity to express their ideas. The debriefing might explore whether this procedure seemed more fair than a free-for-all discussion. Some questions for discussion are as follows:

1. Participants from which cultures tend to speak less in an open discussion?
2. Participants from which cultures tend to speak more in an open discussion?
3. Did the group rules inhibit free discussion?
4. Did people speak out opinions that might otherwise have gone unstated?
5. If people don't want to contribute to a discussion, should they be encouraged to do so?

INSIGHT

Sometimes the group members with the best ideas are not assertive in expressing their ideas unless they are given permission to do so.

60 SEPARATING EXPECTATIONS FROM BEHAVIOR IN 10 SYNTHETIC CULTURES

Objective: To describe the expectations of 10 different synthetic cultures as those synthetic cultures match their different behaviors to the same expectations.

TIME REQUIRED   About an hour

RISK LEVEL   High

PARTICIPANTS NEEDED   Any number of students, plus one facilitator

PROCEDURE   Please take the following steps:

1. Divide the class into 10 or fewer small groups of two or more people each, and assign to each group one of the synthetic culture perspectives described in Exhibit 3.14. It would also be possible to have individuals select which synthetic culture they want to portray. Assign at least two people to each synthetic culture so that each can reinforce the behaviors of the others in that culture.
2. Once the participants have been assigned to synthetic cultures, organize a town meeting of the whole group on a particularly important or controversial issue locally. Each participant will participate in the town meeting in the role of her or his synthetic culture.
3. Allow the meeting to proceed, and discuss the local issue. Serve as the meeting moderator to keep the discussion moving along.

Note. From *Culture-Centered Counseling and Interviewing Skills*, by P. B. Pedersen and A. E. Ivey, 1993, Westport, CT: Greenwood/Praeger. Copyright 1993 by Greenwood/Praeger. Adapted with permission. More information on the synthetic cultures is available from Hofstede, Pedersen, and Hofstede (2002), *Exploring Culture: Exercises, Stories, and Synthetic Cultures*, Yarmouth, ME: Intercultural Press.

Exhibit 3.14 *Ten Synthetic Cultures*

High Power Distance

The primary directive of this culture is respect for status.

Behavior	Meaning
Is soft-spoken, polite, and listens	Friendliness
Is quiet and polite, but does not listen	Unfriendliness
Asks for help and direction	Trust
Does not ask for help and direction	Distrust
Is positive and animated, but makes no eye contact	Interest
Is expressionless and unanimated, but makes eye contact	Boredom

Low Power Distance

The primary directive of this culture is that all people are equal.

Behavior	Meaning
Is loud, direct, and very verbal	Friendliness
Is loud and direct, but does not say much	Unfriendliness
Offers help and direction	Trust
Does not offer help and direction	Distrust
Challenges with direct eye contact	Interest
Is passive and makes no direct eye contact	Boredom

High Uncertainty Avoidance

The primary directive of this culture is respect for the truth.

Behavior	Meaning
Gives detailed responses; is formal, specific, and unambiguous	Friendliness
Gives generalized, ambiguous responses; is anxious to end interview	Unfriendliness
Separates right from wrong unambiguously	Trust
Is openly critical; challenges the credentials of others	Distrust
Is verbal and task-oriented; questions with direct eye contact	Interest
Is passive and quiet; makes no direct eye contact	Boredom

Low Uncertainty Avoidance

The primary directive of this culture is tolerance for ambiguity.

Behavior	Meaning
Is ambiguous, informal, and general	Friendliness
Is specific, rude, and antagonistic	Unfriendliness
Sees rightness and wrongness as relative to the situation	Trust
Is secretive and nondisclosing	Distrust
Is quiet, relationship oriented, and empathic	Interest
Is aggressive and direct	Boredom

(continued)

DEBRIEFING   In debriefing this experience, it is useful to make three observations:

1. The same behavior may have different meanings, and different behaviors may have the same meaning.

Exhibit 3.14   *Ten Synthetic Cultures (Continued)*

High Individualism

The primary directive of this culture is respect for individual freedom.

Behavior	Meaning
Is verbal and self-disclosing	Friendliness
Is critical and likely to subvert or sabotage	Unfriendliness
Aggressively debates issues and controls the interview	Trust
Is noncommittal, passive, ambiguous, and defensive	Distrust
Is loudly verbal and questioning; engages in touching and physical contact	Interest
Maintains physical distance, asks no questions, and makes no eye contact	Boredom

High Collectivism

The primary directive of this culture is respect for friendship.

Behavior	Meaning
Is nonverbal and modestly polite	Friendliness
Is disengaged and likely to withdraw from contact	Unfriendliness
Listens carefully and shows respect	Trust
Is nondisclosing and nonresponsive but polite	Distrust
Listens carefully, seeks to learn, and is respectful	Interest
Is nonresponsive, disengaging, and distant	Boredom

High Masculine

The primary directive of this culture is to win at all costs.

Behavior	Meaning
Engages in physical contact; is seductive and loud	Friendliness
Maintains physical distance; is sarcastic and punishing	Unfriendliness
Is competitive, challenging, and dominating	Trust
Is openly critical and disparaging and is eager to end the interview	Distrust
Is sports oriented, eager to debate, and engaging	Interest
Engages in no eye contact; is discourteous and drowsy	Boredom

(continued)

2. The primary directive of each culture can be achieved without contradicting the primary directive of any other culture.
3. The common ground shared by all participants, such as finding a constructive solution to the local problem, is difficult to identify when participants behave in different and presumed hostile ways.

Once the students have learned their synthetic culture role, there are any number of ways the spectrum of 10 contrasting synthetic cultures can be used. Because the cultures are synthetic (that is, artificial) and do not exist in such an extreme form outside the laboratory classroom, the interaction is relatively safe and also relatively comprehensive. Some questions for discussion might include the following:

1. Were you able to express your synthetic culture role accurately?
2. Can you find aspects of all 10 synthetic cultures in yourself?
3. Can you find common ground across these synthetic cultures?

Exhibit 3.14 *Ten Synthetic Cultures (Continued)*

High Feminine

The primary directive of this culture is respect for the weak.

Behavior	Meaning
Is modest, quiet, and receptive to the other person's ideas	Friendliness
Is polite but disengaged, nonresponsive, and distant	Unfriendliness
Is cooperative and trusting and seeks to please	Trust
Is noncommittal, cold, and nondisclosing	Distrust
Is relationship oriented, warm, and receptive to others	Interest
Is distant, preoccupied, and nonreceptive	Boredom

Long-Term Perspective

The primary directive of this culture is delay of gratification.

Behavior	Meaning
Is direct, questioning, and cooperative	Friendliness
Is disengaged, distant, and exclusionary	Unfriendliness
Is sharing, invested, and purposeful	Trust
Is separate, uptight, stressed, and restrained	Distrust
Is hard working, future oriented, and idealistic	Interest
Is nondisclosing, quiet, distant, and judgmental	Boredom

Short-Term Perspective

The primary directive of this culture is immediate gratification.

Behavior	Meaning
Is extravagant, generous, happy, and smiling	Friendliness
Is blaming, angry, distressed, and rude	Unfriendliness
Is warm, formal, and eager to work with others	Trust
Is disappointed, betrayed, and disengaged	Distrust
Is eager to please, generous, and respectful of traditions	Interest
Is blaming, disrespectful, and eager to end the interview	Boredom

Note. From *Culture-Centered Counseling and Interviewing Skills,* by P. B. Pedersen and A. E. Ivey, 1993, Westport, CT: Greenwood/Praeger. Copyright 1993 by Greenwood/Praeger. Adapted with permission. More information on the synthetic cultures is available from Hofstede, Pedersen, and Hofstede (2002).

4. Were you able to maintain integrity while interacting with other synthetic cultures?
5. Did you find aspects of some synthetic cultures in stereotypes of different cultures?

INSIGHT   It is possible to find common ground without sacrificing cultural integrity or giving up the synthetic culture's primary directive in the process.

61 GIFT GIVING ACROSS CULTURES

Objective: To explore the importance of "ownership" of private property across cultural groups.

TIME REQUIRED About an hour or less

RISK LEVEL High

PARTICIPANTS NEEDED Any number of participants, plus one facilitator

PROCEDURE Please take the following steps:

1. Ask everyone to bring a gift costing less than $1 or $5 depending on the situation.
2. Make sure there are as many gifts as there are participants.
3. Pile the gifts under the tree or in some appropriate place.
4. Put numbers on small slips of paper ranging from #1 to the total number of gifts.
5. Scramble the numbers in a bowl and ask each person to draw a number from the bowl.
6. Have the person who drew #1 go to the pile and select any box or gift he or she wants.
7. The person who drew #2 chooses either to select a gift from the pile or to take away person #1's gift.
8. If person #1 loses his or her gift, that person can select a new gift from the pile.
9. Continue in this manner with those who drew #3, #4, #5, and so forth, until everyone has selected a gift either from the pile or from one of the other participants.

DEBRIEFING The facilitator will need to monitor the experience carefully so that none of the participants become upset at having their gift taken away from them, reminding them when necessary of the spirit of the experience. In the debriefing, the importance of ownership and of taking away someone's private property may be explored as a cultural value. Once a gift has been given, then the recipient usually feels a sense of ownership that is stronger in some cultures than in others. Some discussion questions may include the following:

1. What did the gift symbolize as it was taken away from you or as you took it away from someone else?
2. Did you have a sense of personal ownership as soon as you selected your gift?
3. Does this experience reflect values favoring the right to private property in our culture?
4. Did you feel upset taking away someone else's gift?
5. How would a collectivist culture with a sense of corporate ownership experience this activity differently from an individualistic culture?

INSIGHT   The ownership of private property is a highly emotional issue in many cultures.

62 ROLE-PLAYING A HYPOTHETICAL PROBLEM IN A GROUP

Objective: To examine real controversial cultural issues in the safety of a hypothetical situation.

TIME REQUIRED   About an hour

RISK LEVEL   High

PARTICIPANTS NEEDED   At least five to eight students, including one or more observers, plus one facilitator

PROCEDURE   Please take the following steps:

1. Select a controversial cultural issue, event, or interaction that is of interest to the participants. Take advantage of expertise within the group, such as using a relevant newspaper story or some recent event that the group has actually experienced but never debriefed.
2. Identify the key persons and roles involved in the cultural issue, making sure that all competing sides of the controversy are represented.
3. The facilitator will assign each role to a participant who will role-play that identity during the hypothetical interaction.
4. In assigning roles to participants, it is important to select people likely to know the particular role requirements as closely as possible.
5. The facilitator can initiate or invent new roles as the hypothetical event develops to take advantage of opportunities that will arise.
6. At least one or two participants will have the role of observer to analyze the insights from the group's interaction.
7. The facilitator will monitor the participant's interaction to make sure the interaction is lively but not out of control.
8. After the hypothetical role-play, you can ask the group to share what new insights they learned about the controversial cultural issue or event as a result of the interaction.

The students are likely to "get into" the role-play experience as they experiment with different viewpoints about the problem or conflict assigned to them. The role-play is limited only by the imagination of participants. Some discussion questions might include the following:

1. Did you agree with the viewpoint you role-played?
2. Did you get a new view of the problem by personalizing it?
3. What patterns of behavior did the observer or referee see?
4. Will this method work better with some problems than others?
5. Will this method work better in some cultures than others?

INSIGHT Multicultural problems look different when you take them upon yourself.

63 ROLE-PLAYING A NEWSPAPER INCIDENT

Objective: To demonstrate how people from different backgrounds see everyday events differently by involving people from more than one culture.

TIME REQUIRED   About an hour

RISK LEVEL   High

PARTICIPANTS NEEDED   Any number of participants, plus one facilitator

PROCEDURE   Please take the following steps:

1. Distribute one or more newspapers to the group and ask members to examine them.
2. Instruct the group members to select a story from the paper involving a group (e.g., Asian Americans, international travelers, female students) with which they can identify and that could possibly involve them personally.
3. Have each member of the group project himself or herself into the role of one main person in the selected story and tell the group about what happened as though it had happened to him or her personally.
4. Next, tell the group members to ask questions to explicate aspects of the story that they find difficult to understand.

DEBRIEFING   It is important to keep the students on task and not allow their imaginations to run away with them; they must take their task seriously in order for the experience to work. The facilitator will monitor the role-play and be ready to stop the role-play when necessary. Some questions for discussion might include the following:

1. How did you select the newspaper story to role-play?
2. Did taking on the role of a person in the article change your opinion?
3. Was it difficult to be authentic in your role-play?

4. What were the best questions other classmates asked of you when you were in role?

5. What were your feelings during the experience?

Learning about your own multiculturalism will cause you to read the newspapers with greater insight.

64 LISTENING TO THE VOICES

Objective: To hear the advice of internal voices.

TIME REQUIRED   About an hour

RISK LEVEL   High

PARTICIPANTS NEEDED   Any number of participants, plus one facilitator

PROCEDURE   Please take the following steps:

1. Divide the participants into two groups of equal size.
2. Ask one group to be seated in a circle and the other group members to stand behind a seated member. There should be quiet music suitable for meditation playing in the background to facilitate concentration.
3. Have those standing place their hands on the shoulders of the seated members and stand quietly waiting for a message, thought, insight, or suggestion to come into consciousness.
4. Indicate when the standing person should move to the next seated person in the circle, usually after about 1 to 2 minutes.
5. Tell the standing person to whisper the thought or message that has come to his or her mind to the seated person before moving to the next person.
6. When each standing person has completed the circle, have the standing people and seated people exchange places and repeat the same experience.
7. At the end of the experience, ask members to describe what they experienced both as a standing speaker and as a seated listener (if they would like to share their experiences).

DEBRIEFING   This experience was developed by Native American groups for whom spiritual resources are a profoundly important source of advice and energy. In directing this experience, the leader should be sensitive to the fact that it is based on a spiritual activity designed for use among participants who have respect for the spiritual process. The leader should verify that no participant would be offended by this adaptation of that spiritual experience before proceeding. Debriefing needs to be done with sensitivity so that participants do not reveal more of their feelings than they might want to. At the same time, participants should be allowed to comment spontaneously. Discussion questions may include the following:

1. Did you feel any special connection with your partners during the experience?
2. Were you apprehensive about this experience?
3. Which was more powerful for you, listening to comments or giving comments?
4. What function might this experience serve in a culture?
5. What might be some negative consequences of this experience?

INSIGHT   Taking time to listen to one's internal voices can teach important insights.

65 CULTURAL PERSPECTIVE TAKING

Objective: To see an incident from the perspective of someone from another culture by means of group sculpturing techniques, in which the leader introduces new people or new information to the group, who must adapt to the new and changing conditions with a changed perspective.

TIME REQUIRED　　About an hour

RISK LEVEL　　High

PARTICIPANTS NEEDED　　Any number of students, plus a facilitator

PROCEDURE　　Please take the following steps:

1. Have one group member describe a fairly safe incident that occurred to him or her a day or so ago.
2. Next, ask the other members to describe the same incident from the perspective of other people (e.g., family, friends, observers) and from other cultural roles mentioned in the incident to see how those "cultural" perspectives might be different. This incident can then be role-played by group members with alternative endings as appropriate.
3. Remember to be sensitive to the talents and the fears of individual students as they are assigned different roles in the sculpturing of the multicultural incident.
4. The facilitator can introduce new people and new information into the group role-play so participants are required to adapt to the ever-changing situation.

DEBRIEFING　　This experience is similar to "group sculpturing" exercises. In debriefing it will be important to protect the person who contributed the incident from embarrassment and to be sensitive to real-world concerns that might be implicit within the incident. Some discussion questions might include the following:

1. Why did different people see the same incident in different ways?
2. Were you able to take the cultural perspective of others in this incident?
3. Have you changed your mind about the incident based on this experience?

4. How do you decide what really happened when everyone disagrees?
5. What have you learned from this experience that will help you manage other incidents?

INSIGHT   Perspective taking is essential to accurate cross-cultural communications.

66 GETTING FEEDBACK FROM OTHER GROUP MEMBERS

Objective: To get direct but anonymous feedback from other members in the group regarding how one is being perceived.

TIME REQUIRED   About an hour

RISK LEVEL   High

PARTICIPANTS NEEDED   Any number of participants, plus a facilitator

PROCEDURE   Please take the following steps:

1. Circulate a list of positive characteristics related to multicultural skill to each group member. Include beside each characteristic a seven-point scale beside each characteristic with 1 indicating a low score and a 7 indicating a high score.
2. Ask group members to sign their name at the top of the page and indicate using the scale where they see themselves on each of the 8 to 10 characteristics.
3. When they have scored themselves, have members pass the paper to the right (and receive someone else's paper from the left).
4. Instruct each member to estimate and record on the paper a combined score for all 8 to 10 characteristics for the person whose name is at the top of the page, and to again pass the paper to the right. Ask members not to sign their name to the other members' papers, so their scores of others are anonymous.
5. Have everyone continue scoring other individuals' papers until they receive their own completed score sheet back.
6. Ask the participants to review the scores to see how well their perception of themselves fits with how they are being perceived by other group members. The

---

Note. From *Instructor's Manual for Intentional Group Counseling: A Microskills Approach* (p. 87), by P. B. Pedersen, A. E. Ivey, M. B. Ivey, and Y. Y. Kuo, 2001, Belmont, CA: Brooks/ Cole. Copyright 2001 by Brooks/Cole. Adapted with permission of Wadsworth, a division of Thomas Learning.

same experience can be applied to specific populations defined by ethnographic, demographic, status, or affiliation variables.

In debriefing this experience, it will be important for the leader to help members interpret their scores in a nondefensive way, particularly if others see a member less positively than the member sees himself or herself. This experience provides an opportunity to self-disclose and to give feedback that will help each member check out how he or she is being perceived. Some discussion questions might include the following:

1. Which ratings of you by other group members surprised you?
2. Which ratings of other group members surprised you?
3. Did you understand why you were rated as you were?
4. Did your ratings of other group members surprise them?
5. How might this experience be helpful to you?

INSIGHT Others may see us differently than we see ourselves.

67 CULTURAL VALUE SYSTEMS IN A COUNSELING RELATIONSHIP

Objective: To demonstrate the cultural complexity of a counseling relationship.

TIME REQUIRED   About an hour

RISK LEVEL   High

PARTICIPANTS NEEDED   Any number of participants, plus one facilitator

PROCEDURE   Please take the following steps:

1. Identify on the culture grid in Exhibit 3.15 the multiple salient cultures interacting in a particular counseling interview.
2. Describe on the grid how these multicultural factors influence the counselor, client, problem, environment, and significant others.
3. Discuss how these multicultural factors can enhance the counseling interview.
4. Discuss how these multicultural factors can complicate the counseling interview.

DEBRIEFING   Discuss the implications of the statement that all counseling interviews are multicultural. Does this mean that multicultural competencies are generic for all counselors? Some questions for discussion are as follows:

1. How do you learn to manage all of the different cultures in a counseling interview?
2. What happens if you pretend that the cultural differences are unimportant?
3. How do you prepare to work with other cultures in counseling?
4. Are all behaviors learned and displayed in a cultural context?
5. What has to happen for counseling to accept multicultural complexity?

INSIGHT   It is important to acknowledge the cultural complexity of every counseling interview.

Exhibit 3.15   *Culture Grid*

Multiple cultures affecting the interview	Influence of culture on actors				
	Counselor	Client	Problem	Environment	Significant others
1.					
2.					
3.					
4.					
5.					
6.					
7.					
8.					
9.					
10.					

68 THE TRIAD TRAINING MODEL

Objective: To hear the unspoken self-talk that culturally different clients are thinking but not verbalizing.

TIME REQUIRED   About an hour

RISK LEVEL   High

PARTICIPANTS NEEDED   Any number of participants, plus a facilitator

PROCEDURE   Please take the following steps:

1. Instruct students to review the brief transcript excerpts in Exhibit 3.16 and write in what they believe an anticounselor and a procounselor might say in the blanks provided. You may choose to have students role-play the scripted dialogue in a training session. The anticounselor articulates the negative thoughts the person might be thinking but not saying about what is going on, such as a "devil" making things go wrong. The procounselor articulates the positive thoughts the person might be thinking but not saying about what is going on, such as an "angel" making things go right.
2. When all the students have written in the responses of an anticounselor and procounselor for the transcript segment, compare the different responses.
3. Choose small groups of three to four students to work together to discuss what a procounselor and anticounselor would say.
4. When the students have finished discussing their responses, move to the next transcript segment and repeat the process.

Note. From *Hidden Messages in Culture-Centered Counseling: A Triad Training Model* (pp. 165–177), by P. B. Pedersen, 2000, Thousand Oaks, CA: Sage. Copyright 2000 by Sage. Adapted with permission.

Exhibit 3.16 *Sample Transcripts*

Transcript 1

The first dialogue is transcribed from an interview between a White male counselor and a Black female client discussing relationship problems the client is having at the university.

Identity

Client: OK, my problem is that I don't seem to be able to trust the White people here on campus. Being a Black person, I seem to have sort of a problem with this sort of thing, and I don't know what to do about it and somebody recommended you. Said that you were a good counselor, so I decided to come and get some help from you.

Counselor: Do you have any problems relating to the Black students on campus?

Client: No, not really. You know, there are people everywhere. Some you don't like, some you do like.

Anticounselor:

Procounselor:

Relationship

Counselor: How do you feel in terms of our relationship now? You came here, and we have been talking for about 2 to 3 minutes. How do you feel about the way we've been talking?

Client: Well, you haven't helped me, for one thing. I mean you just . . .

Anticounselor:

Procounselor:

Comfort Evaluation

Counselor: Do you feel uncomfortable with me?

Client: Um, not now, not yet.

Counselor: I um . . . I, ah, . . . *(pause)* I don't feel any discomfort with you at all.

Client: Oh, well, 'cuz I'm a friendly person, I suppose. *(laughs)*

Anticounselor:

Procounselor:

Counselor's Culture

Counselor: Are you getting a little uncomfortable? . . . Perhaps because I'm White? In sharing some of these things with me?

Client: Um . . . Not really, and it's like I said, you know, I try to be pretty open-minded about what I'm talking about. But the thing I want to know is, can you really understand where I'm coming from? What kind of things I'm really dealing with?

Anticounselor:

Procounselor:

(continued)

DEBRIEFING

Have students review the statements they made as a procounselor or as an anticounselor in dyads or small groups. Direct them to pay attention to how their responses were similar to or different from those of others in the group. Consider the following questions in a group discussion:

1. Were the statements of the anticounselor and procounselor accurate? Why or why not?
2. How might the counselor respond on hearing the anticounselor or procounselor statements?

Exhibit 3.16 *Sample Transcripts (Continued)*

Transcript 2

The second dialogue is transcribed from an interview between a White male counselor and a Latin American female client discussing relationship problems the client is having at the university.

Identity

Client: Yeah, they treat me like dirt, that's it, you know? And I feel divided inside. Like they don't care for me as a whole person.

Counselor: U— . . . You said divided. What is the division?

Client: The division is that they just want sex. They don't want to see me as a whole person.

Anticounselor:

Procounselor:

Relationship

Counselor: Could you tell me what you would rather have from them? How you would like a man to treat you when you go out with him?

Client: Well, it's just that, especially the first time . . . for some time . . .

Counselor: Um-— . . .

Client: I like to get to know the person in a different way.

Anticounselor:

Procounselor:

Comfort Level

Counselor: OK, I better ask you another question then. How comfortable are you with me? Should . . . maybe I'm not the right person to work with you . . . because I'm an American man.

Client: So far you're OK because you are far enough . . .

Anticounselor:

Procounselor:

Counselor's Culture

Client: Yeah, you see this thing, these things for me are very intense for me right now because I just came. I've been here for only about a month.

Counselor: Would you feel better if I got back behind the desk and we sort of had that between us?

Client: No, then you remind me of my father.

Anticounselor:

Procounselor:

Note. From *Hidden Messages in Culture-Centered Counseling: A Triad Training Model* (pp. 165–177), by P. B. Pedersen, 2000, Thousand Oaks, CA: Sage. Copyright 2000 by Sage. Adapted with permission.

3. How might the client respond on hearing the anticounselor or procounselor statements?
4. How might it be useful for multicultural counselors to monitor the anticounselor and procounselor messages in a client's internal dialogue?
5. Can you listen to the dialogue among the procounselor, anticounselor, client, and your own internal dialogue at the same time?

INSIGHT

The culturally different client will not verbalize everything he or she is thinking in a counseling interview.

69 CULTURE-CENTERED GENOGRAM

> *Objective:* To identify similarities and differences within a person's family over three generations according to ethnographic, demographic, status, and affiliation categories as a useful way of learning the sources of one's cultural identity.

TIME REQUIRED About an hour

RISK LEVEL High

PARTICIPANTS NEEDED Any number of participants, plus one facilitator

PROCEDURE Please take the following steps:

1. Identify your own family context by constructing a genogram for three generations including yourself, your parents on both sides, and all of your parents' parents. Use Exhibit 3.17.
2. Compare the similarities and differences in your family backgrounds. Feel free to include qualitative commentary in each of the culture categories for each of your family members, especially regarding the salience, or particular importance, any of these categories had for that individual family member.

DEBRIEFING Significant or salient identities in your family probably served a positive function in the formation of your own cultural identity. Other salient identities in your family probably served a negative function in the formation of your cultural identity. How would you describe the identity of each family member? What patterns were reinforced in men and women by family members? What would you say are the enduring cultural values across generations in your family? Some additional questions are the following:

1. What will be your unique and special contribution to the family for the future?
2. To what extent was career important to the cultural identity of family members?
3. What are the myths or traditions that emerge from your family background?
4. What boundaries are defined by your family background?

Exhibit 3.17   *Genogram Worksheet*

Use the following grid to complete your culture-centered genogram.

Culture category	Paternal Grandfather	Paternal Grandmother	Maternal Grandfather	Maternal Grandmother
Ethnographic				
Demographic				
Status				
Affiliation				
Culture category	Father and Siblings		Mother and Siblings	
Ethnographic				
Demographic				
Status				
Affiliation				
Culture category	Self and Siblings			
Ethnographic				
Demographic				
Status				
Affiliation				

5. What would you like to change about your family, and what would you like to keep the same?

INSIGHT   Family background is more important in some cultures than in others.

■ CHAPTER FOUR ■

TWO-HOUR LABORATORY EXPERIENCES

The laboratory experiences described in this chapter might be used in a separate weekend workshop or even a separate class for an extended class period. These experiences are more complex and self-contained than the experiences in previous chapters, and it might be useful to combine several of the previously described shorter experiences with one of these larger laboratory experiences. The same precautions mentioned as important for the previous experiences are also important for these longer experiences.

Like the shorter experiences, those described in this chapter each have a special focus. The students will be required to prepare prior to the experience and to participate in debriefing following the experience to ensure that the learning objectives are met. An instructor might want to modify the focus of the experience to fit the needs and priorities being studied in a particular class. As a general rule, facilitating the longer self-contained laboratory experiences will require a higher level of experience and expertise than facilitating the shorter experiences.

The laboratory model of intensive learning works better for skill-based objectives than for other curricula. The advantage of an extensive and concentrated experience is that it will have a stronger impact than shorter weekly meetings. The impact is likely to be remembered more vividly than a more casual or occasional approach to learning. The disadvantages of a laboratory design are that it requires a larger block of time, usually outside the regular instruction schedule, and the interaction is sometimes more intense than anticipated by unprepared participants. An instructor will need to be prepared and trained to take full advantage of the laboratory format.

70 ORIENTATION FOR A CROSS-CULTURAL EXPERIENCE

> *Objective:* To define the kinds of roles that are important for people new to a culture through an orientation and to learn whether their suggested solutions to problems are appropriate to their new culture.

TIME REQUIRED   Several hours to a half day

RISK LEVEL   Low

PARTICIPANTS NEEDED   Any number of participants, plus a facilitator

PROCEDURE   Please take the following steps:

1. Provide participants with the list of images in Exhibit 4.1 that people from other cultures could manifest (others may be added). Discuss and clarify each image.
2. Each image is an abstraction that presents one alternative identity that the person might experience in the host culture.
3. The "rehearsal" is to try on many different images from which they will need to choose when they get to the host culture.
4. Each image will be defined or perceived differently in each cultural context.
5. Discussing the images in the home and host culture will get participants thinking about the choices they will be making in the future.
6. Each participant will discover which "images" they want to project or assume in the transfer from their home to their host culture context.
7. Have participants select three images that they feel are most appropriate to themselves most of the time.
8. Provide participants with problems and five solutions prepared ahead of time by the facilitator. Exhibit 4.1 contains examples of problems and solutions illustrating two of the images listed.

Note. From "Dress Rehearsal for a Cross-Cultural Experience," by R. T. Moran, J. A. Mestenhauser, and P. B. Pedersen, 1974, *International Educational and Cultural Exchange,* *X*(1). Adapted with permission by the authors. In the public domain.

Exhibit 4.1   *Cultural Images*

Images

- Internationalist, nationalist
- Traditionalist, progressive
- Insider, visitor guest
- Deserving, poor
- Disoriented, oriented
- Competitor
- Culture sharer
- Elitist

Example 1: Insider, Visitor Guest

Description of Problem

A male foreign student had a series of arguments with his host family. He felt that the whole family was demanding too much of his time and attention. The family in turn felt that the guest was being discourteous and demanding special treatment that they would not give to their own children. The arguments became so oppressive that they affected the student's grades.

Alternative Solutions

1. I would make some excuse, leave the host family, and find another place to live.
2. I would confront the host family and tell them they are taking too much time and to give me more time to study.
3. I would rearrange my schedule and try to study more at the university and continue to let the family take up time.
4. I would do nothing and would accept it and do my best in school.
5. Or I would [students can propose other solutions].

Example 2: Disoriented, Oriented

Description of Problem

A female foreigner fails in her attempt to mix socially with Americans and puts the blame on her ethnic identity. She debases the values of her own culture and rejects her compatriots, who in turn reject her. At the same time, she is no more successful in communicating with Americans. She is isolated and feels lonely.

Alternative Solutions

1. I would accept living in a foreign country and realize that I will be lonely.
2. I would seek help, preferably from compatriots and counselors.
3. I would socialize with people from my own country and try to show them the stupidity of our values.
4. I would start over and try to mix socially with another group of Americans.
5. Or I would [students can propose other solutions].

Note. From "Dress Rehearsal for a Cross-Cultural Experience," by R. T. Moran, J. A. Mestenhauser, and P. B. Pedersen, 1974, *International Educational and Cultural Exchange, X*(1). Adapted with permission by the authors. In the public domain.

9. Ask participants to select from the five solutions the one that most appeals to them and consistent with the three images they already selected.
10. Have participants discuss each other's solutions in terms of whether they feel the solution helps or hinders the person's image and is appropriate to the situation.
11. Assign roles appropriate to the problems; then role-play the situations.

12. Following the role-playing, allow each person to defend his or her position and take a vote of all participants regarding the best overall solution.
13. To rehearse solutions to students' own present and future problems, form small groups (8 to 10 people) and discuss, role-play, and vote on possible solutions.

DEBRIEFING

The role-played situations will generate a great deal of discussion, especially among the international students in the small groups. The instructor should let the international students take the lead in interpreting the consequences of alternatives. Some discussion questions are as follows:

1. Was there a pattern in the alternatives selected for each example?
2. Is being from another country always a disadvantage?
3. How would one proceed to change unfair treatment of international students?
4. How does an international student deal with feeling helpless?
5. Which image was the most difficult, and why?

INSIGHT

Each multicultural situation presents choices, some better and some worse.

71 MICHIGAN INTERNATIONAL STUDENT PROBLEM INVENTORY

Objective: To define problems or areas of conflict that an international student may be experiencing.

TIME REQUIRED   Several hours to a half day

RISK LEVEL   Low

PARTICIPANTS NEEDED   Any number of participants, plus a facilitator

PROCEDURE   Please take the following steps:

1. Have the students read the Michigan International Student Problem Inventory in Exhibit 4.2 carefully, pausing at each problem, and if the problem suggests a situation that troubles them, have them circle the number to the left. Remind the students that there are no right or wrong answers and that this is a list of problems that occasionally trouble, perturb, distress, annoy, grieve, or worry students from other countries who are attending college in the United States.
2. Have the students go back over the numbers circled and place an X in the circle of the problems that are of most concern.
3. Monitor the students as they complete the inventory, and be ready to answer their questions.
4. Organize small groups to compare the problems that students checked.
5. Organize a large group to discuss the most frequently identified problems.

Note. From *Decisional Dialogues in a Cultural Context: Structured Exercises* (p. 79), by P. B. Pedersen and D. Hernandez, 1997, Thousand Oaks, CA: Sage. Copyright 1997 by Sage. Adapted with permission. For more information see *Michigan International Student Problem Inventory*, by J. W. Porter and A. O. Haller, 1962, International Programs, Michigan State University, East Lansing.

Exhibit 4.2   *The Michigan International Student Problem Inventory*

1. Evaluation of my former school
2. Concern about value of U.S. credentials education
3. Choosing college subjects
4. Treatment received at orientation meetings
5. Unfavorable remarks about home country
6. Concept of being a "foreign" student
7. Frequent college examinations
8. Compulsory class attendance
9. Writing or typing term (semester) papers
10. Concern about becoming too "Westernized"
11. Insufficient personal–social counseling
12. Being in love with someone
13. Taste of food in United States
14. Problems regarding housing
15. Being told where one must live
16. Poor eyesight
17. Recurrent headaches
18. My physical height and physique
19. Religious practice in the United States
20. Attending church socials
21. Concern about my religious beliefs
22. Speaking English
23. Giving oral reports in class
24. Ability to write English
25. Regulations on student activities
26. Treatment received at social events
27. Relationship of men and women in U.S.
28. Lack of money to meet expenses
29. Not receiving enough money from home
30. Having to do manual labor (with hands)
31. Finding a job upon returning home
32. Not enough time in U.S. for study
33. Trying to extend stay in United States
34. Getting admitted in U.S. college
35. Registration for classes each term
36. Not attending college of my first choice
37. Relationship with foreign student
38. Leisure time activities of U.S. advisor students
39. Law enforcement practices in the U.S.
40. Competitive college grading system
41. Objective examinations (true–false, etc.)
42. Insufficient advice from academic advisor
43. Being lonely
44. Feeling inferior to others
45. Trying to make friends
46. Costs of buying food
47. Insufficient clothing
48. Not being able to room with U.S. student
49. Hard to hear
50. Nervousness
51. Finding adequate health services
52. Finding worship group on own faith
53. Christianity as a philosophy
54. Variety of religious faith in U.S.
55. Reciting in class
56. Understanding lectures in English
57. Reading textbooks written in English
58. Dating practices of U.S. people
59. Being accepted in social groups
60. Not being able to find "dates"
61. Saving enough money for social events
62. Immigration work restrictions
63. Limited amount U.S. dollar will purchase
64. Becoming a citizen of the U.S.
65. Changes in home government
66. Desire to not return to home country
67. Understanding college catalogs
68. Immigration regulations
69. Lack of knowledge about U.S.
70. Campus size
71. U.S. emphasis on time and promptness
72. Understanding how to use the library
73. Too many interferences with studies
74. Feel unprepared for U.S. college work
75. Concerned about grades
76. Sexual customs in U.S.
77. Homesickness
78. Feeling superior to others
79. Bathroom facilities cause problems
80. Distances to classes from residence
81. Relationship with roommate
82. Dietary problems
83. Need more time to rest
84. Worried about mental health
85. Having time to devote to own religion
86. Spiritual versus materialistic values
87. Doubting the value of any religion
88. Understanding U.S. slang
89. My limited English vocabulary
90. My pronunciation not understood
91. Activities of International Houses
92. U.S. emphasis on sports
93. Problems when shopping in U.S.
94. Finding part-time work
95. Unexpected financial needs
96. Money for clothing
97. Uncertainties in the world today
98. Desire enrolling at another college
99. U.S. education not what was expected

(continued)

100. Differences in purposes among U.S. education
101. Difference in U.S. and home education
102. Not being met on arrival at campus
103. College orientation program insufficient
104. Trying to be student and tourist
105. Attitude of some students/foreigners
106. Doing laboratory assignments
107. Insufficient personal help from U.S. professors
108. Relationship between students and faculty
109. U.S. emphasis on personal habits of cleanliness
110. Not feeling at ease in public
111. Attitude of some U.S. people to skin color
112. Finding a place to live between college terms
113. Changes in weather conditions
114. Lack of invitations
115. Feeling under tension
116. Service received at health center
117. Health suffering due to academic pace
118. Criticisms of homeland religion
119. Accepting differences in great religions
120. Confusion about religion and morals in U.S.
121. Insufficient remedial English services
122. Having a non-English speaking roommate
123. Holding a conversation with U.S. friend
124. Activities of foreign student organization
125. Lack of opportunities to meet more people
126. Concern about political U.S. "ambassador" discussions
127. Costs of an automobile
128. Finding employment between college terms
129. Finding jobs that will pay well
130. Insufficient help from placement office
131. Staying in U.S. and getting a job
132. Wonder if U.S. education is useful for job at home

Note. From *Decisional Dialogues in a Cultural Context: Structured Exercises* (p. 79), by P. B. Pedersen and D. Hernandez, 1997, Thousand Oaks, CA: Sage. Copyright 1997 by Sage. Adapted with permission. For more information see *Michigan International Student Problem Inventory,* by J. W. Porter and A. O. Haller, 1962, International Programs, Michigan State University, East Lansing.

DEBRIEFING

This inventory was first constructed in the 1960s and provides a list of problem areas identified by international students. It is useful to have both international students and domestic students in the same group so that each can learn from the other. The facilitator should be sensitive to the danger of an international student revealing more about a personal problem than he or she intends to. Some discussion questions include the following:

1. Which problems were most frequent, and why?
2. Were there similarities among the problems identified?
3. How would you approach managing some of the more serious problems?
4. Did students from some countries or cultures have more or different problems?
5. What did you learn from this experience that surprised you?

INSIGHT

Some problems occur to international students with greater frequency than to other students.

72 CRITICAL INCIDENTS IN AIRLINE TRAVEL

Objective: To identify the barriers to intercultural communication in intercultural situations involving airline travel.

TIME REQUIRED About a half day

RISK LEVEL Low

PARTICIPANTS NEEDED Any number of participants with some experience in airline travel, plus one facilitator

PROCEDURE Please take the following steps:

1. Explain to students that the situations in Exhibit 4.3 occurred aboard international airline flights and were collected to illustrate the dynamics of intercultural communication for a training program.
2. Instruct students to read each situation and briefly reflect on the perspectives of the people involved.
3. Then, have students indicate which of the intercultural communication barriers listed at the beginning of the exhibit apply to the listed elements of the situation. The answers are given at the end of the exhibit.

DEBRIEFING In debriefing the instructor should review the situations and the communication barriers in each situation to make sure the students understand each barrier in the incident. Students may have additional examples of barriers to communication from the incidents or from their own experiences. The instructor should monitor the emotional level of participants carefully so that the discussion is not sidetracked in a destructive direction. Some questions for discussion are as follows:

Note. From *Decisional Dialogues in a Cultural Context: Structured Exercises* (pp. 127–137), by P. B. Pedersen and D. Hernandez, 1997, Thousand Oaks, CA: Sage. Copyright 1997 by Sage. Adapted with permission.

1. What are some of the unique problems that come up in international air travel?
2. Have you personally experienced a critical incident during an international flight?
3. Which situations aboard an airline are the most difficult?
4. How would you describe a multiculturally skilled flight attendant?
5. How can flight attendants best be trained in multicultural skills?

INSIGHT   People behave differently when they are airplane passengers on an international flight than they would otherwise.

Exhibit 4.3   *Identifying Barriers to Intercultural Communication Using Airline Incidents*

The following descriptions of situations involving airline passengers and flight attendants can help you learn to identify barriers to intercultural communication. There are five such barriers: language differences, stereotyping, evaluation, use of nonverbal communication, and stress.

Situation 1: Last Rites

1. Read the situation.

As the passengers boarded the plane, a new flight attendant noticed that several Latin American passengers crossed themselves and seemed to say a small prayer, as though they were expecting to crash and were preparing to die. When one of the U.S. passengers called the flight attendant's attention to this behavior and asked what it meant, the flight attendant was not sure enough of the accurate interpretation to respond, even though the flight attendant felt it was his responsibility to respond in some way.

2. Identify the perspectives.

From the Latin Americans' perspective, they were practicing their religious beliefs as they had learned them to provide comfort in a stressful or unfamiliar situation.
  From the U.S. passenger's perspective, there was some suspicion associated with a group of persons speaking a foreign language and performing an unfamiliar ritual.
  From the flight attendant's perspective, he had to explain a cultural behavior that he didn't really understand.

3. Indicate which barriers apply to the following five elements of the situation:

1. the use of a foreign language
2. religious beliefs that seem strange to some and familiar to others
3. suspicion of foreigners
4. an unfamiliar way to cope with a situation
5. an unfamiliar gesture with ambiguous meaning.

Situation 2: A Money Tip

1. Read the situation.

During a flight through the Middle East, one wealthy Middle Eastern passenger was very pleased with the service he received from the flight attendant and wanted to show his appreciation. As the flight was preparing to land, he handed the flight attendant a sealed envelope and asked her not to open the envelope until she reached her hotel that night. The flight attendant agreed not to open the envelope and accepted his explanation that it was a card with a poem of appreciation in it and that he would be embarrassed if the flight attendant opened it in his presence. When the flight attendant opened the envelope later, she discovered that it contained a large amount of money.

(continued)

2. Identify the perspectives.

From the Middle Eastern passenger's viewpoint, he was used to giving a gift of appreciation for special occasions, and to have the gift rejected would be a serious insult to him.

From the flight attendant's point of view, it was not according to regulations to accept money gifts, but she didn't want to offend the passenger either, and she would like to keep the money.

3. Indicate which barriers apply to the following five elements of the situation:

1. the money itself and what it symbolizes
2. the possible expectation that the passenger might want special favors
3. airline regulations prohibiting both accepting money and offending passengers
4. Middle Eastern customs regarding giving and receiving gifts
5. anxiety in wanting to please both the airline and the passenger.

Situation 3: Left-Handed Flight Attendant

1. Read the situation.

A flight attendant happens to be left-handed and normally uses her left hand in whatever task she performs. On one flight, a Middle Eastern passenger traveling first class became extremely upset when the flight attendant served him his drink with her left hand, and he refused to accept the service. Furthermore, the passenger insisted on filing a formal complaint against the flight attendant for being extremely insulting and failing to acquaint herself with Middle Eastern customs.

2. Identify the perspectives.

The Middle Eastern passenger expected the flight attendant to know Middle Eastern customs because the airline flies to that part of the world. He was insulted when the flight attendant used her left hand, which is considered both ritually and literally unclean in Middle Eastern culture.

The flight attendant did not understand what she had done wrong and saw herself as treating all passengers alike. If the rest of the passengers were happy with the service, she felt, why should this passenger be unhappy?

3. Indicate which barriers apply to the following five elements of the situation:

1. Middle Eastern customs about the left hand being unclean
2. the passenger's expectation that flight attendants are culturally knowledgeable
3. the flight attendant's habit of using her left hand
4. the anger of the Middle Eastern passenger
5. stress at having made the Middle Eastern passenger angry enough to write a complaint letter.

Situation 4: Finger Snapping

1. Read the situation.

A well-dressed and apparently wealthy Latin American man was sitting in the first class section, demanding special attention from the flight attendant. He would call for the flight attendant by snapping his fingers repeatedly until the flight attendant turned around and came over to his seat. The flight attendant had experienced more than enough difficulty during the day and was getting irritated at his calling by snapping his fingers.

2. Identify the perspectives.

From the Latin American passenger's point of view, he was calling for service as he would call for any servant back home, and he was required to show only the courtesies he would show those of lesser rank in society.

From the flight attendant's viewpoint, the passenger's snapping his fingers was demeaning and offensive in the extreme and suggested his wanting immediate and very special attention beyond the attention given to other passengers.

(continued)

3. Indicate which barriers apply to the following five elements of the situation:

1. snapping fingers as a mode of asking for service
2. a superior attitude toward inferior ranks of society
3. anger at being looked down upon
4. stereotypes of servants and inclusion of flight attendants in the category of servant
5. unwillingness to adapt to other forms of calling for service, like using the call button.

Situation 5: European Style

1. Read the situation.

One of the European flight attendants was being criticized by the other flight attendants for being blunt and discourteous in her treatment of passengers and in her relations with other flight attendants. When the European flight attendant was confronted with this criticism, she defended herself as being appropriately formal in her relationships according to the guidelines of professional behavior. She interpreted any less formal behaviors as unprofessional. Several of the U.S. flight attendants discussed ways of dealing with this difference of opinion.

2. Identify the perspectives.

From the European flight attendant's point of view, she should be allowed to conduct her work independently in a formal and professional style as she had learned from her culture, without interference from coworkers.

From the U.S. flight attendants' point of view, it is necessary to be informal and friendly to all passengers and for flight attendants from all cultures to work together as a team on that basis.

3. Indicate which barriers apply to the following five elements of the situation:

1. the learned meaning of professional behavior
2. the interpretation of formal behavior as unfriendly
3. isolation of a culturally different coworker
4. stereotypes of passenger reactions to formal behavior by a flight attendant
5. the giving of negative feedback to a coworker from another culture.

Situation 6: Everybody Looks Alike

1. Read the situation.

A U.S. passenger called one of the Asian flight attendants and asked her to return her bag to her. The Asian flight attendant insisted that she had not taken the woman's bag, but the passenger became more and more angry, insisting that the Asian flight attendant was lying. At this point, one of the other Asian flight attendants came up to the woman and said that she had been the flight attendant who had stored the woman's bag and would get it immediately. The U.S. passenger excused herself, saying that "all Asians look alike anyway."

2. Identify the perspectives.

From the U.S. passenger's point of view, she was a bit suspicious of the foreign flight attendants and was anxious to make sure that she was not being taken advantage of in any way.

From the flight attendant's point of view, people of Asian origin were being unfairly stereotyped as all alike and not being acknowledged as individuals, just because they were from a different culture.

3. Indicate which barriers apply to the following five elements of the situation:

1. stereotypes about Asian flight attendants
2. anger at believing she was being lied to by the flight attendant
3. embarrassment of both passenger and flight attendants
4. similarity between the two Asian flight attendants
5. the passenger's anxiety about her bag.

(continued)

Situation 7: Knife, Fork, and Spoon

1. Read the situation.

The very traditional Japanese passenger was obviously uncomfortable during the meal service and was not touching any of the food. The passenger had indicated earlier that she was very hungry, so the flight attendant was surprised when he picked up her full tray at the end of the meal service. Later, the person sitting next to the passenger talked with the flight attendant and confided that the passenger did not eat, even though she was hungry, because she was not used to using a knife and fork, but preferred chopsticks.

2. Identify the perspectives.

The Japanese passenger wanted to avoid the embarrassment of either asking for chopsticks or trying to eat with a knife and fork and doing it improperly, so she chose to withdraw.

The flight attendant did not know that the passenger preferred chopsticks and served her the way he had served all the other passengers, assuming that all passengers would prefer knives and forks.

3. Indicate which barriers would apply to the following four aspects of the situation:

1. the unfamiliar custom of eating with a knife, fork, and spoon
2. the embarrassment of requiring special attention
3. the expectation that all passengers eat with a knife, fork, and spoon
4. the lack of fluency in English by the passenger or in Japanese by the flight attendant.

Situation 8: Saying Yes or No

1. Read the situation.

A Chinese passenger who did not speak English was flying alone and was shy among so many strangers. The flight attendant was trying to help the passenger to be more comfortable, but every time the flight attendant would ask her a question, the passenger would shake her head up and down, as though saying yes, while moving her open palm from side to side in front of her face, as though saying no. The more the flight attendant tried to interpret her gestures, the more embarrassed and uncomfortable the passenger became.

2. Identify the perspectives.

From the Chinese passenger's point of view, she was more interested in reducing embarrassment than in getting service. She was trying to respond appropriately in a neutral way that left the interpretation up to the flight attendant.

From the flight attendant's viewpoint, she was trying to get a simple yes or no answer from the passenger so she could get on with the job of providing service. She was determined to get a response without regard for the embarrassment that resulted.

3. Indicate which barriers apply to the following five elements of this situation:

1. the ambiguous hand signal
2. the expectation that the passenger wants service
3. the method of saying yes or no to a question
4. anxiety at flying by herself
5. the embarrassment of not being able to respond appropriately as the flight attendant expected a passenger should respond.

(continued)

Answers

Situation 1: (1) language differences, (2) stereotyping, (3) evaluation and stereotyping, (4) stress, and (5) use of nonverbal communication.

Situation 2: (1) use of nonverbal communication, (2) stereotyping and evaluation, (3) evaluation and stress, (4) use of nonverbal communication and stereotyping, and (5) stress.

Situation 3: (1) use of nonverbal communication and evaluation, (2) stereotyping, (3) use of nonverbal communication, (4) stress, and (5) stress and evaluation.

Situation 4: (1) use of nonverbal communication, (2) evaluation and stereotyping, (3) stress, (4) stereotyping, and (5) use of nonverbal communication and stereotyping.

Situation 5: (1) stereotyping, (2) use of nonverbal communication, (3) evaluation, (4) stereotyping, and (5) evaluation.

Situation 6: (1) stereotyping, (2) stress and evaluation, (3) stress and evaluation, (4) stereotyping, and (5) stress.

Situation 7: (1) use of nonverbal communication, (2) stress and evaluation, (3) stereotyping and evaluation, (4) language differences, and (5) stress.

Situation 8: (1) use of nonverbal communication, (2) stereotyping, (3) language differences, (4) stress, and (5) stress and stereotyping.

Note. From *Decisional Dialogues in a Cultural Context: Structured Exercises* (pp. 127–137), by P. B. Pedersen and D. Hernandez, 1997, Thousand Oaks, CA: Sage. Copyright 1997 by Sage. Adapted with permission.

73 POTLUCK DINNER

Objective: To eat together as a valuable example of common ground across cultures.

TIME REQUIRED   An evening

RISK LEVEL   Low

PARTICIPANTS NEEDED   Any number of participants

PROCEDURE   Please take the following steps:

1. Discuss the possibility of a potluck dinner with the group, and get their support before scheduling the meal. It might be a way to provide closure to a series of regular meetings.
2. Decide who should bring which food, perhaps emphasizing foods with cultural meaning.
3. Schedule an appropriate place for the meal, which could be the regular classroom, someone's home, or some other setting.
4. Consider bringing in entertainment; entertainment by group members might be a good idea.
5. Prepare a 2 to 3 minute thank-you talk in case it is appropriate to use during the meal event.

DEBRIEFING   In debriefing the leader will want to give each member an opportunity to talk about their experiences in the group thus far, about what the symbol of eating together means

---

Note. From *Instructor's Manual for Intentional Group Counseling: A Microskills Approach* (p. 66), by P. B. Pedersen, A. E. Ivey, M. B. Ivey, and Y. Y. Kuo, 2001, Belmont, CA: Brooks/Cole. Copyright 2001 by Brooks/Cole. Adapted with permission of Wadsworth, a division of Thomas Learning.

to them, and about the symbolic significance of the food they brought to dinner. Some questions for discussion are as follows:

1. Which time and place would be most appropriate for this potluck dinner?
2. Which foods would be most appropriate?
3. Can cultural traditions from group members be incorporated in the meal?
4. Do you want to invite guests, such as resource people from other class meetings?
5. How can this potluck dinner best and most meaningfully fit in with other activities of the group?

INSIGHT   Food and eating together are an excellent example of common ground across cultures.

74 EVALUATING A WORKSHOP WITH A PRETEST AND A POSTTEST

> *Objective:* To provide an example of pretesting and posttesting to evaluate learning from training activities.

TIME REQUIRED   An hour at the beginning and an hour at the end of a workshop

RISK LEVEL   Low

PARTICIPANTS NEEDED   Any number of participants, plus a facilitator

PROCEDURE   Please take the following steps:

1. Give the participants a pretest before the training experience. Ask them to indicate where they rate themselves currently and to estimate where they expect to be at the end of the training.
2. After the training experience is over, ask the participants again to rate where they are currently and to indicate where they were before the training activity. In this way it is possible to identify change resulting from the training activity at several levels. First, the comparison of scores indicates one aspect of change resulting from training. Second, the comparison of where trainees expected to be after training and where they actually are indicates a second aspect of change. Third, the comparison of the trainee's pretest ratings made before and after the training also indicates an aspect of change.

DEBRIEFING   In some cases the trainees may have overrated or underrated their abilities before training, so it would be possible for a successful training program to result in lower but more realistic ratings. In other cases, the trainee may have overestimated or underestimated where they would be after training. This evaluation format is useful in comparing perceptions, expectations, and actual self-ratings to measure change resulting from the training activity. Some discussion questions are as follows:

1. What are the criteria for evaluating a multicultural training workshop?
2. How do you know that the same score has the same meaning across individuals from different cultures?
3. Why is evaluation of multicultural training activities important?
4. Do some cultures put more emphasis on formal evaluation than others?
5. How might you conduct an informal evaluation?

INSIGHT   Evaluating multicultural training activities is especially difficult.

75 SCRIPTS FOR TRIGGER VIDEOTAPES

Objective: To rehearse managing conflict by creating brief videotapes to trigger a discussion on differences.

TIME REQUIRED   About a half day

RISK LEVEL   Moderate

PARTICIPANTS   Any number of participants, plus a facilitator
NEEDED

PROCEDURE   Please take the following steps:

1. Ask local resource people to read the statements in Exhibit 4.4 while being recorded with a video camera.
2. Fade to black after each statement. A less complicated version could be produced on audiotape.
3. Once you have created the stimulus videotape or audiotape, present the stimulus to the students, and ask them to respond by writing down their reactions. A more powerful version would be to have students view and respond to each stimulus in private.
4. When all students have had an opportunity to respond, organize small groups to discuss their responses.
5. Next, organize a large group discussion.

DEBRIEFING   The trigger videotapes present highly emotional statements out of context, and participants respond to the statements in an imagined context. These potentially explosive

Note. From *Decisional Dialogues in a Cultural Context: Structured Exercises* (p. 81), by P. B. Pedersen and D. Hernandez, 1997, Thousand Oaks, CA: Sage. Copyright 1997 by Sage. Adapted with permission.

Exhibit 4.4 *Statements Indicating Emotions for Use as Scripts for Trigger Videotapes*

Fear Statements

1. Don't tell my supervisor I'm here!
2. My supervisor is going to have my butt when he finds out I filed this complaint.
3. There's no way I'd confront him!
4. I can't tell my boss to get off my back!
5. Bosses are not supposed to have these types of problems!

Anger Statements

1. Go straight to hell!
2. If that honky ever crosses my path again, I'll kill him!
3. I'm looking at you, knot head!
4. Every time he even comes near me, I could scream!
5. Get your act together.
6. I could have had that job if a pretty girl hadn't applied!
7. You've always got some kind of problem.
8. I don't care what my boss does; I'm not going back to the job!
9. You can take this job (or place) and shove it!

Contempt Statements

1. I can't stand to be near him.
2. Don't you realize what's going on around here?
3. You're just protecting the system and don't give a damn.
4. What do you care, you're just like all the rest.
5. If I had my way, I'd cram them all in this engine and blow them out the afterburner.
6. He (or she) is a weasel.
7. You don't really know what I'm getting at, do you?
8. You're reprehensible.

Frustration Statements

1. Just what do you want from me?
2. I feel like I'm going in circles.
3. I give up.
4. Please repeat that, and talk slower.
5. If I see this one more time, I'll scream.
6. Why do you keep interrupting me?
7. Man, I just got to get out of this place.
8. Every time I suggest a new idea, I get shot down.
9. The women in my section get away with murder.

Note. From *Decisional Dialogues in a Cultural Context: Structured Exercises* (p. 81), by P. B. Pedersen and D. Hernandez, 1997, Thousand Oaks, CA: Sage. Copyright 1997 by Sage. Adapted with permission.

emotional statements may trigger a reaction among students who have experienced such statements in the real world. The facilitator needs to be cautious in exploring the students' responses to these stimuli and not press the students to disclose more than they want. Some discussion questions are as follows:

1. Which statements inspired the most emotional reactions, and why?
2. Have you ever experienced situations where similar statements were made?
3. How do different cultures express emotion differently?

4. How should one react to each statement in the U.S. culture?
5. Are "direct" cultures more verbally abusive than "indirect" cultures?

It is usually more difficult to respond to a highly emotional statement than to one showing less emotion, especially in a multicultural situation.

76 INTERCULTURAL COMMUNICATION SKILLS FOR HELP PROVIDERS IN THE MILITARY

Objective: To view military rank and service branch as cultural groups.

TIME REQUIRED   About a half day to a full day

RISK LEVEL   Moderate

PARTICIPANTS NEEDED   Any number of participants, plus one facilitator

PROCEDURE   Please take the following steps:

1. Prepare copies of the seven situations in Exhibit 4.5 and distribute them to participants.
2. Instruct participants to read one or more of the situations and to provide several responses to each situation, indicating which is most appropriate. Then, ask them to explain why they chose the response as most appropriate in the following way: Is it what they feel they would *like* to do, *should* do, or would actually do?
3. Ask the students to identify which of the five intercultural barriers are relevant to each situation: language differences, use of nonverbal communication, stereotypes, evaluation, and stress.

DEBRIEFING   The facilitator needs to be sensitive to the unique situation of military culture, particularly if the training group includes people of different rank and service branch, so that no participant is embarrassed or put in a difficult situation with consequences in real life outside the training situation. Some discussion questions are as follows:

1. How is the military culture uniquely different from other cultural groups?
2. Were you able to identify barriers to communication?

Note. From *Decisional Dialogues in a Cultural Context: Structured Exercises* (pp. 109–115), by P. B. Pedersen and D. Hernandez, 1997, Thousand Oaks, CA: Sage. Copyright 1997 by Sage. Adapted with permission.

3. Were you able to identify strategies for decreasing intercultural communication barriers?
4. Which barriers were the most difficult to overcome?
5. Have you had actual experience with these communication barriers?

INSIGHT Barriers to communication are viewed differently by those outside the military culture than by those inside that culture.

Exhibit 4.5   *Critical Incidents in the Military*

Sexual Harassment

Complainant: Chief Master Sergeant (CMS) White male

Offender: White female secretary

Complaint: A secretary in my office has lodged a sexual harassment complaint against me with the civilian equal opportunity office (EEO). She claims I sexually harassed her by using endearing terms and derogatory comments. She lodged this complaint yesterday based on a statement I made that she claims was offensive. The statement was made in pure jest. She usually carries a key to the duplication machine that is tied to a large metal hook. She appeared to be in a good mood, and I was in a good mood, so I said, "Hey, here comes my favorite hooker." There were two other individuals standing by, and they chimed in, saying, "Yeah, ours, too." Everybody laughed, including her, then went on with his or her business. Yesterday I received notice of a complaint being lodged against me.

Military Dependents: National Origin

Complainant: Asian female dependent

Offender: Black female dependent

Complaint: We bowl every Friday night. I'm on a bowling team with three other ladies from Korea and Thailand. There is a Black woman on one of the other teams who continually talks about us. She calls us names and stares at us the whole time we are bowling. She slapped her husband one night because he was talking to me about Korea. She told me that she didn't want me nowhere near her husband. I don't know him and didn't start the conversation that night. I don't mind the stares so much, but I get embarrassed at the way she talks about us. I reported her to the manager at the bowling alley, but he said there was nothing he could do. My husband is in the Navy and has been at sea for 5 months, so he can't help me. The woman says we have no right to bowl in the Air Force Bowling Alley, but the rule only states that we be military dependents to join the league. I want her to stop talking about me and stop staring at me. Can you help?

Racism Complaint

Complainant: Black male Half Sergeant (SSgt)

Offender: SSgt. Marine

Complaint: I went into the marine enlisted club looking to have a beer and cool off. This marine sitting at the bar began to stare at me. I ordered a drink and some chips and began to watch TV at the bar. The Marine SSgt made a comment that I should use the Air Force Club; they usually cater to my kind. I tried to ignore him, but he continued to make racial slurs directed at me. The bartender tried to quiet him down without success. Finally, I reported him to the night manager. They appeared to know each other well. Finally, the guy left. The night manager informed me there might be trouble if I left by the front entrance and suggested I leave by a side door. I decided to have another drink and left by the front door. The SSgt was waiting, and we got into a fight. The police arrested both of us, releasing me to my commander. I want you to get the marine charged with racial prejudice and get my record wiped clean.

(continued)

Exhibit 4.5 *Critical Incidents in the Military (Continued)*

Commander Religion

Complainant: Female First Lieutenant

Offender: Male Lieutenant Colonel

Complaint: I have a young female First Lieutenant assigned to my unit who said she was going to lodge a complaint against me. She claims I will not allow her an opportunity to participate in various religious activities involving her church. The Lieutenant is an excellent musician, I'm told, and is in charge of her church choir. She claims that I've prevented her from attending various functions by changing her shift schedules. The Lieutenant is one of three officers assigned to the unit. We are required to have one officer on call each night, ready to respond at a moment's notice. The Lieutenant, aside from being the newest member on board, single, and living on base, was recently trained on some delicate equipment that one other officer is temporary duty (TDY) receiving training for. Prior to her arrival, duties were covered by my two male officers. With one being TDY, I felt the Lieutenant must shoulder a larger role of responsibility. My remaining Captain has long been involved in some off-duty education and is nearing completion. I do not feel I should hinder him in his endeavors at this time. The problem will be resolved within 2 months with the return of the Captain who is TDY and the completion of the second Captain's education. I feel my actions are correct based on the circumstances. How can I prevent her from filing an equal opportunity training (EOT) complaint against me?

Racism Complaint

Complainant: Black male Sergeant

Offender: White male Technical Sergeant (TSgt)

Complaint: Three days ago I was involved in a name-calling incident with one of the guys in my dorm. He called me a name, I called him a name, we both went into our rooms, and that ended it. Last night a TSgt came into the dorm looking for the guy I previously had the name-calling incident with. I came out of my door as he was going by. The TSgt asked me if I knew where the other guy lived. I said yeah, down the hall. The TSgt asked me to show him the room. I said I was in a hurry and really didn't want to have anything to do with the guy. The TSgt insisted by grabbing me by the arm. I jerked my arm back, telling him not to grab me. At that time the administrator I'd had the problem with stuck his head outside the door and yelled, "Sarge, that's the. . . . I was telling you about. He's always starting trouble." I yelled back at him, saying he should mind his own business. The TSgt said he'd handle this dumb . . . . Based on the TSgt's statement about the incident, I received a letter of reprimand for insubordination. I want the letter of reprimand withdrawn and the TSgt cited for prejudice. Can you help me?

Sexual Discrimination by Supervisor

Complainant: Female security policeman

Offender: Male supervisor

Complaint: In October I was called into my supervisor's office and informed that my application for dog handler training was being disapproved. I had applied for this training 3 months prior. At the time I applied, two men requested the same training. The three of us have approximately the same time in service and the same rank and experience in the Security Police. I am friends with the two men and was informed by them that their applications were approved at base level and sent forward to the commander with recommendation for approval. My supervisor informed me that my application was disapproved in the squadron because they did not feel I was strong enough to control a dog. He further stated that, in their opinion, I had shown an abnormal fear of large dogs and possibly would wash out of school because of this. The supervisor could have only gotten this information through conversation with one of the other applicants. He has never observed me around animals. I've got a good working relationship with the supervisors and most of the people in the section. I don't want to ruin it. I would like a shot at the school, but I don't want to cause trouble in the squadron. What should I do?

(continued)

Exhibit 4.5   *Critical Incidents in the Military (Continued)*

Sexual Harassment

Complainant: White woman (military)

Offenders: Two civilian contractors

Complaint: They are painting some empty houses on my street. Since I live on base, I go home for lunch each day. When I get out of my car, they will usually come to the door of the house they are painting and whistle or yell at me. I have reported them, but nothing has come of it. I want them to leave me alone and, if possible, have the contractor thrown off base for not taking action. What should I do?

Note. From *Decisional Dialogues in a Cultural Context: Structured Exercises* (pp. 109–115), by P. B. Pedersen and D. Hernandez, 1997, Thousand Oaks, CA: Sage. Copyright 1997 by Sage. Adapted with permission.

77 REHEARSAL DEMONSTRATION MODEL

Objective: To rehearse the role of an Alter Ego with someone from another culture.

TIME REQUIRED — About a half day

RISK LEVEL — Moderate

PARTICIPANTS NEEDED — Any number of participants, plus a facilitator

PROCEDURE — Please take the following steps:

1. Assemble a multicultural group of participants.
2. Organize the group so that half sit in a circle of chairs and the other half stand behind the seated members. The standing person will become the Alter Ego of the seated partner. Every time the seated person speaks or might have a viewpoint, the Alter Ego will express that implicit message to the group. For example, if the person smiles and agrees with the leader, the Alter Ego might say, "That doesn't make any sense at all, but since you are giving me a grade, I had better pretend to accept what you say and not make waves." Help students generate new situations and scripts to rehearse managing conflict in its multicultural context.
3. When the group discussion has continued for a while, ask the members to pause and discuss what they have learned before continuing.

DEBRIEFING — In debriefing this experience, it is important to point out that the Alter Ego might not always be right. However, the Alter Ego gives an alternative interpretation, and by

Note. From *Hidden Messages in Culture-Centered Counseling: A Triad Training Model* (pp. 132–133), by P. B. Pedersen, 2000, Thousand Oaks, CA: Sage. Copyright 2000 by Sage. Adapted with permission.

observing the member's reaction to that interpretation, it will be possible to judge whether the Alter Ego was on target or not. Some discussion questions are as follows:

1. Were some Alter Egos more accurate than others?
2. Were Alter Egos that were from the same culture as their partners more accurate?
3. Why were some messages not made explicit in the discussion except through the Alter Ego?
4. How would multicultural communication be changed if people understood what others are thinking but not saying?
5. How will you use what you learned in this experience?

INSIGHT   People from different cultures do not always say everything they are thinking.

78 ROLE-PLAYING A TRANSCRIPT

Objective: To bring a multicultural transcript to life by taking on the different roles.

TIME REQUIRED   About a half day

RISK LEVEL   Moderate

PARTICIPANTS NEEDED   Any number of participants, plus a facilitator

PROCEDURE   Please take the following steps:

1. Obtain transcripts of multicultural interviews from books or other sources, and distribute the transcripts to each class member.
2. Ask group members to volunteer to role-play each of the characters in the transcript and to be interviewed (in role) by the other group members about what he or she thought about the people in the transcript. By interviewing each of the characters in the transcript, the group members will have a chance to analyze and evaluate the process comments accompanying the transcript and to personalize the transcript for themselves. You may want to do several different transcripts.
3. Limit the interviews of characters to no more than 10 minutes each to reduce stress for the role-player.

DEBRIEFING   In debriefing this experience, the leader will want to have group members identify how the interaction changed their opinion about the character in the transcript. Some questions for discussion are as follows:

1. What do you like and not like about each character in the role-play?
2. Who did you identify with?

3. What do you think the different characters wanted out of their transcript conversation?
4. Were the different cultural groups presented authentically?
5. How will you apply what you learned in this experience?

INSIGHT   Taking on the role of a stranger provides insight into that person's perspective.

79

A SYNTHETIC CULTURE
TRAINING LABORATORY

Objective: To simulate the interaction of four contrasting groups discussing problems caused by outsiders who attempt to find common ground without sacrificing their integrity.

TIME REQUIRED   A half day

RISK LEVEL   Moderate

PARTICIPANTS NEEDED   Any number of participants and a facilitator acquainted with the Synthetic Culture Lab or Hofstede's (2001) research

PROCEDURE   Please take the following steps:

1. Distribute the time schedule in Exhibit 4.6.
2. Announce the objective of this experience as this: to role-play four contrasting synthetic cultures in a simulation demonstrating the importance of identifying cultural similarities and differences.
3. Introduce the four synthetic cultures. Guidelines are presented in Exhibit 4.7.
4. Have students select a synthetic culture identity for themselves either because it fits with or contrasts with their own viewpoint or for any other reason they choose.
5. Have students assemble in a small group with their synthetic culture co-members to socialize one another into the new synthetic culture identity.
6. As students discuss the written rules for their synthetic culture, they should incorporate those very same rules into their communication with other group members.

Note. From *Culture-Centered Counseling and Interviewing Skills* (pp. 67–75), by P. B. Pedersen and A. E. Ivey, 1993, Westport, CT: Greenwood/Praeger. Copyright 1993 by Greenwood/Praeger. Adapted with permission.

Exhibit 4.6 *Schedule for a Synthetic Culture Training Laboratory*

1:30 p.m.	Introduction to four synthetic cultures: Alpha (high power distance), Beta (strong uncertainty avoidance), Gamma (strong individualism), and Delta (high masculine). Participants will be divided into four corresponding groups to

- learn the assumptions and rules of their synthetic culture;
- discuss the problems created by the "outsiders" in each synthetic culture; and
- select a team of two consultants from each synthetic culture who will visit the other three host cultures to help them deal with the problem of outsiders.

2:30 p.m.	By this time, the four small groups should have completed the above three tasks and be ready to do the following:

The first rotation will require sending teams of consultants from each synthetic home culture to each synthetic host culture for a 10-minute consultation in role, followed by a 10-minute debriefing out of role and 10 minutes to report back to their home synthetic culture on what they learned.

3:00 p.m.	The second rotation will follow the same pattern as the first with the next synthetic host culture.
3:30 p.m.	The third rotation will follow the same pattern as the first two with the final synthetic host culture.
4:00 p.m.	Each synthetic culture group will report back to the assembled participants on how to find common ground and agreement between their own culture and persons from different cultural backgrounds.

The instructor will lead a synthesis of learning for the day and completion of evaluation forms.

4:30 p.m.	End of day.

7. Direct students to take on their new synthetic culture identity in everything they say and do.
8. Have the synthetic culture groups review the list of problems created in their synthetic culture because of "outsiders." Each synthetic culture community has a problem with outsiders from the other three synthetic culture communities who move into other communities as refugees, visitors, tourists, students, and immigrants. These outsiders have caused serious problems in the schools, institutions, and community because they disregard that culture's way of doing things. They do not believe the same things as people from that culture. Ask students to write a list of two or three specific problems that have resulted from interacting with outsiders.
9. Direct each group to select a team of two consultants who will be sent to another synthetic culture to help them work on the problems caused by outsiders. Have groups send the team to the next synthetic host culture and receive a team from a different synthetic culture.
10. Instruct the groups to complete the three rotations so that each home culture has sent a team to each of the three other host cultures in turn.

Exhibit 4.7   *Guidelines for the Four Synthetic Cultures*

Alpha Culture: High Power Distance

Power distance indicates the extent to which a culture accepts that power is unequally distributed in institutions and organizations. Alpha culture accepts a large degree of unequal distribution of power.

Alpha Behaviors

Language

Alphas will use the following words with a positive meaning: *respect, father* (as a title), *master, servant, older brother, younger brother, wisdom, favor, protect, obey, orders,* and *pleasing.*

   Alphas will use the following words with a negative meaning: *rights, complain, negotiate, fairness, task, necessity, co-determination, objectives, question,* and *criticize.*

Behaviors and Their Meanings

The following behaviors by Alphas will express the corresponding meanings:

Behavior	Meaning
Is soft-spoken and polite and listens	Friendliness
Is quiet and polite but does not listen	Unfriendliness
Asks for help and direction	Trust
Does not ask for help and direction	Distrust
Is positive and animated, but makes no eye contact	Interest
Is expressionless and unanimated, but makes eye contact	Boredom

Barriers to Communication

- *Language differences:* Alphas are very verbal but usually soft-spoken and polite.
- *Use of nonverbal communication:* Alphas are usually restrained and formal.
- *Stereotypes:* Alphas are hierarchical and seek to please.
- *Evaluation:* Alphas tend to blame themselves for any problems that come up.
- *Stress:* Alphas internalize stress and express stress indirectly.

Gender Roles

Role of Gender

Leadership roles may be held by either men or women. If the society is matriarchal, the visible power of women in decision making is likely to be more obvious than in patriarchal societies, where the visible power of men would be more obvious.

Role of Women

In home and family affairs, women are likely to be very powerful, even though that power might be less visible than the more visible male roles. Although women may seem subservient, they may not in fact be so.

Role of Men

Men in leadership roles are often held accountable for the consequences of their decisions. If they lose the support of the women, new leaders will emerge. Although men may be the visible traditional leaders, the men may be much more subservient in less visible and more private social roles in a balance of power.

Beta Culture: Strong Uncertainty Avoidance

Uncertainty avoidance indicates a lack of tolerance of uncertainty and ambiguity. Beta culture members seek to avoid such uncertainty.

(continued)

Exhibit 4.7   *Guidelines for the Four Synthetic Cultures (Continued)*

Beta Behaviors

Language

Betas will use the following words with a positive meaning: *structure, duty, truth, law, order, certain, clear, clean, secure, safe, predictable,* and *right.*

Betas will use the following words with a negative meaning: *maybe, creative conflict, tolerant, experiment, spontaneous, relativity, insight, unstructured, loose,* and *flexible.*

Behaviors and Their Meanings

The following behaviors by Betas will indicate the corresponding meanings:

Behavior	Meaning
Gives detailed responses; is formal, specific and unambiguous	Friendliness
Gives generalized, ambiguous responses; is anxious to end the interview	Unfriendliness
Separates right from wrong unambiguously	Trust
Is openly critical; challenges the credentials of others	Distrust
Is verbal and task oriented; questions with direct eye contact	Interest
Is passive and quiet; makes no direct eye contact	Boredom

Barriers to Communication

- *Language:* Betas are very verbal and well organized and are somewhat loud.
- *Use of nonverbal communication:* Betas are animated in using hands but make little or no physical contact.
- *Stereotypes:* Betas have rigid beliefs that don't change easily.
- *Evaluation:* Betas quickly evaluate a situation to establish right and wrong, sometimes prematurely.
- *Stress:* Betas externalize stress and usually make the other person feel the stress rather than themselves.

Gender Roles

Role of Gender

The right and appropriate roles of men and women are rigidly defined without ambiguity. The dress, behavior, and functions of men and women are defined by rules, traditions, and carefully guarded boundaries.

Role of Women

Women tend to be in charge of home, family, children, and religious or traditional spiritual rituals as guardians of society through a romantic and idealized role of who the woman should be. Society can be very unforgiving to women who rebel or violate those rules, although elderly women may take on traditional power roles otherwise reserved for men.

Role of Men

Men are expected to take care of the women and to protect the home and family by providing for material needs and demonstrating strength in their public posture. Men are expected to be more visible in their public roles than women, and women—especially younger women—might have difficulty sharing power with men in public or work roles.

(continued)

Exhibit 4.7   *Guidelines for the Four Synthetic Cultures (Continued)*

Gamma Culture: High Individualism

Individualism indicates the extent to which a culture believes that people are supposed to take care of themselves and remain emotionally independent from groups, organizations, and other collectivities. Gamma culture places a high value on individualism.

Gamma Behaviors

Language

Gammas will use the following words with a positive meaning: *self, friendship, do your own thing, contract, litigation, self-respect, self-interest, self-actualizing, individual, dignity, I and me, pleasure, adventurous,* and *guilt.*

Gammas will use the following words with a negative meaning: *harmony, face, we, obligation, sacrifice, family, tradition, decency, honor, duty, loyalty,* and *shame.*

Behaviors and Their Meanings

The following behaviors by Gammas reflect the corresponding meanings:

Behavior	Meaning
Is verbal and self-disclosing	Friendliness
Is critical and likely to subvert or sabotage	Unfriendliness
Aggressively debates issues and controls the interview	Trust
Is noncommittal, passive, ambiguous, and defensive	Distrust
Is loudly verbal and questioning; engages in touching and physical contact	Interest
Maintains physical distance, asks no questions, and makes no eye contact	Boredom

Barriers to Communication

- *Language differences:* Gammas are verbal and self-centered, using *I* and *me* a lot.
- *Use of nonverbal behaviors:* Gammas touch a lot and are somewhat seductive.
- *Stereotypes:* Gammas are defensive and tend to be loners who see others as potential enemies.
- *Evaluation:* Gammas use other people and measure the importance of others in terms of how useful they are.
- *Stress:* Gammas like to take risks and like the challenge of danger to continually test their own ability.

Gender Roles

Role of Gender

Power might as easily be held by men as by women, especially in urban and modernized areas. Gender roles are less rigidly defined, with each gender taking on the roles of the other—to serve his or her self-interests—in public or private activities.

Role of Women

Women are free as long as they have the power to protect themselves. Attractive women can gain power by being manipulative and taking advantage of their beauty. Less assertive and particularly older women are likely to become victims of exploitation by both younger men and women.

Role of Men

Men excel in areas requiring physical strength. Younger, taller, and physically attractive men can be expected to be aggressive in asserting their power over others. Men who are uncomfortable being competitive, especially older men, are likely to be ridiculed as weak and losers.

(continued)

Exhibit 4.7   *Guidelines for the Four Synthetic Cultures (Continued)*

Delta Culture: High Masculinity

Masculinity indicates the extent to which traditional masculine values of assertiveness, money, and things prevail in a culture, as contrasted to traditional feminine values of nurturance, quality of life, and people.

Delta Behaviors

Language

Deltas will use the following words with a positive meaning: *career, competition, fight, aggressive, assertive, success, winner, deserve, merit, balls, excel, force, big, hard, fast,* and *quantity.*

Deltas will use the following words with a negative meaning: *quality, caring, solidarity, modesty, compromise, help, love, grow, small, soft, slow,* and *tender.*

Behaviors and Their Meanings

The following behaviors by Deltas will indicate the corresponding meanings:

Behavior	Meaning
Engages in physical contact; is seductive and loud	Friendliness
Maintains physical distance; is sarcastic and sadistic	Unfriendliness
Is competitive, challenging, and dominating	Trust
Is openly critical and disparaging and is eager to end the interview	Distrust
Is sports oriented, eager to debate, and engaging	Interest
Engages in no eye contact; is discourteous and drowsy	Boredom

Barriers to Communication

- *Language differences:* Deltas are loud and verbal, with a tendency to criticize and argue with others.
- *Use of nonverbal communication:* Deltas like physical contact, direct eye contact, and animated gestures.
- *Stereotypes:* Deltas are macho, are hero and status oriented, and like winners.
- *Evaluation:* Deltas are hard to please, tend to be overachievers and defensive, and blame others for their mistakes.
- *Stress:* Deltas are type A personalities, generating stress through fast-paced lifestyles.

Gender Roles

Role of Gender

Men and more masculine women are typically more powerful and are highly favored in leadership roles. Passive and facilitating behaviors are tolerated in women but not in men. Men are stereotyped as strong and women as weak.

Role of Women

Women tend to be either masculine in their personal style as "one of the guys" or completely subservient and docile, with few women in between. Young and attractive women can use their beauty to win, but without romantic illusions. Older or less attractive women are at a great disadvantage.

Role of Men

Young, strong, tall, and attractive men are idealized as heroes and are admired or envied by others. Men see life as a game played by men, with women as cheerleaders.

(continued)

Exhibit 4.7   *Guidelines for the Four Synthetic Cultures (Continued)*

Brief Comparison of the Behaviors of the Four Synthetic Cultures

Meaning	Behavior			
	Alpha	Beta	Gamma	Delta
Friendliness	Polite and listening	Formal and specific	Verbal and disclosing	Physical and loud
Unfriendliness	Polite and not listening	General and ambiguous	Critical and attacking	Sarcastic and distant
Trust	Asks for help	Actively listens	Debates all topics	Challenges and competes
Distrust	Does not ask for help	Attacks and challenges	Is noncommittal and passive	Is critical and insulting
Interest	Positive, no eye contact	Active, eye contact	Loud and physical	Playful
Boredom	Passive and direct	Passive, no eye contact	Distant, eye contact	Detached, quiet, and distant

Barriers to Communication and the Behaviors of Synthetic Cultures

Barrier	Synthetic Cultures			
	Alpha	Beta	Gamma	Delta
Language differences	Verbal and soft-spoken	Loud and verbal	Verbal and self-centered	Critical and arguing
Use of nonverbal communication	Restrained and formal	Animated and nonphysical	Seductive and physical	Physical and direct
Stereotypes	Hierarchical and pleasing	Promoting of rigid beliefs	Defensive and paranoid	Macho and hero oriented
Evaluation	Self-blaming in evaluations	Premature and selfish	Utilitarian	Overachieving
Stress	Internalizes stress	Externalizes stress	Takes risks	Generates stress
Organizational constraint	Follows formal rules	Is highly structured	Is disorganized and chaotic	Competes to win

Mediating Conflict Between Synthetic Cultures

The following sections examine examples of conflict between synthetic cultures and identify examples of similarities and differences in positive expectations and values that persons from both synthetic cultures share.

Conflict Between an Alpha and a Beta

Alphas emphasize a hierarchy of power where each person has his or her place, showing respect to those above and expecting obedience from those below their own level. Betas dislike uncertainty and do not tolerate ambiguity, so there is a structure of laws that must be obeyed that go beyond the needs of individuals or society. A possible conflict between Alpha and Beta might occur when a high-power-level group of Alphas do whatever they like and disregard the rules, in spite of the objections by Betas in that society.

(continued)

Exhibit 4.7   *Guidelines for the Four Synthetic Cultures (Continued)*

Conflict Between an Alpha and a Gamma

Alphas emphasize a hierarchy of power where each person has his or her place, showing respect to those above and expecting obedience from those below their own level. Gammas are individualistic and believe that everyone should take care of himself or herself and remain emotionally independent from groups, organizations, and society. A possible conflict between Alphas and Gammas might be a group of Gammas who fail to show proper respect for the Alpha leaders.

Conflict Between an Alpha and a Delta

Alphas emphasize a hierarchy of power where each person has his or her place, showing respect to those above and expecting obedience from those below their own level. Deltas are assertive, materialistic, and success oriented, seeking rapid progress and ultimate domination in their relationships with others. A possible conflict would be a group of Deltas who attack the Alpha hierarchy as uneconomic and inefficient and attempt to remove the Alphas from power.

Conflict Between a Beta and a Gamma

Betas avoid uncertainty whenever possible and prefer a structure of clear, unambiguous rules to define truth and duty in their relationships. Gammas are individualistic and believe that everyone should take care of himself or herself and remain emotionally independent from groups, organizations, and society. A possible conflict between Betas and Gammas might be the increased power of Gammas, who promote individual freedom where anybody can do whatever they want and where nobody has a right to control their behavior.

Conflict Between a Beta and a Delta

Betas avoid uncertainty whenever possible and prefer a structure of clear, unambiguous rules to define truth and duty in their relationships. Deltas are assertive, materialistic, and success oriented, seeking rapid progress and ultimate domination in their relationships with others. A possible conflict between Betas and Deltas might be the increased power of a small clique of Deltas who interpret the rules to their own advantage or find ways around the rules to increase their own power in society.

Conflict Between a Gamma and a Delta

Gammas are individualistic and believe that everyone should take care of himself or herself and remain emotionally independent from groups, organizations, and society. Deltas are assertive, materialistic, and success oriented, seeking rapid progress and ultimate domination in their relationships with others. A possible conflict between Gammas and Deltas might be a power struggle where the Deltas use teamwork in their organization to destroy individualistic Gammas and take over power in society.

Outsider Problems

Outsiders cause problems in Alpha culture by emphasizing the equality of all persons, demanding accountability to the community of powerful people, encouraging shared responsibility in the family, promoting shared authority in classrooms, and advocating the decentralization of power.

Outsiders cause problems in Beta culture by emphasizing the importance of uncertainty, the dangers of stress and assertiveness, leniency of rules, interest in things that are different, open-ended learning situations, taking time off, flexibility in use of time, moderation, and the value of human rights.

Outsiders cause problems in Gamma culture by emphasizing the importance of the group, welfare guarantees, the dominant role of government, harmony and consensus, avoidance of confrontations, diplomas as measures of credibility, and relationships prevailing over task goals.

Outsiders cause problems in Delta culture by emphasizing caring for others, warm relationships, modesty, equal rights for men and women, tenderness in relationships, sympathy for the weak, androgyny of gender roles, compromise, negotiation, permissiveness, preservation of the environment, and helping the less fortunate.

Note. From *Culture-Centered Counseling and Interviewing Skills* (pp. 67–75), by P. B. Pedersen and A. E. Ivey, 1993, Westport, CT: Greenwood/Praeger. Copyright 1993 by Greenwood/Praeger. Adapted with permission.

DEBRIEFING   The Synthetic Cultures are based on four dimensions of Geert Hofstede's 55-country database. Each culture represents tendencies of those cultures but each synthetic culture is an abstraction. In this experience, it is useful to have each group discuss and present a report to the larger group on their advice to people coming to their culture and their feedback to the other three synthetic cultures. Some discussion questions are as follows:

1. Were you able to discover elements of all four synthetic cultures in your own culture?
2. Were you able to find common ground without sacrificing integrity?
3. Which synthetic cultures did you work with most constructively?
4. Which synthetic cultures were most difficult to work with?
5. How will you use what you learned from this experience?

INSIGHT   If the training context is safe and if you take some risks, you can learn to find common ground across cultures without sacrificing integrity.

80 CRITICAL INCIDENTS IN MULTICULTURAL ETHICS

Objective: To identify four different ethical perspectives on the same ethical dilemma.

TIME REQUIRED   About a half day

RISK LEVEL   Moderate

PARTICIPANTS NEEDED   Any number of participants, plus one facilitator

PROCEDURE   Please take the following steps:

1. Gather examples of multicultural critical incidents that occurred in a brief 5- to 6-minute period, required a decision to be made, had serious consequences if a wrong decision was made, but had no clearly right decision that was obvious ahead of time.
2. Analyze each critical incident by identifying each behavior that might be interpreted in a negative or potentially hostile way by other individuals or groups but without judging or evaluating the behavior out of context.
3. Analyze each example of different and potentially negative or hostile behavior in terms of the possibility of shared positive common-ground expectations between individuals or groups as a basis for comparing and evaluating the individuals' or group's behavior.
4. Develop an intervention strategy for building on the common ground, shared perceptions of trust, respect, safety, success, or ultimate effective behavior without disregarding the culturally learned interpretations by which those perceptions are manifested.
5. Collect 20 or 30 critical incidents and develop a brief description of the incident plus your analysis of how the individuals or groups are both similar and different and your suggested strategy for evaluating the ethical behavior of the individuals or groups.

6. Divide participants into several small groups of about five people per group. Give each group copies of all the incidents to work with.

7. Give each group an equal amount of time (5 or 10 minutes) to discuss each incident and evaluate your intervention strategy in terms of its ethical adequacy. If the group believes they have a more adequate ethical intervention strategy for the critical incident, ask them to identify that strategy.

8. When all the groups have evaluated each critical incident and your intervention strategy in terms of ethical adequacy, introduce the four classical ethical positions based on consequences, intentions, absolute truth, and culturally relative truth (see Exhibit 3.12 in chap. 3, this volume), and ask the group to discuss the perceptual strategy they judged as most ethically adequate in terms of these four interpretative dimensions.

9. Ask each group to report on how the same critical incidents were evaluated differently to demonstrate the influence of each individual or group's indigenous ethical standards.

10. Lead a general discussion on "doing the right thing" in multicultural situations, demonstrating that ethical decision making is not only "right," but it often is more efficient and leads to more effective action as practicing professionals make accurate judgments.

DEBRIEFING   The facilitator will want to emphasize the importance of common ground in "doing the right thing." Focus on the four classical ethical traditions of making ethical judgments based on consequences, intentions, absolute truths, or cultural relativity. Some discussion questions are as follows:

1. Were you able to see how all four classical ethical traditions apply to doing the right thing?

2. In what ways do different cultures have different ways of making ethical judgments?

3. Identify one incident where two different cultures would make quite different decisions.

4. Are you now more aware of your own ethical decision-making process?

5. Why is common ground essential to making ethical judgments?

INSIGHT   Each cultural context defines its own ethical criteria for judging right and wrong behavior.

81 AMERICAN AND CONTRAST-AMERICAN VALUES

> *Objective*: To identify American values, as well as "contrast-American" values, that determine conflicting points of view in a cross-cultural encounter as a means to better understand the variety of worldviews in cultures outside the American context. (Contrast-American is an artificial identity constructed by establishing opposite alternatives to the typical American perspective.)

TIME REQUIRED   About a half day

RISK LEVEL   Moderate

PARTICIPANTS NEEDED   Any number of participants, plus a facilitator

PROCEDURE   Please take the following steps:

1. Ask students to identify a specific conflict situation of their own experience between two people from different cultural backgrounds.
2. Have students check the values and behaviors that distinguish the people who were involved in that situation against the information provided in Exhibit 4.8.
3. Lead a class discussion of their conclusions about how those values may be understood, modified, or directed to reconcile the conflict toward greater harmony and productivity.
4. When all items have been reviewed, have students count up the number of American and contrast-American items they checked and report these data.

DEBRIEFING   The instructor will compile data from participants on the board to examine the importance of American and contrast-American values and assumptions. The discussion

---

Note. From material by Edward Stewart, who wishes to acknowledge the contributions of Dr. Jasper Ingersoll, Department of Anthropology, Catholic University, to the development of Exhibit 4.8 and described in *A Manual of Structured Experiences for Cross-Cultural Learning* (pp. 34–39), by W. H. Weeks, P. B. Pedersen, and R. W. Brislin, 1977, Yarmouth, ME: Intercultural Press. Copyright 1977 by Intercultural Press. Adapted with permission of publisher and author.

Exhibit 4.8 *Summary of Cultural Assumptions and Values*

Cultural area	Issue	American assumptions and values	Contrast-American assumptions and values
Definition of activity	How do people approach activity?	Concern with doing, progress, change External achievement Optimistic, striving	Concern with being Spontaneous expressions Fatalistic
	What is the desirable pace of life?	Fast, busy Driving	Steady, rhythmic Noncompulsive
	How important are goals in planning?	Stress means, procedures, techniques	Stress final goals
	What are important goals in life?	Material goals Comfort and absence of pain Activity	Spiritual goals Fullness of pleasure and pain Experience
	Where does responsibility for decisions lie?	With each individual	Function of a group or a role (dual contrast)
	At what level do people live?	Operational; goals evaluated in terms of consequence	Experimental truth
	On what basis do people evaluate?	Utility (does it work?)	Essence (ideal)
	Who should make decisions?	The people affected	Those with proper authority
	What is the nature of problem solving?	Planning behavior Anticipation of consequences	Coping behavior Classification of the situation
	What is the nature of learning?	Learner is active (student-centered learning)	Learner is passive (aerial rote learning)
Definition of social relations	How are roles defined?	Attained Loosely Generally	Ascribed Tightly Specifically
	How do people relate to others whose status is different?	Stress on equality Minimization of differences Stress on informality and spontaneity	Stress on hierarchical ranks Stress on differences, especially with superiors Stress on formality, behavior more easily anticipated
	How are sex roles defined?	Similar, overlapping Sex equality Friends of both sexes Less legitimized	Distinct Male superiority Friends of same sex only Legitimized

(continued)

Exhibit 4.8 *Summary of Cultural Assumptions and Values (Continued)*

Cultural area	Issue	American assumptions and values	Contrast-American assumptions and values
	What are members' rights and duties in a group?	Assumes limited liability Joins group to seek own goals Active members can influence group	Assumes unlimited liability Accepts constraint by group Leader runs group, members do not
	How do people judge others?	Specific abilities or interests Task centered Fragmentary involvement	Overall individuality of person and his or her status Person centered Total involvement
	What is the meaning of friendship?	Social friendship (short commitment, friends shared)	Intense friendship (long commitment, friends are exclusive)
	What is the nature of social reciprocity?	Real only Nonbinding (Dutch treat) Equal (Dutch treat)	Ideal and real Binding Unequal
	How do people regard friendly aggression in social interaction?	Acceptable, interesting, fun	Not acceptable, embarrassing
Motivation	What is motivating force? How is person–person competition evaluated?	Achievement As constructive, healthy	Ascription As destructive, antisocial
Perception of the world (worldview)	What is the (natural) world like?	Physical Mechanical Use of machines	Spiritual Organic Disuse of machines
	How does the world operate?	In a rational, learnable, controllable manner Chance and probability	In a mystically ordered, spiritually conceivable manner (fate, divination) No chance or probability
	What is the nature of man?	Apart from nature or from any hierarchy Impermanent, not fixed, changeable Good is unlimited	Part of nature or of some hierarchy (dual contrast) Permanent, fixed, not changeable Good is limited
	What are the relationships between man and nature?	Man should modify nature for his ends Good health and material comforts are expected and desired	Man should accept the natural order Some disease and material misery are naturally to be expected
	What is the nature of truth and goodness?	Tentative (working type) Relative to circumstances Experience analyzed in separate components, dichotomies	Definite Absolute Experience apprehended as a whole

Perception of the world (worldview) (continued)	How is time defined and valued?	Future (anticipated)	Past (remembrance) or present experience (dual contrast)
		Precise units	Undifferentiated
		Limited resource	Not limited (not resource)
		Lineal	Circular, undifferentiated
	What is the nature of property?	Private ownership important as extension of self	Use for "natural" purpose regardless of ownership
Perception of the self and the individual	In what sort of terms is self defined?	Diffuse, changing terms	Fixed, clearly defined terms
		Flexible behavior	Person is located in a social system
	Where does a person's identity seem to be?	Within the self (achievement)	Outside the self in roles, groups, family, clan, caste, society
	What is the nature of the individual?	Separate aspects (intent, thought, act, biographical background)	Totality of person
	On whom should a person place reliance?	Self	Status superiors, patron, others
		Impersonal organizations	Persons
	What qualities of a person are valued and respected?	Youth (vigor)	Age (wisdom, experience)
	What is the basis of social control?	Persuasion, appeal to the individual	Formal, authoritative
		Guilt	Shame
Generalized forms	Time	Lineal	Nonlineal
		Efficient and material cause-and-effect thinking	Formal causes, correlative thinking
	Essence and energy	Material, substantive	Spirit, energy
		Operationalism	Direct apprehension or formalism (dual contrast)
	Implied observer	Induction	Deduction or transduction (dual contrast)
		Judgment by comparison	Judgment against an absolute standard
		World stuff expansive (unlimited good)	World stuff restricted (limited good)

Note. From material by Edward Stewart, who wishes to acknowledge the contributions of Dr. Jasper Ingersoll, Department of Anthropology, Catholic University, to the development of this Exhibit and described in A Manual of Structured Experiences for Cross-Cultural Learning (pp. 34–39), by W. H. Weeks, P. B. Pedersen, and R. W. Brislin, 1977, Yarmouth, ME: Intercultural Press. Adapted with permission.

will not value one system as better than the other but will discuss the consequences of both systems. Questions for discussion are as follows:

1. To what extent is there an "American" system of values?
2. What would be some national or cultural examples of "contrast-American" values?
3. Which values are more important than others?
4. Were you surprised by your own score?
5. How will this experience be of help to you?

INSIGHT   There are alternatives to the American cultural values.

82 DECREASING CULTURAL BARRIERS

> *Objective:* To identify barriers to cross-cultural communication and develop ways to decrease those barriers.

TIME REQUIRED   A half day

RISK LEVEL   Moderate

PARTICIPANTS NEEDED   Any number of participants, plus a facilitator

PROCEDURE   Please take the following steps:

1. Select a brief case study relevant to the interests of the group.
2. Ask participants to read the case study carefully.
3. Where possible, it will be useful to role-play the case example to the group.
4. Distribute Exhibit 4.9, and help participants systematically evaluate those barriers that are most salient in each situation and develop strategies to cope with each barrier in turn.

DEBRIEFING   A discussion of the six communication barriers will identify additional examples of each barrier in the case study and additional strategies for crossing those barriers. The instructor should be sensitive to emotional issues that may arise during the discussion. The class can also examine ways that familiarity with these barriers might be helpful. Some discussion questions are as follows:

1. How does each barrier function differently in different cultures?
2. Can you give an example of overcoming the barriers in a particular situation?
3. Which barrier is the most difficult to lower, and why?
4. How do you identify cultural barriers in yourself?

Exhibit 4.9   *Overcoming Barriers to Cross-Cultural Communication*

Lowering Language Barriers

1. Learn the language.
2. Find someone who can speak the language as a go-between.
3. Ask for clarification if you are not sure what was said.

Lowering Nonverbal Communication Barriers

1. Do not assume that you understand any nonverbal communication.
2. If the communication is insulting, don't take it personally.
3. Develop an awareness of your own nonverbal patterns and their interpretation by others.

Lowering Stereotype Barriers

1. Make every effort to increase your awareness of your own stereotypes.
2. Reinterpret the behavior of others from their cultural perspective.
3. Test, adapt, and change your stereotypes to fit real-life situations.

Lowering Evaluation Barriers

1. Maintain objectivity.
2. Recognize that change over time moves slowly.
3. Do not judge others until you know their cultural values and patterns.

Lowering Stress Barriers

1. Reduce the ambiguity of those factors causing you stress.
2. Monitor your level of stress and the consequences of stress on communication.
3. Re-evaluate your expectations for the situation toward more realistic and modest outcomes.

Loosening Organizational Constraints

1. Identify the limitations on an organization's ability to control events.
2. Identify the best interests of an organization from that organization's viewpoint.
3. Identify new ways that the organization can fulfill its needs and the needs of others.

5. Would people from a minority culture be more sensitive to these barriers than people from a majority culture?

INSIGHT   The barriers to cross-cultural communication can be bridged to increase win–win outcomes of cultural conflict.

83 AMERICAN AUCTION

Objective: To raise money for a project while exploring the importance of money as a cultural perspective.

TIME REQUIRED   An evening

RISK LEVEL   Moderate

PARTICIPANTS NEEDED   Any number of participants, plus a facilitator or auctioneer

PROCEDURE   Please take the following steps:

1. Organize a fund-raising activity in the form of an auction of donated goods.
2. Instruct the participants that they will be responsible to pay each amount they bid for an item whether or not their bid is the highest bid for the item.
3. If participants make more than one bid, they will be responsible for paying the sum total of all their bids, whether or not their final bid is the highest bid for the item.
4. The objective of the auction is to raise a large amount of money from the participants rather than on the attaining of items being auctioned.
5. Each bid will be recorded as an independent contribution to the cause.

DEBRIEFING   Money in the majority culture is normally exchanged for some kind of commodity of equal value and seldom given away without getting something in return. This experience will be useful to raise money while also providing a training activity. The experience is focused on the symbolic role of money in different cultures and how it has a potentially positive as well as negative meaning. Make sure all participants know the rules before doing the experience. In debriefing the facilitator will want to explore how money is valued in different cultures as experienced by the participants. Some discussion questions are as follows:

1. Do some cultures emphasize money more than others, and if so, why?
2. Were participants shocked by how much they owed when all their separate bids were added up?

3. What was the feeling among participants about this experience?
4. Has money become a cultural symbol?
5. How will you use what you learned in this experience?

INSIGHT   Money has an important symbolic value in many, if not most, cultures.

84 HEARING THE SOUNDS OF A CULTURAL CONTEXT

Objective: To accurately interpret the sounds of a cultural context from a tape recording.

TIME REQUIRED A half day to make audiotapes and a half day to play them in class

RISK LEVEL Moderate

PARTICIPANTS NEEDED Any number of participants, plus a facilitator

PROCEDURE Please take the following steps:

1. Ask individual participants prior to the experience to carry an audiotape recorder to a distinctly cultural context and record the sounds occurring in that context in 3- to 5-minute segments.
2. With the group, listen to the tapes without allowing the participants to reveal the context of their recordings.
3. Ask the group members to glean as much information as possible and ask each other questions about the cultural context based on cues from the recordings. Some of these questions might include the following:
   - Who were the people in the recording?
   - Where was it recorded?
   - When was it recorded?
   - What was happening at the time of the recording?
4. Have students reveal the events taking place at the time the recordings were made.

DEBRIEFING The facilitator will guide the discussion about the cues that were evident in the tape recordings played back in class. The focus might be to encourage participants to observe and listen to the world around them more carefully. Some discussion questions are the following:

1. Were you able to identify the context of the tape recordings?
2. How carefully do you listen to what is going on around you?
3. Are some cultures more focused on silence than others?
4. Can you match typical sounds with particular cultures?
5. How will you use what you learned in this experience?

INSIGHT

Audio cues are important to understanding the interactions in a multicultural group.

85 CRITICAL INCIDENTS INVOLVING ETHNIC MINORITIES

Objective: To examine brief hypothetical critical incidents involving cultural groups.

TIME REQUIRED   A half day or full day

RISK LEVEL   High

PARTICIPANTS NEEDED   Any number of participants, plus a facilitator

PROCEDURE   Please take the following steps:

1. Discuss an incident in Exhibit 4.10 by looking for similarities and differences between and among the participants.
2. Diagram the conflict in each of the brief critical incidents using the Interpersonal Cultural Grid in Exhibit 4.11 to find examples of common ground where the individuals shared the same positive expectations but expressed their expectation using culturally different behaviors.

DEBRIEFING   Students will no doubt find that one or more critical incident in this experience is similar to something they have experienced in the past. The facilitator should be sensitive to the emotions students may connect to such incidents and should not force the students to reveal more than they might want. Use the incidents themselves as a springboard for a discussion on constructive multicultural problem solving. Some questions for discussion are as follows:

Note. The critical incidents were developed by Daniel Hernandez. From *Decisional Dialogues in a Cultural Context: Structured Exercises* (pp. 97–109), by P. B. Pedersen and D. Hernandez, 1997, Thousand Oaks, CA: Sage. Copyright 1997 by Sage. Adapted with permission of publisher and author.

1. Which incidents seemed most powerful, and why?
2. Were you able to find examples of common ground using the Interpersonal Cultural Grid?
3. Were you tempted to focus on behavior in managing the conflict before you had established a foundation of common ground?
4. Can you see how conflict moves quickly from being cultural to becoming personal?
5. How will this experience help you solve problems in a multicultural context?

INSIGHT   Each critical incident in life is a valuable educational resource.

Exhibit 4.10 *Critical Incidents Involving People From Ethnic Minorities*

Incident 1

At a rally protesting the lack of Black, Hispanic, and Native American professors at a state university campus, students gathered and listened to speakers as they expressed their concerns about the inequalities. The rally was a part of a week of events creating cultural awareness in higher education. Issues discussed centered around the slow recruitment of minority professors, admissions standards that were biased against minorities, and the lack of ethnic studies on campus.

The rally received a great turnout. Minority students applauded and cheered as the lectures continued. Nonminority students began gathering at the rally to listen to the many speeches being delivered. A Hispanic man, excited at seeing a large nonminority population attend the rally, commented to a White student, "I'm glad to see you attend the rally. It makes me feel good to see you support our cause." The student turned and said, "These issues of inequality are important to me. Being Jewish has not always been easy."

Incident 2

A Hispanic couple living in California hired a live-in nanny to care for their two daughters. Ana, a 19-year-old undocumented immigrant, came to California to seek employment in order to earn money for surgery that her ill father needed. The Hispanic couple were both professionals; the husband was an educator, and the wife worked in marketing in the computer industry.

One day the couple informed Ana that the family would be relocating to the East Coast in 3 months. Ana declined to move with the family, feeling insecure about leaving a large Hispanic population and fearing that the move would bring her into closer contact with immigration agents at state borderlines.

Two weeks before leaving, the couple located a job for Ana with another family. Ana was pleased to have another family to care for but was worried about having to readjust to another environment. Complicating matters further was the fact that the new family spoke little Spanish. A month after relocating to the East Coast, Ana notified the couple that her younger sister had been killed in an auto accident. Ana was facing many hardships—adjustment to a nonbilingual family, not having saved enough money for her father's surgery, and now the loss of her sister. She was offered free counseling services, but she refused because of lack of trust and fear of deportation. Two weeks later, Ana suffered a nervous breakdown and was hospitalized.

Incident 3

A Mexican American doctoral student, Jorge, was having a conversation with the director of the retention program while interviewing for a graduate assistantship position in a student service program. The director discussed the role and responsibility of the assistantship position. The primary responsibility would be outreach targeted specifically toward Hispanic students on campus who were not using the services that were available to them. The director believed that Jorge would be a good role model for the Hispanic students and that he could help convince these students to use the services more frequently.

During the course of the interview the director stated his belief that due to biological factors, some people are able to learn more and are more intelligent than others. The director informed Jorge that he wanted to be open and honest to avoid uneasiness down the road.

Incident 4

Susan, a White student at a small liberal arts college, recently ended a 3-year relationship with her high school boyfriend. Her roommate, Jill, noticed that Susan began sleeping in and eating less. Jill believed that this type of behavior was just a phase and that soon Susan would be herself again.

One night after returning from a late-night movie, Jill noticed that there was a small container of pills on Susan's nightstand. Jill shared her concerns about the pills with Susan and recommended that she seek free counseling available through the campus counseling center. Susan replied that she had thought about counseling but felt uncomfortable because the counselors at the center were all men, and she preferred to meet with a female counselor.

(continued)

Incident 5

A Vietnamese high school student, Anh, was experiencing difficulty in concentrating on her schoolwork due to issues at home. Hesitant in talking to someone about family issues, she felt she had no choice but to meet with her school counselor because her studies were suffering.

Anh informed the counselor that because of financial hardships, her father had started drinking and had become physically violent toward the family. Anh also stated that she was staying up late at night comforting her 3-year-old sister, who was scared and had regressed to bed-wetting.

The counselor said that she was saddened to hear of the situation and conveyed to Anh the importance of continuing school so that she could go on to college, graduate, and contribute at home by helping out financially. The counselor informed Anh that her situation was common for recent immigrants and tried to reassure her that things would get better.

Incident 6

A Chinese American student transferring to a 4-year university was invited to an orientation for new students. The new students were given a schedule of spring classes and instructed to tentatively select their classes and then meet with a department advisor for approval.

After completing the instructions, the student, Anthony, met with his advisor. As he left the advisor's office, the advisor attempted to welcome Anthony by saying, "You know, the restaurant across the street sells the best won ton soup around."

Incident 7

A Taiwanese student returned to her home country after receiving her graduate degree in counseling in the United States. Li Ming's initial work consisted of explaining the process of counseling and how counseling was used in the United States. Many of her contacts could not believe that Americans would tell their personal stories to a stranger and that they paid the stranger to listen.

After a short period in Taiwan, Li Ming returned to the United States in hopes of working as a counselor in a university setting. She explained that it was difficult to do counseling in a culture that did not believe in discussing personal or family matters outside the home.

Incident 8

A 50-year-old Mexican woman, Marta, was referred to a counselor by her physician after Marta related her chest pains to being unable to attend her mother's funeral. The counselor, a Mexican American, learned that Marta did not receive notice of her mother's death until months later, because her family in Mexico had no phone.

The counselor believed that Marta's pain was caused by the guilt she carried. The counselor also learned that Marta had no family or relatives nearby. The counselor contacted a local parish that gave mass in Spanish; he spoke with the priest and informed him of Marta's situation. The priest was able to meet with Marta that afternoon.

A few weeks later Marta contacted the counselor and thanked him for his help. She said that the priest was able to say a rosary and a mass for her mother.

Incident 9

A Chinese graduate student, Chen, recently finished his master's degree in counseling psychology and was preparing to apply to a doctoral program. Chen received many invitations to attend numerous universities throughout the country. In addition, he received fellowship offers from several prestigious universities.

Chen visited the doctoral programs at universities that were within reasonable driving distance. From universities that were out of state, Chen was able to do research through the mail.

After narrowing the selection to five universities, Chen met with his advisor to decide on which school to attend. After a lengthy conversation with his advisor, Chen finally made a decision. One important factor that he had overlooked, however, was the fact that none of the five schools had faculty of color, specifically professors of Chinese descent.

(continued)

Incident 10

María, a 17-year-old first-generation Mexican American high school student, was angry and upset because her parents did not give her permission to attend a field trip to visit a local university. María's friends were concerned about her and informed a counselor at the counseling and guidance center. Ms. Bustamante, the Mexican American counselor, met with María to find out what was troubling her. María explained that she would like to attend college but that her family did not support her decision. María mentioned that her father wanted her to stay home and help her mother around the house and that maybe, in a few years when she was older, she could possibly go on to school. María believed that her father's real reason for not being supportive of her continuing her education was the rapes that were occurring on college campuses.

Ms. Bustamante shared with María that she too had not had the support of her parents when she went to college. She was not angry at her parents, though, because she knew that they really loved her, and she found a way to convey to her parents the benefits of attending college.

Ms. Bustamante advised María to do the same and suggested that she share with her parents information about the different colleges. In addition, Ms. Bustamante suggested that María gather information about housing and, if possible, the security services the campuses offer students.

Incident 11

A counselor at an urban high school was leaving his office after school to meet with a teacher in another building. As he approached the school library, he heard two people screaming and shouting. The counselor went to see what the commotion was all about and witnessed a Vietnamese woman hitting a Vietnamese student with an umbrella. The counselor immediately stopped the woman from hitting the student and escorted them to the administration office.

Mrs. Troung, a volunteer teacher's aide of Vietnamese origin, was called in to assist with the matter. After a long discussion with the mother and student, Mrs. Troung shared with the counselor the following: The older Vietnamese woman was the mother of the student. She was upset because the daughter had told her mother that she was studying at the school library, and that was why she had arrived home late for the past several nights. That day the mother had come to the school to make sure her daughter was studying. When she arrived at the school, however, the mother found her daughter talking with a Vietnamese boy. The mother began hitting her daughter for lying. The rule was that the student was not to have a boyfriend until she was ready to marry.

Incident 12

A Korean family met with a family therapist because the parents were having difficulty controlling their oldest son. The parents were immigrants and were referred to family services via a community agency. The therapist, a Hispanic woman, was experiencing difficulty in establishing a smooth session. Although she was aware of the cultural factors in counseling Asian families, she realized that for some reason the session was not going as well as she wanted.

As the session came to an end, the therapist scheduled the family for the following week. A couple of days later, the family canceled the appointment and asked if they could have a referral. The therapist asked if she had upset them in any way, and the mother responded that she did not; however, she did comment that her husband would feel more comfortable if the therapist were an older Korean man.

Incident 13

Jessica, a 22-year-old Mexican American woman from central Illinois, left home to attend college in California. A few weeks into the semester, she began to notice the cultural differences between herself and other Hispanics on campus. Jessica noticed that the majority of the Hispanics were able to speak both English and Spanish fluently. Although her parents spoke Spanish at home, they did not insist that the children be bilingual.

In her English class, composed predominantly of White students, Jessica felt comfortable and relaxed. However, in a Chicano studies course that fulfilled the cultural pluralism requirement for graduation, she felt out of place because she did not share the experiences of other Hispanics in class.

(continued)

Jessica shared her feelings with the Chicano studies professor, who was very sensitive to her issue. The professor responded by telling Jessica that not all Mexican Americans share the same sociocultural experience and that people need to understand and respect the values of others.

Incident 14

Raquel, a 29-year-old Hispanic college student, recently received her bachelor of arts in English. Raquel graduated with honors and was the first of seven siblings to finish college. Raquel was married and had two children ages 2 and 4. Her husband worked the swing shift at a supermarket, and she worked as a teacher's aide at an elementary school. During the day Raquel's husband would take care of the children, and in the afternoon he would leave them with his mother. Raquel attended classes three nights a week, and after class she would pick up the children.

A couple of weeks before graduation, Raquel was informed that the faculty in her department had nominated her for an award that recognized outstanding students in comparative English literature. In addition, the department chairperson met with Raquel to discuss graduate school. Raquel was offered a scholarship to attend the master's program in English for the following fall.

Raquel was torn between her conflicting desires to go to graduate school and to be at home with her children. After several days of thinking about the offer, she decided that she would take a year off from school to be with her family. Coincidentally, Raquel did not receive the award for which she had been nominated.

Incident 15

Leonard, a Lakota Indian, returned home to the reservation after serving 3 years in the armed services. During Leonard's stay in the Marines, he was stationed at several bases in the United States and was sent to Germany for 1 year. At a sweat lodge, many of Leonard's friends and older members of the tribe shared stories of their ancestors. When Leonard was a child, he remembered listening to his father tell stories about his great-grandfather, and he had always enjoyed learning about his family history. However, Leonard realized that now these stories did not mean anything to him and that he could not understand the importance that his tribe placed on talking about individuals who no longer existed.

After several weeks at home from the service, Leonard found himself in conflict with his parents and siblings. Many of his friends claimed that Leonard was acting as though he was too good to be a Lakota Indian. The conflict with family and friends caused Leonard much pain. He felt that no one understood him. He felt alone. Leonard wanted to leave the reservation to find work so that he could save his money and travel through Europe; however, he knew that with only a high school education, getting a job would be difficult.

Leonard became more depressed about the conflict that he was experiencing at home. He realized he could no longer live on the reservation and be happy. After 2 months at home, Leonard left the reservation and reenlisted in the Marines for another full term.

Incident 16

In the book *Silent Language*, Edward T. Hall talked about his experience working for the Soil Conservation program at a Navajo reservation. In his experience supervising the construction of small earth dams, he noticed that the Navajo workmen operated at a relaxed pace, as though they had no worries at all. He recalled sharing his American values about hard work and how working hard today will bring rewards tomorrow. Hall noticed that this had no effect on their work behavior.

After discussing this problem with a friend who had spent all his life on a reservation, Hall decided to approach the Navajo workmen in a different manner. He recalled talking with the work crew and telling them how the American government was helping them get out of debt by providing them jobs near their families and giving them water for their sheep. Hall stressed the fact that in return, they had to work hard for 8 hours a day. He noticed that the change in approach altered their work performance.

(continued)

Incident 17

A Middle Eastern student attending an East Coast university was experiencing difficulty in meeting American students. One day after Walid's chemistry class, he decided to talk with a student who sat next to him in class. The classmate was an American woman who easily engaged in a conversation with Walid. After a few minutes of conversing, the American student on several occasions glanced at her watch. Walid noticed her behavior and felt as though he was intruding or boring her with his conversation.

On another occasion, Walid was having lunch at the campus cafeteria. While he ate, he noticed that many American students were eating and reading at the same time. Others were eating and writing letters or doing their schoolwork. He found it very interesting that American students rarely relaxed.

Incident 18

Pélin, an international student from Taiwan, was asked to share her experiences with students who had recently arrived in the United States from China. Pélin shared that when she first arrived, she was excited about attending an American university. In her spare time she went to see American movies and ate a variety of American foods. After some time, she began noticing the major differences in the behavior of American students and how their beliefs, values, and lifestyles conflicted with hers.

Pélin lived in the residential halls and had an American roommate. She spoke of how offended and embarrassed she was when her roommate's boyfriend came by to visit and how openly they would kiss and hug each other. She also shared the difficulty she experienced when using the community showers for women. Her sense of privacy and personal space was constantly being challenged.

Pélin shared with the group that at first, her adjustment as a student at an American university was difficult, and although many of the values were different from hers, she was able to adjust. Pélin ended by saying that her biggest growth was being able to appreciate her own values by learning to appreciate American values.

Incident 19

An admissions counselor at a California state university was reviewing an admissions application submitted by Thanh, a Vietnamese refugee student. Sections of the admissions application requested parental information and asked specific questions about the family history. Because these sections were left blank, the admissions counselor asked Thanh to make an appointment.

During their meeting the counselor learned that Thanh and his sister were living with an aunt and that they had no knowledge of the whereabouts of their parents. Thanh hesitantly shared with the counselor that his parents were taken prisoner by the communist regime in Vietnam, and he was left behind with his younger sister. Through the Vietnamese Immigration Agency, the refugee program, he was able to locate his aunt in California.

It had been 10 years since Thanh had last seen his parents. He expressed that it was important for him to go to college, because with a college degree he would be able to take care of his younger sister and not be such a burden to his aunt.

Incident 20

A Hispanic social worker in Colorado was assigned a client who had been raped by her employer. The client, Teresa, was a 25-year-old Salvadoran woman who came to the United States so that she could work and save money to pay for an operation that her son needed.

Teresa had answered an ad in the paper to work as a live-in nanny. The employer was a successful dentist who was married and had two children. Within days after Teresa had started working, she was raped by the dentist. Unable to speak English and fearful of the consequences of deportation, Teresa could not report the incident to authorities.

In desperation, Teresa went to see a priest for help. The priest contacted a clinic, which later contacted the social work agency. The social worker discovered that Teresa had been raped on 11 different occasions within a 5-day period.

(continued)

Incident 21

A counselor at a rehabilitation center for juveniles was assigned to a case in which the minor, Will, had a history of aggressive behavior. Will was sent to the rehabilitation center for 8 months because of violation of probation. After a few counseling sessions, the counselor and Will were able to identify situations that caused Will to act aggressively. The counselor learned in the counseling session that as a young child Will had witnessed his father physically abuse his mother. Will described his father as a man who had a short fuse and vented his anger at his mother.

Will internalized his feelings and developed an intense hatred toward his father. Will grew up not knowing how to deal with his anger, and he would act out when confronted with stressful situations. Through additional counseling the counselor discovered that Will had an uncle whom he respected very highly and always called whenever he was in trouble. Will shared with the counselor that his uncle was someone who was always there when he needed someone to talk with. The uncle, who was the mother's older brother, was self-employed and often traveled.

Through further counseling Will and the counselor were able to develop strategies for Will to use in dealing with stressful situations. Rewards were granted in the form of additional visitation time with his mother on Sundays when Will was able to control his anger. The counselor trained Will to use breathing exercises to help him control his emotions in a stressful event. The counselor also arranged special visitations with Will's uncle. In addition, the counselor worked with Will's mother in teaching him prosocial skills in preparation for release.

Incident 22

A married couple met with a counselor to discuss the difficulties they were having with their oldest daughter. The daughter was 15 years old and a sophomore in high school. The parents' primary concern was that the daughter was always yelling at her parents and disobeying them. The parents were worried that they had no control over their daughter.

The counselor spoke to the parents in detail about areas that could be worked on; however, it required that the parents receive instruction and training in anger control skills. The parents were very hesitant and shared with the counselor that it would be difficult to actively take part in the process.

Incident 23

In a small community in Texas, parents of Mexican American children were upset when several of the students were placed in a specialized classroom for students with learning disabilities. Several parents received a letter from the teacher stating that their children had been given very low scores on a standardized intelligence test. The letter stated that the exam provided evidence that their child was borderline mentally retarded.

After much pressure from the parents, consultants from a nearby university evaluated the exam and found that it was biased. The test did not take into account the linguistic and cultural factors of the students tested.

The students were retested with an intelligence test that was not biased and was sensitive to linguistic and cultural elements. The results of the exam indicated that the Mexican American students did not differ from White students, and in several areas the Mexican American students scored higher than their counterparts.

Incident 24

An African American woman, Aisha, met with a counselor because she was feeling depressed about being unemployed. Aisha expressed that she felt worthless and useless. Unemployed for the past 4 months, she could not understand why, with a business degree and 4 years of professional experience, she had been unable to find a job.

Aisha stated that for the past 3 months she had been sending out six resumes a week and had not received any responses. Aisha began questioning her own ability and self-confidence and began to feel that she did not have the right stuff.

(continued)

Incident 25

A White female school counselor, Linda, recently moved to Los Angeles from Ohio with her husband, who had accepted a principal's position at a high school. Linda experienced culture shock when she met the parents of a Hispanic student who were concerned about their son's truancy problem. The parents spoke limited English, but sufficient enough to be able to communicate with those who did not speak Spanish.

Understanding the demographics of the school where she worked and in anticipation of working with Hispanic parents with limited English fluency, Linda thought it beneficial to enroll in a Spanish class. For the next 6 months she studied Spanish at a community college near her residence.

At work Linda would practice her Spanish with students whenever possible, and she found that Hispanic students were less inhibited around her. On several occasions, Linda was able to speak Spanish with parents who spoke limited English. She noticed that by speaking Spanish with the parents, they felt relaxed and comfortable. Linda realized that by being able to communicate in the language of her clients, she was able to establish trust and rapport.

Incident 26

A family who had immigrated from India was experiencing difficulty with their oldest daughter and met with a family therapist to discuss their concerns. The family informed the counselor that they did not approve of their daughter having boyfriends and had difficulty getting her to obey their rules.

The therapist spoke with the parents about relationships and what they meant to a teenage girl. The therapist informed the parents that it would probably be best if the daughter could attend their next meeting so they could all work out a solution together.

The parents were somewhat taken back by what the therapist told them. They told the therapist they did not think it was possible for the family to meet. All they wanted was for the therapist to tell them how to handle the situation.

Exhibit 4.11   *Interpersonal Cultural Grid: What Was Done?*

Reasons for action	Perceived positive action	Perceived negative action
Perceived positive reasons	1	2
Perceived negative reasons	3	4

1. Cell #1 describes a situation where the behavior/action was considered positive by both parties and the expectation/reason for doing the behavior/action was also positive. Two people are both smiling, and they both want to be friends.
2. Cell #2 describes a situation where the behavior/action was judged negatively by one of the two parties, even though the expectation/reason for doing the behavior/action was in fact positive. Two people both want to be friends and one is smiling but the other is not smiling as an example of a "cultural" misunderstanding.
3. Cell #3 describes a situation where the desired behavior/action is presented as demanded by the stronger party, but now the expectation by the weaker party is negative. One of the two "pretends" to agree with the other but actually does not agree as an example of "personal" misunderstanding.
4. Cell #4 describes a situation where the behavior/action is negative and the expectation is also negative for both parties. Both parties have gone to war against the other.
5. Conflict that can be contained in Cell #2 is potentially positive, but conflict in Cell #3 and ultimately #4 is negative and destructive.

Note. The critical incidents were developed by Daniel Hernandez. From *Decisional Dialogues in a Cultural Context: Structured Exercises* (pp. 97–109), by P. B. Pedersen and D. Hernandez, 1997, Thousand Oaks, CA: Sage. Copyright 1997 by Sage. Adapted with permission of publisher and author.

86 CRITICAL INCIDENTS WITH INTERNATIONAL STUDENTS

Objective: To experience the problem situations of international students as an educational event.

TIME REQUIRED About a half day

RISK LEVEL High

PARTICIPANTS NEEDED Any number of students, about half of whom or more are international students, plus a facilitator

PROCEDURE Please take the following steps:

1. Allow the international student resource person to select an incident from Exhibit 4.12 with which he or she is already familiar and comfortable. The more time the resource person has to consider the incident, the more realistic the student will be in projecting himself or herself into the role.
2. Ask the international student resource person to come to the front of the room and briefly read or summarize the situation.
3. Then invite the student to speak for 1 or 2 minutes about how he or she felt in that dilemma.
4. Invite the audience to ask questions, give advice, comment, or respond to the student in some helpful way.
5. After about 8 or 10 minutes, end the discussion.
6. Have the resource person go out of role and highlight those comments from the audience that seemed particularly helpful.

Note. From "International Students and International Student Advisors," by P. B. Pedersen, 1994, in R. W. Brislin and T. Yoshida (Eds.), *Improving Intercultural Interactions* (pp. 148–167), Thousand Oaks, CA: Sage. Copyright 1994 by Sage. Adapted with permission.

Exhibit 4.12   *International Student Incidents*

The Faculty Advisor

You came to the international student counselor for help with academic problems. It soon became apparent that you are having a difficult time communicating with your academic faculty advisor. You described the advisor as always busy and as impatient with your questions when you asked for clarification. As a result, you often agreed to decisions you did not really understand because you felt your advisor wanted you to answer that way. You are terrified of the academic advisor. The advisor is totally unaware of your feelings, and because you seldom sought him out for help, he assumed you were doing fine. You are your academic advisor's only international student advisee. Usually international students are advised by two other faculty members in the department who are already overloaded with advisees. You want to change advisors to one of these other two faculty members, but they are too busy to accept new advisees.

Working Without Permission

You were caught working illegally by the Immigration and Naturalization Service (INS) and called to a deportation hearing. You claimed that you applied for work permission during the academic year but did not hear from the INS for 2 months. When summer came, you thought that international students were allowed to work without permission because they do not need to be in school. However, the INS claimed that you knew that accepting the job was illegal, or you would not have applied for permission to work. Because you had never received a denial letter, you felt INS was being unfair. The procedure was lengthy and humiliating for you. You felt that whatever offense you might have committed did not justify the expense of time and effort by either the INS or yourself. The job you took was in a nursing home for a small amount of pay after they had tried desperately but unsuccessfully to find someone else to work there. Finally, the INS relented and let you stay, but they gave you a scolding about the problems this country is facing with unemployment and made it plain that international students should never displace U.S. nationals. You listened to the lecture but felt bitter about it.

Failing Grade

You asked the international student advisor to talk to your instructor to see if there was any way your grade in a particular course could be raised to a C. You believed you knew the material even though you did badly on the exam. You are already on probation, so a failing grade would cause the university to drop you. As a consequence, the INS would require you to return home or transfer to another program of study. Because it is in the middle of the year, no other university or program would be likely to accept transfers, especially from a failing student. After seeing both the faculty member and you, the advisor arranged a meeting for the three of you in the faculty member's office to identify alternatives. From your point of view the issue should be whether or not you know the material rather than how well adjusted you are to the U.S. environment. The advisor seemed intimidated by the system and unable to advocate your case as you would have liked.

(continued)

7. Then applaud the resource person and introduce the next resource person.
8. After responding to the critical incidents, organize the students into small groups or one large group for a discussion of the experience.

DEBRIEFING   This experience allows international students the opportunity to teach students from the host country the nature of the problems international students encounter. The facilitator will need to carefully monitor levels of emotion in the group discussion

Exhibit 4.12 *International Student Incidents (Continued)*

The International Student Office

You are a U.S. student who wrote a letter to the campus newspaper suggesting that the International Student Office (ISO) be eliminated. You wrote,

> If we have to save money and cut budgets in the university, the least painful way is to abolish the position of the international student advisor and the supporting budget. For one thing, we cannot really maintain a separate office for a relatively small group of students. The time has come that we must treat all students alike and not have services for any "special" group.
>
> Second, we really will not hurt anybody by this decision, because international students are just students like any other student and thus can enjoy the same services as are available to any other student. This action might actually work better for international students, because having a special international student advisor probably isolates international students from other students. International students will be more integrated with other students on campus.
>
> The great majority of international students on our large campus reportedly don't visit the ISO office anyway unless they have to. It is only a small minority of international students that have difficulties, and they are often marginal students who possibly should not have been brought here to begin with. We must make sure that these students make a realistic decision about leaving here if they can't make it on their own. The ISO often protects these students, asking for more and more exceptions when in fact these extensions only delay a decision to terminate them eventually. The money we save by eliminating the ISO can be redirected to important programs related to the special problems of our own society.

Financial Aid

You were refused financial aid and made an appointment with the director of financial aid to learn why. You were told there was barely enough money to meet the needs of U.S. minorities such as Blacks, Native Americans, and Hispanics, whose needs came first. You became angry, because international students were being evaluated by a more strictly defined need criteria than other students. You came to the international student advisor and said the reason minorities were getting aid was their militancy and organizational pressure. You described this policy as part of an anti-foreign bias in admissions, in awarding teaching or research assistantships, and at every other point where international students always came last. You threatened to organize international students to demonstrate against the university. You complained that international students are being treated unfairly and inequitably. You asked the international student advisor to decide which side he is on, the students' or the institution's.

Note. From "International Students and International Student Advisors," by P. B. Pedersen, 1994, in R. W. Brislin and T. Yoshida (Eds.), *Improving Intercultural Interactions* (pp. 148–167), Thousand Oaks, CA: Sage. Copyright 1994 by Sage. Adapted with permission.

and prevent the discussion from being sidetracked in a destructive direction. Some questions for discussion are as follows:

1. What are some unique problems faced by international students in the United States?
2. Do students from some countries have an especially difficult time? Why?
3. Do students from other countries have an especially easy time? Why?
4. How do international students typically respond to the problems they encounter?
5. How can international students be prepared for the problems they will encounter?

INSIGHT

International students experience problems differently from students from the host country.

87 CRITICAL INCIDENTS IN TOURIST GROUPS

Objective: To identify appropriate responses to critical incidents of intercultural interaction in a host culture.

TIME REQUIRED About a half day

RISK LEVEL High

PARTICIPANTS NEEDED Any number of participants, some of whom have been tourists, plus a facilitator

PROCEDURE Please take the following steps:

1. Distribute copies of the critical incidents in Exhibit 4.13 to students. These incidents are grouped into four categories: lifestyle differences; dehumanizing biases, discrimination, and prejudices; learning environments; and respect for human diversity and personal rights.
2. Ask the students to write out their responses to each incident.
3. Have students individually indicate the appropriate response for each incident.
4. Organize the students into small groups to discuss their responses in all four categories of critical incidents.

DEBRIEFING The four categories of critical incidents during tourism provide a structure for discussing the incidents and the student's responses to each incident. In debriefing the group discusses how well the students' responses fit the title of each category. Some discussion questions include the following:

1. Which of the four categories of incidents was the most difficult, and why?
2. Which of the four categories was less difficult, and why?

Note. From *Decisional Dialogues in a Cultural Context: Structured Exercises* (pp. 123–127), by P. B. Pedersen and D. Hernandez, 1997, Thousand Oaks, CA: Sage. Copyright 1997 by Sage. Adapted with permission.

3. Have you experienced similar incidents as an international tourist?
4. What is the best way to prepare tourists before they go abroad?
5. Are some cultures easier to visit than others? Why?

INSIGHT Experience is a pretty good, if not the best, teacher for developing multicultural awareness.

Exhibit 4.13 *Critical Incidents Involving Tourists*

Lifestyle Differences

Incident 1

You are acquainted with a student from a foreign culture whose lifestyle does not emphasize time consciousness. The student's failure to meet deadlines had downgraded his otherwise adequate assignments and alienated the student from his teachers. Neither the school nor the student seem willing to adapt their style to one another. The student's father asks you what to do.

Incident 2

You find that the inhabitants of a small village where you are staying resent Americans a great deal because of previous bad experiences with the U.S. military and tourists. You discover that you have been grossly overcharged at your hotel and taken advantage of in other ways. Your plan was to spend the whole summer in one place rather than tour around so that you would get to know the people and not be an ordinary tourist. Now you find they are taking out their hostility toward Americans on you as an individual. You seek the advice of a casual friend who seems better accepted by the people than yourself.

Incident 3

The person with whom you are traveling, a friend from back home, seems to be turning into the classic Ugly American. He is condescending in his treatment of others, suspicious that he is being cheated, concerned that nothing is clean enough, and generally obnoxious toward non-Americans. You want to help him make a better adjustment both for his sake and yours, because his behavior is embarrassing. You take him aside for a "little talk."

Dehumanizing Biases, Discrimination, and Prejudices

Incident 4

You are in a mixed group of new acquaintances. The elections have just been held, with the political parties divided along Protestant and Roman Catholic lines. The discussion is extremely intense and likely to erupt into violence. You are not well enough acquainted with the issues to recognize which of the persons in your group belong to which political party and which religious group. One of the leaders in the group asks you for your opinion.

Incident 5

In becoming acquainted with your host family, you discover that the women in this society are in a very subservient role, having to work very hard and being completely dominated by men. Cautious inquiries suggest that this style of life is well accepted and normal, even though it seems extremely unfair to you as a woman. Your anger over this unfair treatment is beginning to show, and the members of your host family are starting to make fun of you for being a "women's lib" type.

Incident 6

In spite of your best efforts to learn the foreign language, you find that your ability to express yourself is very inadequate. The persons with whom you talk on the street seem very impatient and somewhat irritated by the way you mangle their language. You refuse to use English, even though their English

(continued)

Exhibit 4.13 *Critical Incidents Involving Tourists (Continued)*

is very adequate, and are beginning to resent their lack of sympathy with your attempts to enter their culture. You catch yourself becoming unreasonably angry with a complete stranger who doesn't understand you when you ask him a simple question.

Learning Environments

Incident 7

You are Jewish and find yourself in a large German city where everyone seems prejudiced against you. You had many relatives who suffered under the Nazis in concentration camps, but you were never aware of any strong anti-German bias in yourself until now. It seems impossible to separate your feelings about them as a group from your relationship with them as individuals. You can understand and explain your bias, but you cannot seem to control your feelings, which are coming out in your behavior toward Germans. A German casual acquaintance asks you if you are Jewish because you "look" Jewish, and you become extremely angry with him.

Incident 8

You are Black and have been invited to speak before a class of secondary school students in a foreign country who have never seen or talked with a Black person. A friend of yours invited you to come and explain to them about the racial problem in the United States and what is being done to combat racism.

Incident 9

The leader of your tour group is a very authoritarian man who succeeds in dominating, planning, and controlling the activities of the group. He is very jealous of any threat to his control. Other members of the group are able to tolerate his domination, but you find it increasingly impossible. The other group members have begun looking to you, a woman with considerable international experience, for advice and guidance on what to do. You believe that the leader is doing a bad job and resents your threat to his authority. You sit down to have it out with him for the sake of the group as well as yourself.

Respect for Human Diversity and Personal Rights

Incident 10

One of your friends on the tour is planning to marry a foreign national who is of a different religion as well as a different nationality. Neither set of parents agrees to the marriage, and the engaged couple is not sure they will be able to overcome the differences in both culture and religion. At the same time, they are unwilling to separate and are hopeful that once they are married, their families will somehow come to agree. They ask your advice.

Incident 11

Your new friends from abroad insist on borrowing things from you and neglect to return them unless you ask for them back. They appear much more casual about ownership of personal belongings than you would like and assume that they have a right to your things as your friends. You try to set an example by not borrowing anything from them, but they continue to borrow from you and don't acknowledge the subtle hints you make. They seem to be using you to their own advantage, although among themselves they seem to have developed a satisfactory arrangement.

Incident 12

You have been caught with a group of friends who were in possession of marijuana. The police have placed all of you in jail and are not allowing you to contact anyone outside the jail. The conditions are impossible, and you feel that you are entirely at the mercy of the jailor. You are ready to do just about anything to get out of the jail and are angry because you didn't even break the law in the first place. You need to find some way to get help.

Note. From *Decisional Dialogues in a Cultural Context: Structured Exercises* (pp. 123–127), by P. B. Pedersen and D. Hernandez, 1997, Thousand Oaks, CA: Sage. Copyright 1997 by Sage. Adapted with permission.

88 HEARING THE DEVILS AND THE ANGELS

> *Objective:* To hear the negative and positive messages that someone is thinking but not saying.

TIME REQUIRED   About a half day

RISK LEVEL   High

PARTICIPANTS NEEDED   Any number of participants, plus a facilitator

PROCEDURE   Please take the following steps:

1. Organize the students into four-person multicultural groups. Each person in the group is assigned a role as interviewer, client, angel, or devil.
2. Instruct the person in the interviewer role to begin talking to the person in the client role. Have the interviewer continue for about 5 to 8 minutes while the angel and the devil provide continuous and immediate feedback.
3. At the end of the interview, ask the four participants to discuss what they learned.
4. After a 5- to 10-minute discussion, set up another interview, with each of the four members taking a different role.
5. Continue with interviews and debriefing until members have experienced all four roles.
6. At the end of the experience, organize a large group discussion.

DEBRIEFING   Because the person providing negative feedback as a devil is deliberately destructive, a skilled leader will need to monitor the effect of that negative feedback on the group so that the participants feel safe enough to take some risks. In debriefing the leader needs to emphasize that this devil and angel are not real people, but rather parts of the member's imagination, so the members role-playing the devil and angel should not be held responsible for deliberately exaggerating what they think the other individual members might be thinking but not saying. Some discussion questions are as follows:

1. Were the devil and the angel on target in what they said?
2. Was it easier to be a devil than an angel? Why?
3. Was it frustrating having the devil and angel talk during the interview?
4. Was the interviewer able to use feedback from the devil and angel in the interview?
5. Can you learn to imagine a client's positive and negative internal dialogue?

INSIGHT   Thought in every culture includes a conversation between devils and angels.

89 ACTION PROJECT

Objective: To work together as a group to influence social change.

TIME REQUIRED   A half day or a series of meetings

RISK LEVEL   High

PARTICIPANTS NEEDED   Any number of participants, plus a facilitator

PROCEDURE   Please take the following steps:

1. Divide the class into small groups and have them identify a multicultural action project, like writing a letter to the editor of a newspaper, that can be done within one session. Other action projects might be volunteering as a group for a soup kitchen, going on a field trip, and cleaning up a park or a section of roadside.
2. Coach the small groups of students through the completion of their action project.
3. Allow students either to present the action project they intend to complete or to report back to the group on a project the group has completed.
4. Help the members see how their small contribution makes a difference when added to others over a longer period of time.
5. Keep the group from being discouraged, and help them find the meaning of taking action.

DEBRIEFING   In debriefing this experience, the leader will want to show how a group moves from talking about a problem to doing something about it. It is also important to point out that change happens in a series of very small wins, and not like a tidal wave. Some discussion questions are as follows:

1. How did you decide on a multicultural action project?
2. How will the project have meaning in a multicultural context?

3. Are all the group's resources being mobilized?
4. Do all group members have a role, and are all involved?
5. What consequences do you expect the action project to have?

INSIGHT   Social change occurs through small wins.

90 LUMP SUM: A BUDGET SIMULATION

Objective: To demonstrate feelings, roles, and attitudes in a simulated conflict among competing special interest groups.

TIME REQUIRED   About a half day

RISK LEVEL   High

PARTICIPANTS NEEDED   Any number of participants, plus a facilitator

PROCEDURE   Please take the following steps:

1. Introduce the participants to the interaction, and give them a copy of the announcement in Exhibit 4.14 to study.
2. Form interest groups either through assignment of roles or by allowing participants to volunteer for membership in designated special interest groups, keeping all groups approximately equal in size. The size of groups may range from 4 to 12 individuals per group and the number of groups from 4 to 6, each group representing a different special interest. The group will simulate a special meeting of representatives from special interest groups assembled to allocate the lump sum of money.
3. Have the special interest groups meet separately to:
   a. Elect a special interest group negotiator.
   b. Decide on the overall division of all funds, with special attention to the sum their interest group plans to request for itself, and prepare an argument defending their allocation both for all groups in general and for their own group in particular.

Note. From *A Manual of Structured Experiences for Cross-Cultural Learning* (pp. 87–93), by W. H. Weeks, P. B. Pedersen, and R. W. Brislin, 1977, Yarmouth, ME: Intercultural Press. Copyright 1977 by Intercultural Press. Adapted with permission.

Exhibit 4.14   *Lump Sum Simulation Handout*

A Special Announcement (Strictly Confidential):
Emergency Meeting of Representatives From Hawaii Schools

You have been called together in this special emergency meeting to represent the unique interests of your constituencies in making an extremely important decision. The future of education in Hawaii may depend on your decision today and the unique opportunity presented to us.

A representative of the U.S. Department of Education Special Fund has today informed me that due to bureaucratic oversight there is US$10,000,000 which has not been allocated in the budget for any specific project and that is available for the use of schools in Hawaii for the prevention of school violence, provided that you can make a rapid decision on allocation of those funds and inform the Secretary of Education in Washington. We have an open telephone line to the Secretary's office to notify him as soon as a decision is made. The Secretary apologized for the urgency of his request, but the fiscal year for the Department of Education ends today, and all funds already appropriated but not allocated to specific projects by that time will revert to the General Fund and will not be available for special projects.

For the sake of speed and the fair allocation of the money, you special representatives from the various aspects of K–12 schools have been called together today to draw up a plan for spending the money. *The DOE wants the money spent to "directly" or "indirectly" reduce violence in schools.* They stipulate *absolutely* that all representatives must come to a unanimous agreement on their decision within the time limit or else lose the money.

The Department of Education agrees to abide by whatever allocations you *unanimously* decide on within the next 2 hours. If, of course, you do not reach unanimous agreement within the time limit, the money will revert to the General Fund.

You are already divided into six groups:

1. Elementary and kindergarten education
2. Middle school education
3. High school education
4. Extracurricular education (such as music and sports)
5. Parents
6. School board

For the sake of a speedy decision, each group will select its own negotiator, and the six negotiators will carry out the actual negotiations for spending the money.

Because only 2 hours can be allowed to reach a conclusion, we have established a timetable that you must rigidly adhere to. You will have adequate time to express the proposal of your delegation, to present your proposal to the group, and to negotiate privately as well as publicly with other delegations toward unanimous agreement. Although the actual negotiations will take place through your selected negotiator, you may, if the majority of the delegation is dissatisfied with his or her performance, replace your representative with someone selected by the majority of your delegation.

Your timetable is as follows:

1. *20 minutes:* Each delegation will meet together and (a) settle among themselves who will be the negotiator representing them and (b) draw up specific plans for how the entire amount ($10,000,000) ought to be divided and allocated according to the needs of the entire state and the special concerns of your constituency.
2. *18 minutes:* In the first negotiation session, each representative will be given 3 minutes to report on how his or her delegation proposes to allocate the money. There will be no discussion among the representatives, but each representative will be given an opportunity to explain the merits of his or her delegation's allocation of the money to the assembled company.
3. *10 minutes:* In the first consultation, representatives will go back to their own delegation for 10 minutes to consult with them on strategy, presentation, any changes in their proposals they may want to make, and private consultation with members of other groups.

(continued)

Exhibit 4.14 *Lump Sum Simulation Handout (Continued)*

4. *10 minutes:* In the second negotiation session, representatives will present any modifications made on the basis of the other representatives' proposals or on the basis of consultations that have just taken place.
5. *10 minutes:* In the second consultation, further modifications in each group's proposals can be made. Also, this is the time to consult again with other groups on any private compromises that may be proposed to secure their cooperation.
6. *20 minutes:* In the third negotiation session, representatives will discuss and present their final and presumably unanimously agreed upon proposal on allocation of the $10,000,000 lump sum of money.

Note. From *A Manual of Structured Experiences for Cross-Cultural Learning* (pp. 87–93), by W. H. Weeks, P. B. Pedersen, and R. W. Brislin, 1977, Yarmouth ME: Intercultural Press. Copyright 1977 by Intercultural Press. Adapted with permission.

    c. Decide on a strategy for securing their portion, that is, on the maximum they hope to obtain and the minimum for which they will settle in later negotiations. The announcement in Exhibit 4.14 should be adequate to stimulate planning within groups and competition among groups. The sum of US$10,000,000 is suggested as enough to encourage serious planning but not enough to give everyone what they might want.

    d. Decide on bargaining strategies and possible coalitions of interest between groups to their mutual benefit.

    e. Groups may be allowed a minimum of 20 minutes and a maximum of 1 hour in which to develop their initial program strategy. The longer a group meets in its initial session, the stronger group identity tends to become, and the less likely the group is to compromise. Because more learning seems to occur among groups that do not compromise, and thus lose the money, the more time individual groups can have in the initial session the better.

4. Begin the first negotiation session with each group's elected negotiator being placed at a bargaining table in such a way that he or she faces his or her own constituency. Negotiators will be given only 3 minutes to report on their delegation's specific proposal for allocation of the money. There must be no discussion among the representatives or debate from the floor while each negotiator presents and defends his or her group's proposal within this first 3 minutes.

5. After the first consultation session, allow the negotiators to return to their group and consult with the special interest group on strategy, presentation, and changes in the group proposal. The consultation will continue for 10 minutes. Private consultation and negotiations with other special interest groups will be permitted at this time.

6. For the second negotiation, bring negotiators back to the bargaining table for at least 10 but no more than 15 minutes. This will be the first public bargaining session where negotiators will be allowed to speak and debate without restriction.

7. After this consultation session, allow the negotiators to return to their groups for 10 minutes. In the second consultation, groups can make further modifications in their proposals. Again, groups may wish to engage in private negotiations with other groups to secure their cooperation toward a solution.

8. For the third negotiation session, bring negotiators back to the bargaining table for the last time for 20 minutes, unless the negotiators come to a unanimous

agreement before that time. Negotiators must reach unanimous agreement in this session or lose the money.

DEBRIEFING   Following the simulation, a minimum of 20 minutes should be allowed for debriefing on the learning that has taken place through the simulation. Discussion should be oriented to the content level (articulation of information and the position of each simulated interest group by participants) and the process level (the interaction of individuals in this simulation as they approached bargaining and negotiations and exercised power). Some discussion questions are as follows:

1. Did the group reach consensus on the budget? If so, how?
2. Did the group not reach consensus on the budget? If so, why not?
3. Were the different special interest groups able to find common ground?
4. Did some special interest groups need to compromise their best interests to reach consensus?
5. How can you use what you learned from this experience?

INSIGHT   People are sometimes willing to sacrifice money to maintain their integrity without compromise.

91 CULTURALLY LEARNED PARENT ROLES FOR IMMIGRANTS AND REFUGEES

Objective: To help immigrant and refugee families identify a variety of parenting roles and compare parenting priorities between the home and host cultures.

TIME REQUIRED   About a half day

RISK LEVEL   High

PARTICIPANTS NEEDED   Any number of participants, plus a facilitator

PROCEDURE   Please take the following steps:

1. Have each participant read the parent role descriptions in Exhibit 4.15 and identify the five most important roles according to their own personal priorities for being a parent, keeping this information private from the group. Feel free to add roles to the 14 that are listed and eliminate or modify roles so the list applies more accurately to the group.
2. Next, have the group members identify those roles that are easier in the host culture than they would be in the members' home culture, discussing this with the group.
3. Next, ask group members to identify those roles that are harder in the host culture than they would be in the home culture, discussing this with the group.
4. Show the group at least 20 pictures of parents you previously cut out from magazine illustrations and advertising; each picture should be numbered.
5. Instruct the group to work together to identify up to three roles they think the parents in the picture are assuming.
6. Select four of the pictures that have been classified in 10 or more of the personally most important roles individual group members identified in step 1.
7. Ask participants to become the person in the picture and answer the questions of the other members of the group, using their imaginations to provide answers that fit the appropriate role. Participants can choose whether to answer the questions as a parent from the home culture or the host culture.

Exhibit 4.15   *Parent Roles*

1. *Provider:* Parents contribute to the welfare of the family in a variety of ways. A provider is a parent who contributes to the economic welfare and well-being of the family.
2. *Celebrant:* The parent as a celebrant adds a dimension of life and enthusiasm, joy, and self-presence quite different from celebrations where the parent is not present. Behind nearly all celebrations is the implicit recognition of the parental role in bringing out the harmony and purpose of the event.
3. *Nurturer:* Parents are important in nurturing ideas and providing the quality of care and comfort that society values for the family.
4. *Technician:* In an increasingly technical world, most parents are technicians. Parents use equipment and facilities to produce a variety of products, and they cope with breakdowns in technology from a broken appliance to a stalled car.
5. *Companion:* The companion role of the parent involves leisure time activity to reinforce family relations. Being a companion means more than doing things together; it means being a part of the family adventure and experience.
6. *Socializer:* A socializer transmits values, ideas, and content of culture from one generation to another. Socializing can include giving the family members advice and teaching what is important.
7. *Symbol:* Much has been written about parents as symbols. Parents represent dominant ideas in the culture. There are both positive and negative aspects in parents as symbols for the family and society.
8. *Manager:* Parents plan, organize, and carry out ideas and evaluate the results. Parents provide both formal management of a group and the less formal management of decisions in the family.
9. *Comforter:* To be a comforter means to know when another person needs aid and comfort, to be able to determine the nature of the other person's problem, and to take appropriate steps to help the other person.
10. *Budgeter:* Parents have various resources at their disposal, such as time, money, endorsement, and organization. Being a budgeter means making careful use of the resources beyond just managing them.
11. *Promoter:* The promotional role of parents is part of the communications system in the community. As promoters, parents translate ideas and values to the community and promote and sell a particular point of view to the community.
12. *Counselor:* The counselor's experience and understanding allow him or her to see problems from different ways. Parents see problems as counselors do and help the family deal with them.
13. *Communicator:* The communicator gives others instructions, information, and reasons. Parents communicate the goals, ideals, and activities of the family to society and of society to the family.
14. *Problem solver:* Crises, emergencies, and situations arise in the family, and the parent takes the role of problem solver. Problem solving involves identifying the appropriate solution to the situations, whether simple and routine or complicated.

---

8. Have participants try and guess, asking yes or no questions, (a) the personally most important role being played by the group member and (b) whether the parent being role-played is in the host culture or the home culture.

DEBRIEFING   This experience was developed from stories of refugees from different countries in the United States who had to learn new "parent roles" in the U.S. culture. Discuss how the role of parent is viewed differently by the group members and their host culture and home culture. Discuss how the parent role of the father is different from the parent role of the mother. Some discussion questions are as follows:

1. How are parent roles similar across cultures?
2. How are parent roles different across cultures?
3. Which pattern of parenting is most familiar to you, and which is least familiar?

4. What special problems arise when a family is in a foreign culture?
5. How can you help families prepare to live in a foreign culture?

The complicated process of role learning is especially difficult for immigrants and refugees and their families.

92 FINDING COMMON GROUND IN SPORTS AND ATHLETICS

Objective: To identify ways that superordinate goals, such as winning an athletic competition, might provide examples of common ground across cultural differences.

TIME REQUIRED   A half day or more

RISK LEVEL   High

PARTICIPANTS NEEDED   Any number of participants, plus a facilitator

PROCEDURE   Please take the following steps:

1. Divide the participants into teams. Explain to the group that constructive conflict management is a priority concern of U.S. society, more perhaps than at any previous time in history. Observe that frequently, conflict between individuals escalates into racial conflict, especially if the people in conflict perceive themselves as culturally different. Consequently, cultural factors are frequently perceived as contributing to the escalation of conflict.
2. Ask each team to generate critical incidents or brief case examples of multicultural conflict that have actually happened or that could have happened, and examine how that conflict was mediated or resolved.
3. Present the case examples for discussion with the larger group, and direct the discussion toward the positive or negative consequences of action taken in each case example. These case examples and notes from the discussion could be collected into a casebook for distribution to the participants after the workshop.

DEBRIEFING   The debriefing discussion on the sports and athletics context will focus on their positive contributions in reframing conflict into a cultural context to find common ground where two people who come from different cultures can disagree without either one being necessarily wrong. Sports provide an excellent example of common ground across cultures as in the Olympics and the peaceful interaction of sports figures from countries or groups who are otherwise hostile to one another. Some discussion questions are as follows:

1. Can you give examples of common ground unique to sports activities?
2. Is "sports" and "athletics" a culture?
3. Why has sports cooperation so often been the first stage of diplomatic contact between conflicting nations?
4. How will a culture metaphor be helpful to an athletic team?
5. Can we generalize peacekeeping from a sports context to other aspects of society?

INSIGHT   The metaphor of teamwork and competition in a sports or athletic context provides an example of common ground that might be transferred to other activities.

93 UNANSWERED QUESTIONS AND KNOWLEDGE GAPS

> *Objective:* To identify those questions about multiculturalism that remain unanswered but that will require answers in the future.

TIME REQUIRED   One or more days

RISK LEVEL   High

PARTICIPANTS NEEDED   Any number of participants with a track record in multicultural research, plus a facilitator

PROCEDURE   Please take the following steps:

1. Begin discussion by asking participants to focus on unanswered questions that will require answers in the future.
2. Help sharpen specific questions and assist the participants in determining questions that may lead to future research and publications by participants.

DEBRIEFING   The debriefing discussion should focus less on answering research questions and more on sharpening the questions in more precise terms. Participants will have an opportunity to work together. Some questions for discussion are the following:

1. Can you list important multicultural research questions that you do not know the answers to?
2. How can you be sure you are asking the right questions?
3. What are the consequences of doing research on the wrong questions?
4. Where do hypotheses come from before they are tested?
5. How can you be sure you have identified the right answers to questions for multicultural research?

INSIGHT   The questions about multiculturalism to which we do not have answers can also provide meaningful information and stimulate future research.

■ CHAPTER FIVE ■

HOMEWORK

This chapter describes multicultural experiences that can be assigned as homework and discussed later in class. In addition, many of the experiences described in previous chapters can also be done outside the classroom with some modification. The advantage of homework is to encourage immersion by the student into community cultures and to blur the boundary between the classroom and the community. Each homework assignment will require debriefing by the instructor either in the classroom or elsewhere.

Homework assignments need to be more tightly structured to guide the students in a particular direction. The higher degree of structure results in less risk for the participants, who have a clear sense of task. The debriefing of homework assignments by the instructor, however, requires a high level of skill. Learning in the outside community is more complicated than learning in the controlled environment of a classroom. For that reason, homework in the community provides a useful supplement to classroom training and teaching.

94 A PERSONAL CULTURAL HISTORY

> *Objective:* To help students become more aware of the role of culture in their lives by systematically describing their own personal cultural history.

TIME REQUIRED   From 1 to 3 hours

RISK LEVEL   Low

PARTICIPANTS NEEDED   Any number of participants, plus a facilitator

PROCEDURE   Please take the following steps:

1. Ask students to complete the following questionnaire:
   a. Describe the earliest memory you have of an experience with a person or people of a cultural or ethnic group different from your own.
   b. Who or what has had the most influence in the formation of your attitudes and opinions about people of different cultural groups? In what way?
   c. What influences in your experience have led to the development of positive feelings about your own cultural heritage and background?
   d. What influences in your experience have led to the development of negative feelings, if any, about your own cultural heritage or background?
   e. What changes, if any, would you like to make in your own attitudes or experiences in relation to people of other ethnic or cultural groups?
   f. Describe an experience in your own life when you feel you were discriminated against for any reason, not necessarily because of your culture.
   g. How do you feel you should deal with (or not deal with) issues of cultural diversity in American society?
2. Organize a small or large group discussion to compare responses to this self-assessment across students. Allow the students to disclose.

DEBRIEFING   Discuss the similarities and differences in group members' responses to the same questions. Allow the students to self-disclose only to the extent they are comfortable;

no student should feel pressure to disclose his or her responses if reluctant to do so. Some discussion questions are as follows:

1. How would you describe your culture?
2. Who was the most significant culture teacher in your life?
3. How has your culture changed over time?
4. Are you aware of how your culture has changed you?
5. How many different cultures do you belong to?

INSIGHT   Each of us belongs to many different cultures.

95 APPLICATIONS OF CRITICAL INCIDENTS

Objective: To develop classroom teaching materials based on events students have seen, heard about, or experienced themselves.

TIME REQUIRED   Several hours

RISK LEVEL   Low

PARTICIPANTS NEEDED   Any number of participants, plus a facilitator

PROCEDURE   Please take the following steps:

1. Ask students to identify an event or occurrence with as much specificity as possible, the problem to be solved, the decision to be made, and the issues involved.
2. Have students produce written descriptions of the relevant details and circumstances surrounding the event so that readers will understand what happened when, how, why, and where.
3. Ask students to list the people involved, describing them and their relationships to the student and to one another.
4. Have students describe their own role in the situation in terms of what he or she did or how he or she acted, identifying the particular multicultural skill or skills involved and the choices made.
5. Ask students to write a brief analysis of the incident telling what they learned from the incident, stating estimates of the students' and other actors' levels of multicultural skill development.
6. Instruct students to identify the specific psychological construct or concept that is illustrated in this critical incident.

Note. From *Decisional Dialogues in a Cultural Context: Structured Exercises* (pp. 91–97), by P. B. Pedersen and D. Hernandez, 1997, Thousand Oaks, CA: Sage. Copyright 1997 by Sage. Adapted with permission.

DEBRIEFING   Critical incidents are like short stories with a specific lesson to be learned. By discussing their incidents in a debriefing session, students can help one another improve the quality of their intercultural interactions. Some questions for discussion are the following:

1. How did you select your critical incident?
2. How many cultures are represented in your incident?
3. How might you use your incident in teaching or training?
4. Did you use the resources of students in your class to develop your critical incident?
5. What is the most important idea that can be learned from your critical incident?

INSIGHT   Students bring a variety of multicultural experiences into the classroom that can become educational resources.

96 ANALYZING A TRANSCRIPT

> *Objective:* To identify the negative and positive subscripts in a multicultural interview by reviewing personal transcripts from other sources.

TIME REQUIRED　Several hours

RISK LEVEL　Low

PARTICIPANTS NEEDED　Any number of participants, plus a facilitator

PROCEDURE　Please take the following steps:

1. Ask each student to collect transcripts of their own counseling interviews. If students do not have transcripts of their own interviews, they can use transcripts of other people's interviews.
2. Ask members to write in on the transcripts the negative things they think each character might be thinking but not saying.
3. When everyone has written in their idea of implicit negative thinking on their transcripts, have each person read to the group the passages of transcript.
4. Repeat the process, having students write in the positive comments that the people in the transcript might be thinking but not saying and report them back to the group.

DEBRIEFING　This process helps group members recognize the implicit messages being generated in the transcript. In debriefing this experience, the leader might suggest that group members might also have negative and positive internal messages about the group and that these internal dialogues will significantly influence the group interaction. Some discussion questions are the following:

1. Are you able to monitor your own negative and positive internal dialogue?
2. To what extent can you monitor the negative and positive internal dialogue of a culturally different client?

3. Are some cultures less likely to reveal their internal dialogue?
4. How will you know whether or not you are accurate in estimating a client's internal dialogue?
5. How will you use what you learned from this experience?

INSIGHT It is possible to read between the lines in understanding a transcript.

97 A CULTURE-CENTERED INTERVIEW GUIDE

Objective: To examine the many different questions that indicate whether or not you really know another cultural group.

TIME REQUIRED   Several days

RISK LEVEL   Low

PARTICIPANTS NEEDED   Any number of participants, plus a facilitator

PROCEDURE   Please take the following steps:

1. Ask the students to estimate how well they could answer the questions in Exhibit 5.1. Although this list of questions is much more comprehensive than any interview could cover, it provides the structure for a comprehensive guided interview between a visitor and a host culture resident informant on the rules of a cultural context.
2. After students have reviewed this list of questions, organize a general discussion.

DEBRIEFING   Cultures are extremely complicated. The list of questions in Exhibit 5.1 was developed by the training office of the U.S. State Department about 25 years ago and demonstrates some of the complicated behaviors that are shaped by culture. Some discussion questions are as follows:

1. How much do you need to know to say you "know" another culture?
2. Which of the questions on this list are most important?

Note. From *Culture-Centered Counseling Interventions: Striving for Accuracy* (pp. 62–69), by P. B. Pedersen, 1997, Thousand Oaks, CA: Sage. Copyright 1997 by Sage. Adapted with permission. Developed from *F.S.I.: A Guide to Self-Taught Skills in Cross-Cultural Communication* (U.S. State Department staff training memo), by J. Wilson and M. Omar, 1978.

3. How can you best learn about another culture?
4. What is the role of resource people in learning about cultures?
5. What are the most important ideas of another culture?

INSIGHT   To really know another culture, you need to know the appropriate responses to a wide
range of different situations.

Exhibit 5.1   *Culture-Centered Interview Guide*

Social Customs

1. Are the people overtly friendly, reserved and formal, or hostile to strangers?
2. What are the formal and informal greeting forms that may be used appropriately by a guest? by a child?
3. What are the appropriate manners for entering a house? Do you remove your shoes or any other items of clothing before entering? Do you wait to be welcomed in by the owner or await the owner inside the door? Do you send a calling card in advance? Do you ring a bell, clap hands, or bang with your fist on the door?
4. What are appropriate manners when shopping? in a bazaar? in an haute couture salon? Do you queue or call for a salesperson or wait until a clerk approaches you? Do you bargain? Are you expected to carry your purchases? Do you provide your own containers for food purchases?
5. What are the appropriate manners at the theater? Do you clap hands or shout "bravo" or hiss or whistle to show approval? Do you seat yourself or await an usher? Do you tip the usher? How do you get a program?
6. What are the appropriate manners in a beauty shop? Do you make an appointment in advance or walk in? Do you bring your own beauty supplies? To whom do you give tips?
7. What are the appropriate manners for entering a room? Do you bow, nod, or shake hands with others there? Do you shake hands with everyone, only men, no one, or only the first person to greet you?
8. What is the appropriate moment in a new relationship to give one's name, ask the other's name, and inquire about occupation or family? How are names used for introductions? When compound names are customary, which elements do you use? How do you introduce Señora María Josefina Melina de Diez de Medina or Señorita Consuelo Vázquez Gutiérrez del Arroyo?
9. Is it proper for a wife to show affection for her husband in public by a term of endearment, holding his hand, or greeting him with a kiss?
10. What is the expected gesture of appreciation for an invitation to a home? Do you bring a gift? what kind? Do you send flowers in advance? afterwards? Do you send a thank you note?
11. When gifts are exchanged, is it impolite to open the gift in the presence of the donor? Are gifts presented or received in a special manner? Is it proper to express appreciation for a gift? Are any gift items taboo?
12. Are there any customs affecting the way one sits or where one sits? Is it impolite to sit with feet pointed toward another person? Is the seat to the right of the host a position of special honor?
13. What are the ways of showing respect (e.g., hat off or on, sitting or standing, bowing, lowering head)?
14. Are there special observances a guest should be familiar with before attending a wedding, funeral, baptism, birthday, or official ceremony?
15. Is it offensive to put your hand on the arm of someone with whom you are talking?
16. Do you offer your arm when escorting someone across the street?
17. What are the reactions to laughing, crying, fainting, or blushing in a group situation?
18. Are any particular facial expressions or gestures considered rude?
19. Do people tend to stand more closely together when talking? What is the concept of proper personal space?
20. What constitute "personal" questions?
21. What is the attitude toward punctuality for social and business appointments?
22. How do you politely attract the attention of a waiter in a restaurant?
23. How can invitations be refused without causing offense? Is a previous engagement an acceptable excuse? What happens if the excuse of illness is used?
24. How does one express condolence when a death occurs in the family of an acquaintance or friend? What is the appropriate expression of concern when a prominent member of the host government dies?
25. What is the appropriate response when an unknown person in apparent need comes to your home and asks for help, food, used clothing, or money?

(continued)

Exhibit 5.1   *Culture-Centered Interview Guide (Continued)*

Family Life

1. What is the basic unit of social organization—the individual, the basic family, the extended family, the tribe, the village, the region, the linguistic group, the national state?
2. What family members, of which generations, live together? If you were invited to a home, whom in the family would you expect to meet?
3. Are the elderly treated with special respect? Are they greeted differently from other adults? Does a young person look forward to or dread old age?
4. Is homemaking considered the preferred role for women? How do women figure in the labor force, the professions, and officialdom?
5. What are the duties in the family of women and men? Who controls the family money? Who makes the decisions about the upbringing of children?
6. How do the inheritance laws work? Can female offspring inherit land? Does the last born have a different legacy from the first born? What arrangements are usual for widows?
7. What do girls aspire to become? What careers are preferred for boys? Do special roles ascribe toys and games to either sex?
8. How are children taught (by role, by precept, by conceptual learning)? Who are their teachers in and out of school? What techniques are used at home and at school to reinforce desirable behavior and to correct disapproved behavior?
9. What are the important events in family life, and how are they celebrated?
10. When does a child become an adult? Is there a ceremony to mark passage from one stage to the next (e.g., debutante ball, circumcision rites, bar mitzvah)?
11. Are marriages planned or by individual choice? What do people look for or want from marriage? Who pays for the wedding ceremony? Is a dowry necessary?
12. At what age do most people marry? What encounters between the sexes are approved prior to marriage? Is chastity a virtue? Is polygamy or concubinage approved? Is homosexuality accepted?
13. Is divorce permitted?
14. What are the symbols used in the marriage ceremony, and what do they signify?

Housing, Clothing, and Food

1. What functions are served by the average dwelling? Is there a separate structure for bathing, cooking, toileting, sheltering animals, or storing foodstuffs?
2. Are there differences in the kind of housing used by different social groups in location or type of building or furnishings?
3. Which textiles, colors, or decorations are identified with specific social or occupational groups and not considered appropriate for others? Special colors are sometimes used only for royalty or for mourning.
4. What occasions require special dress (e.g., weddings, funerals, holidays, religious events)?
5. Are some types of clothing considered taboo for one or the other sex?
6. What parts of the body must always be covered by clothing?
7. How many meals a day are customary?
8. With what implements is food eaten? Is there a common bowl or individual servings? Is there an age or sex separation at mealtimes? Is there a special role for hosts and guests in regard to who eats where, what, and when? Are there any customary expectations about the amount of food guests must be offered or must eat? any special rituals for drinking?
9. Are there any foods unique to the country not eaten elsewhere?
10. Which foods are of importance for ceremonies and festivals?
11. Which are the prestige foods (e.g., in Western culture, champagne and caviar)?
12. What types of eating place and what sorts of food and drink are indicative of appropriate hospitality for relatives, close friends, official acquaintances, and strangers?
13. Is "setting a good table" important for social recognition?
14. When dining, where is the seat of honor?

(continued)

Exhibit 5.1   *Culture-Centered Interview Guide (Continued)*

Class Structure

1. Into what classes is society organized (e.g., royalts, aristocracy, large landowners, industrialists, military, artists, professionals, merchants, artisans, industrial workers, small farm owners, farm laborers)?
2. Are there racial, religious, or economic factors that determine social status? Are there any minority groups, and what is their social standing? Is wealth a prerequisite for public office?
3. Does birth predetermine status?
4. Is class structure in rural areas different from that of urban areas?
5. Is there a group of individuals or families who occupy a predominant social position? Can they easily be identified? Is their status attributable to heredity, money, land, or political influence?
6. Are there any particular roles or activities appropriate (or inappropriate) to the status in which Americans are classified? Does high status imply facility for generous contributions to charitable causes? Does a man lose great face by helping his wife with dishes or changing diapers?

Political Patterns

1. Are there immediate outside threats to the political survival of the country? What protection does the country have against any such threats? what defensive alliances? what technological advantages in weaponry? what traditional enmities that color policy options?
2. How is political power manifested? through traditional institutions of government? through control of military power? through economic strength?
3. What channels are open for the expression of popular opinion?
4. What information media are important? Who controls them? Whom do they reach? What are the sources of information available to the average citizen?
5. What is the political structure for the cities (e.g., mayors, councils) and for the countryside (e.g., village chiefs, town councils)?
6. How is international representation handled? What is the process for formulating foreign policy? Who receives visiting heads of state? Who negotiates treaties?
7. If a profile of the power structure were to be drawn, which individuals or groups, visible or behind the scenes, would figure as key elements?
8. In social situations, who talks politics? Is it a subject in which a guest may show interest?
9. What channels, if any, are available to opposition groups to express dissent?

Religion and Folk Beliefs

1. To which religious groups do people belong? Is one predominant?
2. How can the fundamental religious beliefs be described about, for example, the origin of man, life after death, the source of evil, and the nature of the deity or deities?
3. Are there any religious beliefs that influence daily activities (e.g., noon prayers, begging bowls)?
4. Is religion institutionalized? What is the hierarchy of religious functionaries, and in what ways do they interact with the people?
5. Which places have sacred value? which objects? which events and festivals? which writings?
6. Is there tolerance for minority religions? Is proselytizing or educational activities of minority religions permitted?
7. What is said or done to exorcise evil spirits (e.g., knocking on wood, making the sign of the cross)?
8. What is done with a new child or enterprise or building to ensure good fortune?
9. What objects or actions portend good luck and bad luck?
10. What myths are taught to children as part of their cultural heritage (e.g., sandman, Jack Frost, Pere Noel, fairy godmother)?

(continued)

Exhibit 5.1 *Culture-Centered Interview Guide (Continued)*

Economic Institutions

1. How do geographic location and climate affect the ways food, clothing, and shelter are provided? Has extensive irrigation or hydroelectric development been necessary? Has the terrain facilitated or obstructed the development of air transport?
2. How adequate are the available natural resources? Which must be imported? Which are in sufficient supply to be exported?
3. What foodstuffs, if any, must the country import?
4. What are the principal products? major exports? imports? What is the gross national product?
5. In the marketplaces, what items basic to a minimum standard of living do you find missing? Are luxury items available?
6. What kinds of technological training are offered?
7. Are industrial workers organized in unions, confederations, political parties, or none of these? What about rural workers?
8. Are cooperatives important in the economy?
9. Are businesses generally family owned? large public corporations? government operated? Are multinational corporations significant?
10. What percent of the population is engaged in agriculture, in industry, in service trades?
11. What protection has been developed against natural disasters (e.g., floating construction to minimize earthquake damage, advanced warning systems for typhoons, extensive crop insurance backed by the government, private disaster relief)?

Arts

1. Which media for artistic expression are most esteemed?
2. Are there professional artists? art schools?
3. Which materials are most used? stone, ivory, bone, shell, wood, clay, metal, reed, textile, glass?
4. What art objects would you find in a typical home? in a museum?
5. What kinds of music and musical instruments are unique to the country?
6. What forms of drama and dance are popular?
7. Are there special songs for special occasions?

Value Systems

1. Is life to be enjoyed or viewed as a source of suffering?
2. Is competitiveness or cooperativeness most prized?
3. Is thrift or enjoyment of the moment more exalted?
4. Is work viewed as an end in itself or as a necessary evil to be kept to a minimum?
5. Is face considered more important than fact?
6. Is politeness regarded as more important than factual honesty?
7. Is it believed that destiny is controlled by man's actions or subject to impersonal forces?
8. What killing, if any, is sanctioned (e.g., capital punishment, war, killing of adulterer, infanticide during famine)?
9. How is *friend* defined? What are the responsibilities of friendship?
10. What are the injunctions taught to children?
11. Who are the traditional heroes or heroines? What field of endeavor are they from? Who are the popular idols of the day? What values do they symbolize?
12. How would the virtues and vices be defined?
13. How would work as compared to play be defined?

Note. From *Culture-Centered Counseling Interventions: Striving for Accuracy* (pp. 62–69), by P. B. Pedersen, 1997, Thousand Oaks, CA: Sage. Copyright 1997 by Sage. Adapted with permission. Developed from *F.S.I.: A Guide to Self-Taught Skills in Cross-Cultural Communication* (U.S. State Department staff training memo), by J. Wilson and M. Omar, 1978.

98 THE CROSS-CULTURAL TRADEOFF

> *Objective:* To provide the structure for a programmed series of interactions between a visitor and a host culture resident counterpart for exchanging feedback on their alternative perspectives.

TIME REQUIRED   Several days

RISK LEVEL   Low

PARTICIPANTS NEEDED   Any number of participants, plus a facilitator

PROCEDURE   Please take the following steps:

1. Ask the participants to work through the eight steps listed in Exhibit 5.2. In doing each step, the participants should set aside about an hour free from outside distraction.
2. Advise the participants to do no more than two steps in any one day, but at least one step a week.
3. After the participants have proceeded through the steps, ask them to report back what they have discovered by providing a written report or by discussing learned experiences in a group setting.

DEBRIEFING   The structured experience makes it possible to move step by step in examining an important cross-cultural relationship for both participating partners. After completing the experience, the partners may want to discuss what they learned with the facilitator. Some discussion questions are as follows:

1. How is your culture different from that of your partner?
2. How is your culture similar to that of your partner?

Note. From *A Manual of Structured Experiences for Cross-Cultural Learning* (pp. 15–20), by W. H. Weeks, P. B. Pedersen, and R. W. Brislin, 1977, Yarmouth, ME: Intercultural Press. Copyright 1977 by Intercultural Press. Adapted with permission.

3. Were you able to find common ground across cultures, and if so, how?
4. What problems did you encounter in your discussions?
5. How will you use what you learned in this experience?

Structured interaction provides the opportunity to systematically learn more about another person's culture and how your culture is perceived by that person.

Exhibit 5.2   *Eight Steps in the Cross-Cultural Tradeoff Experience*

Step 1

There is a significant body of research evidence that increased interethnic contact is more likely to occur under unfavorable conditions with negative results than under favorable conditions. Unfavorable conditions apply when the contact situation produces competition between groups, when contact is unpleasant and involuntary, when contact lowers the status of either group, when members of either group are frustrated by failure, when the two groups have conflicting moral standards, and when the minority group is of lower status. The immediate and urgent task facing contemporary society is to match the demographic redistribution of culturally defined groups both nationally and internationally with an appropriate educational response. The Cross-Cultural Tradeoff experience is an attempt to bring two persons from different cultures together in a structured interaction under favorable conditions.

Step 2

The things that one of you hears may not be the same as what the other person is saying. Misinterpretation is particularly likely when the communication is across cultures, when we may easily confuse cultural differences with interpersonal differences. Our culture teaches us about a role we are expected to follow and about the roles we can expect others around us to follow. The problem is that different cultures teach different roles. Think about the culturally defined role you have toward your partner and how that role makes you feel good or bad. Then think about the culturally defined role your partner is expected to have toward you and how that makes you feel good or bad. Because each of you is talking about your own feelings about yourself and one another, it doesn't matter whether those feelings are justified or not. Save your criticism and evaluation until later, when you both better understand each partner's expectations.

Make a list that is as specific as possible about the following:

- things about my cultural role that make me feel good
- things about my cultural role that make me feel bad
- things about my partner's cultural role that make me feel good
- things about my partner's cultural role that make me feel bad

After you have made the list, exchange papers, read what each of you has written, and discuss your feelings with one another until each of you can restate the other person's role to the other's satisfaction.

Step 3

You have to know one another before you can really trust one another. You also have to know yourself. You may think you know yourself and one another, but you may be wrong. In this step you will be able to help one another discover whether or not you see one another in the same way.

Go through the list of adjectives and make a check mark beside the most appropriate adjective in each of the four columns:

- you as you see yourself
- you as your culture would like you to be
- your partner as you see him or her
- your partner as his or her culture would like him or her to be

Make about 10 checks under each column. Also, place an X beside those adjectives that would be least appropriate. Write in any specific comments or explanations that would help your partner understand your choice.

Try not to confuse the picture of you or your partner as you are with the picture of you or your partner as you would like him or her to be. Feel free to add as many new adjectives as you want.

(continued)

Exhibit 5.2 *Eight Steps in the Cross-Cultural Tradeoff Experience (Continued)*

Adjective	Me as I see myself	Me as my culture wants me to be	You as I see you	You as your culture wants you to be
1. Adventurous				
2. False				
3. Affectionate				
4. Ambitious				
5. Anxious for approval				
6. Appreciative				
7. Argumentative				
8. Big hearted				
9. Neat				
10. Competitive				
11. Complaining				
12. Critical of others				
13. Demanding				
14. Distant				
15. Dogmatic				
16. Dominating				
17. Easily angered				
18. Easily discouraged				
19. Easily influenced				
20. Efficient				
21. Encouraging				
22. Enthusiastic				
23. Forgiving				
24. Frank, forthright				
25. Fun-loving				
26. Giving of praise readily				
27. Good listener				
28. Helpful				
29. Indifferent to others				
30. Impulsive				
31. Intolerant				
32. Jealous				
33. Kind				
34. Optimistic				
35. Loud				

(continued)

Exhibit 5.2   *Eight Steps in the Cross-Cultural Tradeoff Experience (Continued)*

Adjective	Me as I see myself	Me as my culture wants me to be	You as I see you	You as your culture wants you to be
36. Independent				
37. Orderly				
38. Needs much praise				
39. Obedient				
40. Rebellious				
41. Resentful				
42. Responsible				
43. Sarcastic				
44. Discourteous				
45. Self-centered				
46. Self-respecting				
47. Self-satisfied				
48. Sentimental				
49. Showing of love				
50. Shrewd, devious				
51. Shy				
52. Sociable				
53. Stern				
54. Submissive				
55. Successful				
56. Sympathetic				
57. Tactful				
58. Talkative				
59. Teasing				
60. Thorough				
61. Thoughtful				
62. Touchy, cannot be kidded				
63. Trusting				
64. Uncommunicative				
65. Understanding				
66. Varied in interests				
67. Very dependent on other				
68. Well mannered				
69. Willing worker				

(continued)

Step 4

First, go back over the adjectives you checked and those your partner checked. Look for similarities and differences. Instead of the two of you, there are really four people. There is you as you see yourself, you as your partner sees you, your partner as he or she sees himself or herself, and your partner as you see him or her. Look for surprises in comparing the adjectives you checked with those your partner checked. Whether you decide to change your views or not is still up to you, but knowing what others think should help you decide.

Place your paper and your partner's paper side by side and compare the following:

- your view of yourself and your partner's view of you
- your ideal for yourself and your partner's ideal for himself or herself
- your real view of yourself and your ideal for yourself

Discuss the way you view yourself and the aspirations or goals you have with your partner. Are you being fair to yourself? Are you being fair to your partner?

Step 5

Conflict-producing elements of a culture are evident where incompatible values coexist, as in valuing ambition and humility, competitive success and sympathy for the loser, or frankness and tact. These dilemmas can be confusing in our home culture and even more disturbing when we seek to understand someone else's culture. The confusion is particularly likely to result in conflict when an individual or minority group is being acculturated to a dominant majority value system foreign to them. Cultures vary in how they deal with these areas of potential conflict. Surrounded by a cocoon of pretended reality, the culturally encapsulated individual is able to evade reality either by saying his or her way is always the best way or by saying that each individual should be allowed to do whatever he or she wants to do. Neither alternative is likely to produce a satisfactory partnership. This step tries to help you and your partner work out a better compromise in your relationship.

Take a look at the differences between your partner and yourself to see if you really want to change or not. If you allow these differences to control you, they may lead you to (a) get mad at the other person over some small detail; (b) give in to the other person even when you believe you are right; (c) deliberately embarrass the other person in some way; (d) not speak to the other person; (e) pretend that you really do not care, although you really do; or (f) run away from the other person. Discuss the differences and come to an agreement that either the differences are too small to bother with or that each of you can compromise your expectations in some way to accommodate the other.

Which is the best way to handle differences? There are a number of cues to help find the best way. Can you still work with the other person? Does the way you and he or she handle differences strengthen your relationship with one another? Can both of you accept this way of handling your differences? Does this way of handling differences solve the problem permanently? Does this way of handling differences hurt you or the other person? Can you think of a better way than you have been using?

Up to now your partner and you have been sharing information. The next few steps will help you to take action. This step has two moves:

1. The first move builds on the positive shared feelings and on things your partner and you have in common. This may set guidelines for conduct that you both want to continue and a basis for the future.
2. The second move focuses on differences, disagreement, and conflict between your partner and yourself. In this move you can seek to clarify the difficulty and find ways to work together.

Complete the following sentences:

- Differences and disagreements between you and I are:
- The source of our disagreement seems to be:
- I handle these disagreements by:

(continued)

- You handle these disagreements by:
- I might try:
- You might try:
- I think this way might work because:

Step 6

In this step you bring together all the information you have collected about yourself and your partner from previous steps and work out a plan for the future. Unless you decide to put what you now know to work in some way, you will be disappointed in the Cross-Cultural Tradeoff experience as well as in each other. From step 2 you might want to do more things that make your partner feel good and avoid things that make him or her feel bad. From steps 3 and 4 you might formulate new goals for yourself or revise your expectations about your partner. From step 5 you might find new ways to prevent misunderstandings.

It is not easy to change what you are used to doing. You might try out several new approaches to see if they make any difference, leaving you and your partner free to change your minds again later. You will need each other's help to make the decision a success.

Besides seeking help on problems or difficulties in the relationship with your partner, you might find that he or she can help you on some of your own personal problems as well. Use the following outline:

- Situation, problem, or difference:
- What I intend to do about it:
- What I might do in spite of myself:
- How I would like you to help me:

Step 7

Now you may review your relationship with your partner. By now you have had a chance to try out the approaches you decided on in step 6 and might want to make additional changes. You might want to review what both of you said in earlier steps or add new ideas to what you wrote.

The whole idea of the Cross-Cultural Tradeoff experience is to help both of you learn from each other and share your feelings and reactions, views and ideals, and areas of agreement and disagreement. You should be able to work together better now than before you started.

Trade ideas with your partner about how the approaches you tried out worked or didn't work. Be willing to change your approach if you find something that might be better.

Step 8

You have completed the Cross-Cultural Tradeoff experience, although you may want to return to one or more of the steps later. You may find that the trust you have together now would make it a completely new game when played again. You may want to apply approaches from the Cross-Cultural Tradeoff experience to your day-to-day relationship.

Conclusion

We spend years of formal study analyzing the history of people and nations, language structure, laws of nature, and mechanics of operating tools and machines. But one of the most important subjects has not been studied. Each of us depends on many intercultural relationships, which we allow to develop haphazardly and spend little time analyzing. We can help ourselves and others by taking a look at these cross-cultural relationships. The Cross-Cultural Tradeoff experience provides an opportunity to do just that.

Note. From *A Manual of Structured Experiences for Cross-Cultural Learning* (pp. 15–20), by W. H. Weeks, P. B. Pedersen, and R. W. Brislin, 1977, Yarmouth, ME: Intercultural Press. Copyright 1977 by Intercultural Press. Adapted with permission.

99 ADAPTING TO THE CULTURE OF A UNIVERSITY

Objective: To compare how different cultural groups adapt to the problems of a university culture in ways that are sometimes similar and sometimes different.

TIME REQUIRED   A half day or more

RISK LEVEL   Low

PARTICIPANTS NEEDED   Any number of new students, plus a facilitator

PROCEDURE   Please take the following steps:

1. Assemble a group of freshmen and discuss the three most likely responses to each issue listed in Exhibit 5.3. Continue discussing until the group reaches consensus on the best response. This list of issues and responses can then be given to parents, counselors, teachers, and others concerned to see how accurately they can guess which response the freshmen chose.
2. Divide up the participants according to ethnic group, gender, international identity, or some other measure of cultural diversity. Ask each subgroup to identify the best possible response to each issue. The total group then reassembles to compare their different best responses for each issue.

DEBRIEFING   After completing this task, the facilitator will organize a general discussion. Possible discussion questions are the following:

1. Is entering the university the same as entering a new culture for incoming freshmen?
2. Does this list of problems adequately reflect the challenges faced by a new student?
3. How can the student best prepare for encountering these problems?

4. How will the student be changed by the university culture?
5. How will you use what you learned in this experience?

INSIGHT New students from different cultural backgrounds will respond to the complex culture of a large university in many unexpected ways.

Exhibit 5.3   *List of Issues for University Students From Other Cultures*

- You are so homesick that you call home every night, and nothing seems to help you feel better.
- You are so homesick that you leave school to go home every weekend.
- All of your friends are going to other schools, and you have lost contact with your group of friends.
- You are having a hard time making new friends because you might be rejected and it might be disloyal to your old friends.
- The things that made you popular and a leader back home are not important here, and you now have a much lower status.
- People don't seem to care or to be friendly here like they were back home, and you feel very lonely.
- You have a hard time finding your way around campus and occasionally get lost on your way to class.
- The many stairs and hills make it hard to get around campus from one meeting to another.
- You missed a class because you couldn't find the building or went to the wrong building.
- You are having a hard time organizing a schedule for the many activities required of you.
- You are shocked and frightened by the lectures about rape, drugs, and potential problems of crime on campus.
- You are exploring new lifestyles regarding religion, sexual attitudes, and social norms.
- You are anxious that you might pick the wrong courses and then waste time and money on a major you don't really want.
- You are having a hard time managing your money to cover all the new expenses.
- You are spending much more money here than you spent back home, and you can't see how to spend less.
- You will have to get a job to supplement your funds if you are going to get by.
- The time commitment of your new job is getting in the way of doing your schoolwork.
- The "hidden tuition," such as the cost of textbooks and equipment, is much more than you expected.
- Your phone bills calling home are consuming all of your extra money.
- There is a lot of peer pressure to spend money, or you might lose friends.
- You have encountered racist attitudes among your friends regarding students from other cultures and countries.
- You want to get involved with people from other countries and cultures but don't know how to arrange it.
- You and your roommate become enemies, and you are unable to get your room changed.
- You have a chance to move in with a friend off campus, but your parents would not approve.
- You are frightened about how well you will do on your tests, and you are afraid you will have bad grades this first semester.
- Your professor seems very ambiguous about what is expected, and you are not sure how to get a clear sense of task.
- It is hard to balance your study time with the other things you want to fit into your free time.
- You are having a hard time including extracurricular activities (like band) into your schedule.
- You are having a hard time finding a computer to use when you have time to use them.
- It is hard to study, and you read the material without really understanding it.
- The university is not as much fun as you expected it to be before you came.
- You are having a hard time trying to decide whether to go out at night or stay home and study.
- You have been going out during the weekends, and now you are getting behind in your studies.
- You are having a hard time getting enough sleep, and it is starting to affect your health.
- You feel like you are late to every class or meeting and are having difficulty being on time.

(continued)

- There is hardly enough time to eat here, and you don't enjoy eating as much as you used to.
- You are anxious about dating and are not sure what your date will expect to happen.
- You would like to go out on dates a lot more often than you have, but nobody seems interested in you.
- You are anxious about getting accepted into the campus organizations of your choice.
- Your values about the role of alcohol, sexual behavior, and how you behave seem to be changing.
- You are having difficulty with your long-distance romantic relationship, and the two of you seem to be growing apart.
- The expense of long-distance phone calls and trips home to see your boyfriend or girlfriend are getting too high.
- You are lonely for your back-home boyfriend or girlfriend and are getting pressure from local friends to start going out.
- You are considering dropping out of school and going home because you miss so many things from back home.
- You have just gotten a bad grade on your midterms, and you need to do better.
- You are not doing as well in your grades as you expected, and now you are feeling like a failure in the rest of your life as well.
- You have started gaining weight and feel like everything that is going wrong in your life is because you are getting fat.
- You are convinced that there is no job market for your major and that you are wasting your money in your major.
- You have developed a serious drinking problem and are afraid that you are becoming an alcoholic.
- You have had contact with gays and lesbians and are considering changing your sexual orientation.
- Your roommate continues to bring a lover in to sleep over, and that makes things awkward.
- Your roommate has filed a complaint against you to the university, and you have been called to appear before a judicial committee.
- Your parents are coming for Parents' Weekend, and you are terrified!
- Your parents don't approve of how you are doing in school and have threatened to discontinue their financial support.
- There are so many activities going on around campus, but there is never time to participate.
- College is not what you expected it to be, and your family doesn't understand.
- Final exams are coming up for the first semester, and you are not ready.
- You feel so burned out you almost don't care anymore whether you do well or not.
- Everybody else has plans for exciting things to do during Thanksgiving, but you have no plans.
- By now everybody has set up networks of friends, but somehow you got left out of everybody's network.
- You have a serious conflict with one of the faculty, who doesn't seem to like you.
- You are working so hard and sleeping so little that you are starting to get sick.
- The gray days and drizzling weather are really getting you down, and you feel depressed.
- You have gotten into a group of friends who do a lot more drinking and partying than you are used to.
- You feel very depressed and don't know why, but there doesn't seem to be anyone you can talk with about it.
- You have considered suicide and thought about different ways you could do that if things get too bad.
- You are not prepared for your final exams and urgently need to get good grades.
- You have put off all your classwork to the end of the semester, and now everything is overdue.
- Friends of yours are pressuring you to experiment with drugs as a way to relax.
- You want to take advantage of the concerts going on, but you don't have the time or money.
- You have become much less interested in religious activities, and your parents are getting concerned.
- You would like to get more involved in social service projects, parties, and campus activities, but there's never enough time.
- You are not going home for the December break, and all of your friends have exciting plans that make you feel left out.

(continued)

- The financial cost of this first semester has been much more than you expected, and you can see that you don't have enough money.
- Stress has resulted in health problems, lack of sleep, eating junk food, and general depression.
- You are frightened to return home after the first term because you feel like you have changed a lot.
- You have been unable to resolve your conflicts with your roommate, and it doesn't look like you can change roommates.
- You heard about another student who tried unsuccessfully to commit suicide.
- You have had to make hard choices during the final exams about whether to spend time with friends or studying.
- You are ready to start the second semester, but several of your friends have flunked out or left school, and you are frightened.
- You are excited about having completed a first semester at school and are eagerly looking forward to the second semester.
- You have just come back after spending the December break at home, and now you are more lonely than ever.
- New students have moved into your residence and taken over some of your friends.
- You have experienced a family tragedy back home, and being so far away you feel hurt and helpless.
- You ate so much during the December break that you are now too fat to fit into your clothes.
- You were not able to find work during the December break, and now you have serious money problems.
- You are interested in getting involved and are running for office in one of the campus organizations.
- You are more confident of yourself, and you are considering living off campus the second semester.
- Campus organizations, such as fraternities and sororities, are making their selections, and you are afraid of being left out.
- The gray and cold winter weather is starting to really get to you, and you stay inside most of the time.
- Academic pressures are increasing more than ever, and you are falling farther and farther behind.
- You are having communication problems with your academic advisor, who doesn't seem to understand you.
- You are afraid you made wrong course choices and should change your major.
- You are having relationship problems with your boyfriend or girlfriend, and that is taking up a lot of your time.
- Spring break is coming, and you don't have any time or money to plan exciting things to do.
- You are starting to worry about getting summer jobs, which will be essential to supplement your financial resources.
- You have considered applying to study abroad during one of your future semesters.
- You have a chance to move off campus to save some money, but you don't know the other students very well.
- You need to find some money for spring break so that you are not left behind on campus all by yourself.
- Your family back home is having problems, and you can't concentrate on your studies because you are worried.
- You need to look better in a swimsuit than you do now before spring break.
- Your friends who did not go to the university seem to have lots of money and have moved on with their lives, leaving you behind.
- You are afraid that you have taken the wrong courses and are wasting your time in the university.
- You feel like you are having a crisis coping; you are depressed, and the university has not met your expectations.
- You are tempted to escape from the daily grind by partying, drinking, or doing drugs.
- The end of the second semester is approaching with lots of deadlines, and you are terrified of doing badly.
- There is lots of social pressure to go to parties, dances, and concerts instead of studying and doing academic work.
- Everybody seems to have found a summer job except for you.
- There is a lot of pressure to go home during the spring vacation, but you want to stay at the university.

(continued)

- You feel so burned out you don't even care whether you are popular or not or successful or not, and you are sick of school.
- Spring weather has started to warm up, and it is harder to stay inside studying when the sun is shining outside.
- A friend of yours was sexually assaulted on a date rape, and you know both persons very well.
- You have fallen in love, and this has taken over your life as a primary focus.
- With the weather getting warmer, you want to look less like a couch potato.
- You have overspent your financial resources and are not sure how you will be able to come back to school in the fall.
- You are frightened about leaving school even for the summer to go back to the "real world" outside.
- You want to change your major for next fall, but you don't want to make the same mistakes in picking the wrong courses.
- You are afraid that you didn't do well in the first year and that your parents and friends will be disappointed.
- There are parties going on all over campus celebrating the end of the school year.
- You now have to return home after the first year at the university, and you have mixed feelings.
- You have developed a new lifestyle regarding personal freedom to experiment with new ideas.
- You are depressed by the thought of leaving your friends at the university for the summer.
- You are afraid that you will lose your boyfriend or girlfriend during the summer when you are apart.
- You wonder what it will be like to move back home to your old room and lifestyle after a year at the university.

Note. Many of the problems were adapted from the "Calendar of Significant Student Issues," Syracuse University, Office of Residence Life, for a class of freshmen students taught by P. B. Pedersen in 1994.

100 No Questions Asked

Objective: To learn from observation rather than interrogation and to collect unobtrusive measures of cultural data.

TIME REQUIRED   A half day or more

RISK LEVEL   Moderate

PARTICIPANTS NEEDED   Any number of participants, plus a facilitator

PROCEDURE   Please take the following steps:

1. Send participants into the community for at least one afternoon with instructions to learn as much about it as possible without asking direct questions, preferably without asking questions at all.
2. Allow the students to carry a turned-on tape recorder through the community to capture sounds as part of the information about the community.
3. Organize a discussion, and ask the students specific questions about the community.
4. Ask the student to identify both similarities and differences between the host culture and the student's own culture.

DEBRIEFING   Students will be reminded that many cultures do not ask questions as much as others. Students need to develop other ways to learn besides by asking questions. Some questions for discussion are as follows:

1. Why might questions not be appropriate in a particular culture?
2. How might other ways of gathering information be more accurate?
3. How do you avoid members of the host culture telling you what they think you want to hear?
4. Why do questions work particularly well in other cultures?

5. Do you prefer to use questions to gather information?
6. What alternative information-gathering strategies do you prefer to use?

INSIGHT   Much can be learned without asking questions by watching and listening in another culture.

101 PARTNERS: A SEX-ROLE TRAINING EXPERIENCE

> *Objective:* To train partners of the opposite sex in awareness of sex-role stereotyped perceptions of one another.

TIME REQUIRED   Several days

RISK LEVEL   Moderate

PARTICIPANTS NEEDED   Two or more participants; a facilitator may be needed to guide discussion on the experience after completion

PROCEDURE   Please take the following steps:

1. Explain to the students that sex roles resemble cultures as they shape individual values, perceptions, and decisions.
2. Divide a larger group of colleagues into male–female partners.
3. Distribute the list of sex-role stereotypes in Exhibit 5.4. Each partner should respond to the questions or tasks in the exhibit and then exchange responses to discuss their perceptions with one another.
4. Tell the participants to confirm or disconfirm each hypothesis as it relates to them and their partners and to write the response on the same page as the statement and question. Remind the participants to not discuss the responses or the items with their partners until each has responded and exchanged text booklets.
5. After they have responded to each of the items, have the partners exchange booklets and discuss their responses.

Note. From *Decisional Dialogues in a Cultural Context: Structured Exercises* (pp. 43–44), by P. B. Pedersen and D. Hernandez, 1997, Thousand Oaks, CA: Sage. Copyright 1997 by Sage. Adapted with permission. Based on materials by Project Born Free, Department of Psychoeducational Studies, University of Minnesota, Minneapolis.

6. After all partner teams have completed their responses and discussed their perceptions, have them assemble into one large group to discuss the effect of sex-role stereotyping in their particular organization or group.
7. Explain that sex-role stereotyping has become a topic of controversy giving rise to accusations, counteraccusations, anger, and victimization of both men and women. This experience will attempt to reduce the conflict between different-sex colleagues in several ways:
   a. The experience will relate to factual, data-based research conclusions about sex-role stereotyping rather than emotional accusations or unfounded generalities.
   b. The experience will be limited to the private and confidential exchange between two different-sex colleagues without involving other outsiders.
   c. The experience requires the two participant colleagues, one male and one female, to apply the research findings to their own and their partner's situation thereby personalizing the otherwise abstract research conclusions.
   d. The objectives of this experience are to facilitate a private, nonformal educational exchange between a man and a woman colleague on sex-role stereotypes in their organization or group.

DEBRIEFING

The research for this list of questions was conducted in the 1970s, but a surprising number of the stereotypes still exist. The statements are intended to provoke a private discussion between partners on the topic of sex-role stereotypes. The optimum outcome of participation in this experience will be to increase the participants' motivation for a more comprehensive training program in sex-role stereotypes; to exchange perceptions with a different-sex colleague on how partners see themselves in relation to the other, and to strengthen the trusting relationship with a colleague from the opposite sex on issues of sex-role stereotyping. Some questions for discussion are as follows:

1. How relevant are the data-based statements, given that they are based on research from the 1970s?
2. How would more recent research be different from what is reported in this list?
3. Do you believe that gender role resembles a "culture"?
4. Were you surprised by your partner's responses to any of the items?
5. Having completed this experience, do you feel that your relationship with your partner is stronger than previously?

INSIGHT

Gender cultural differences are frequently overlooked in judging cultural salience.

Exhibit 5.4   *Sex-Role Stereotypes*

Identical products are evaluated more highly when attributed to a man rather than a woman.

- Can you think of an example where you may have evaluated a behavior by someone from one sex differently than the same behavior by someone from the opposite sex?
- Can you think of an example where your partner may have evaluated a behavior by someone from one sex differently than the same behavior by someone from the opposite sex?

As they grow up, women are taught to value men more and themselves less.

- Can you recall a statement from your own childhood where boys were described as superior to girls by a respected adult?
- Would you expect your partner to teach his or her children that boys are superior to girls, even though he or she may not be aware of having taught that lesson?

Women have greater verbal ability than men, whereas men excel in visual–spatial and mathematical ability and tend to be more aggressive.

- What differences did you first become aware of between yourself and those of the opposite sex?
- How do you think your partner saw himself or herself as different from the opposite sex as a child?

Women with a more innovative role or lifestyle tend to have nonstereotypical views of themselves in terms of sex roles.

- Would you describe yourself and your partner as innovative in your lifestyles?
- Would you describe yourself and your partner as having stereotypical views of yourselves in terms of sex roles?

The learning of adult sex roles is seen primarily as occupation directed for men and family directed for women.

- What did your parents want you to be when you grew up, and why?
- What are some other careers in which you think your partner might have enjoyed success?

Women with nontraditional attitudes toward the family not only fantasized more achievement but actually achieved higher grades in college.

- Would you describe the high-achieving women you know as having nontraditional attitudes toward the traditional family?
- Describe one nontraditional attitude of your partner toward the family.

Women who are competent and achieve are viewed as deviant from women's norms and thus anxious, whereas women who see themselves as lacking these traits may suffer low self-esteem.

- If you were given the choice, would you prefer to be viewed as competent, but deviant, or traditional, but lacking in self-esteem?
- Are competent and achieving men less anxious than competent and achieving women?

Women have a more difficult time seeking a career congruent with their self-concept than men.

- Is your career congruent with your self-concept?
- Is your partner's career congruent with his or her self-concept?

Women who have clearly differentiated concepts of career woman and homemaker are more likely to have work plans congruent with their self-image, whether that is as homemaker or career woman.

- Do you differentiate between career woman and homemaker roles as two legitimate directions for men *and* women?
- Does your partner differentiate between both roles as legitimate for men *and* women?

(continued)

Exhibit 5.4 *Sex-Role Stereotypes (Continued)*

Men who see themselves as competent or successful have higher self-esteem than men who do not.

- What are the criteria by which you might describe yourself as competent?
- What are the criteria by which you might describe your partner as competent?

Men and women do not differ on the perceived locus of control until college, when women tend to score higher on measures of external locus of control than men.

- Do you tend to believe that most of your decisions are controlled by others or by external sources of power?
- Do you think your partner feels that most decisions are controlled by others or by external sources?

High school women who scored higher on internal locus of control measures chose more innovative careers than did those with higher external locus of control scores.

- Are you attracted to unusual and innovative career choices?
- Do you think your partner is attracted to unusual and innovative career choices?

Sex-role stereotypes of greater male control and power occur even in elementary school textbooks, in which male characters cause good things to happen by their own actions, whereas female characters profit from the actions of others or from fortuitous circumstances.

- Give an example of a fictional hero or heroine who would rescue others and whom you admired or enjoyed learning about.
- Give an example of a fictional hero or heroine that reminds you of your partner in some way.

People with higher scores on internal locus of control measures work harder for success.

- Do you consider a high score on internal locus of control measures to be "sex-fair" as an evaluation criterion?
- Do you think your partner would describe this measure as sex-fair or unbiased?

Women who blame sexism on "the system" aspire to less typical feminine roles and are more likely to seek careers outside the home.

- Do you think it is good and right to blame the system for being sexist?
- Do you think your partner would say it is good and right to blame the system?

College students of both sexes who have strong internal locus of control beliefs describe themselves more positively and with more traits seen as stereotypical characteristics of the opposite sex.

- What are some of your personality traits that you would characterize as more typically belonging to the opposite sex?
- What are some of your partner's personality traits that you would characterize as more typically belonging to the opposite sex?

Increases in internal locus of control beliefs are reported following participation in a community action program when links between old successes and new goals are explicitly pointed out and when sources of possible reinforcement are described.

- Do you see yourself as tending to see your decisions more and more controlled by internal or by external factors?
- Do you see your partner's decisions as being more and more controlled by internal or by external factors?

Women do not achieve as much as men in the professions, politics, and sports according to traditional measures of success.

- In what ways would you consider yourself more successful than your partner?
- In what ways would you consider your partner more successful than yourself?

(continued)

Exhibit 5.4   *Sex-Role Stereotypes (Continued)*

Women experience a conflict between success and femininity, but they do not exhibit a greater "fear of success" than men.

- Can you describe a particular incident where you seemed to avoid success?
- Can you describe a particular incident where your partner seemed to avoid success?

Although women have as high an achievement motivation as men, they are more likely to focus their efforts on achievement in traditionally defined feminine tasks, just as men are more likely to focus on masculine task roles.

- In what ways do you think you have a higher achievement motivation than your partner?
- In what ways do you think your partner has a higher achievement motivation than yourself?

When a group of men and women are asked to predict how well they will perform on a specified task, women state lower expectations for their performance than men.

- Describe a particular task that you can do better than your partner.
- Describe a particular task that your partner can do better than yourself.

Women's expectancies of success in various tasks requiring visual–spatial or math abilities decline in adolescence.

- How have your visual–spatial or math abilities contributed or not contributed to your success?
- How have your partner's visual–spatial or math abilities contributed or not contributed to his or her success?

Men and women do not differ significantly in the accuracy of their performance estimations but do differ in the direction of error, with men tending to overestimate their performance and women to underestimate theirs.

- Give an example of when you overestimated your performance and an example of when you underestimated your performance.
- Give two similar examples for your partner.

Women may be underrepresented in many prestigious occupations not only because of external barriers that limit access but also because of internal attitudinal barriers that lead women not to aspire to such professions.

- Give an example of an external barrier and an internal barrier that inhibited your career.
- Give an example of an external barrier and an internal barrier that you think inhibited your partner's career.

Compared to women, men have higher career aspirations and anticipate more successful performance in a variety of tasks.

- Do you have career aspirations that are higher than your partner's aspirations?
- Does your partner have higher career aspirations than you do?

Men and women tend to have different patterns of attribution to explain the outcomes of their performance, with women tending to attribute unexpected success to luck and expected failure to lack of ability.

- Describe a recent success of your own, explaining why it was successful.
- Describe a recent success of your partner's, explaining why it was successful.

Women tend to attribute both success and failure to external causes such as task difficulty or luck, so that they feel less pride in success and less shame at failure than men.

- Describe a recent failure of your own, explaining why it was a failure.
- Describe a recent failure of your partner's, explaining why it was a failure.

(continued)

Exhibit 5.4   *Sex-Role Stereotypes (Continued)*

There is sex discrimination in the awarding of financial assistance for college students so that women get less than their share of available money.

- How much scholarship assistance did you get toward the completion of your post-high school education?
- How much scholarship assistance would you estimate your partner received?

Fields are viewed as being masculine or feminine, with more women in professions stereotyped as feminine and more men in professions stereotyped as masculine.

- List the names of at least six people, known to you and to your partner personally, who are in careers that would traditionally be characterized as more appropriate for the opposite sex.
- Have you ever considered a career that might seem more appropriate for someone from the opposite sex?

Over the past decade the proportion of first-year college women planning to enter previously masculine fields such as business, medicine, law, and engineering has nearly tripled.

- What are the careers you would like to see your sons and daughters strive for?
- What are the careers you would expect your partner to want his or her sons and daughters to strive for?

Counselors of both sexes perceive deviant career goals as less appropriate than conforming goals for their female clients and tend to perceive male or female clients with deviant goals as more in need of further counseling.

- If your son or daughter chose a career counselors describe as deviant, would you encourage your son or daughter to continue?
- If your partner's son or daughter chose a career that counselors described as deviant, would your partner encourage his or her son or daughter to continue?

Traditional counselors impute greater maladjustment to female students than to identically described male students.

- Among the eccentric friends you and your partner may both know, cite one male and one female example, indicating which is the most eccentric.
- In what ways do you see yourself as more or less adjusted to stress situations than your partner?

Male counselors in training, while subscribing to a universal standard for healthy men and adults, hold another stereotypical conforming standard for healthy women.

- Write a brief description of a healthy man and a healthy woman.
- Do you expect your partner's comparison to be similar to yours or dissimilar?

In counseling, men are more likely to be rated as having vocational–educational problems, whereas women are more often rated as having emotional–social problems.

- Describe an educational–vocational problem and an emotional–social problem you have experienced or are experiencing.
- Describe similar problems you think your partner might be facing.

Counselors are less well informed to counsel women, especially innovative women, than they are to counsel men.

- Describe the characteristics of a counselor you would seek out for help on your own problems.
- Describe the characteristics of a counselor that you think your partner would seek out.

(continued)

Exhibit 5.4 *Sex-Role Stereotypes (Continued)*

Career interest measurement inventories contain a sex bias in their use of language.

- Give some examples of how career interest inventories might contain a sex bias in the use of language.
- Would you expect your partner to disregard advice from career interest measurement inventories if it ran counter to his or her preferred career?

Textbooks frequently portray women in a negatively biased stereotypical manner.

- Why do you think this might be true?
- Why do you think your partner would say it might be true?

It has been harder for a woman to get admitted to an undergraduate college than for a man.

- Do you believe a more qualified male applicant should be rejected in preference for a less qualified female applicant to college, or should sex be disregarded in the question of admissions?
- How do you expect your partner to respond to that question?

The majority of professional women (70%) are concentrated in a few professions traditionally considered feminine, such as teaching, nursing, library science, secretarial positions, and social work.

- Do you expect future men and women to move into professional roles reserved for the opposite sex in the past?
- Do you think your partner expects future men and women to move into one another's professional roles?

In 1970, nearly one half of all women were working because of financial necessity rather than for pleasure or self-fulfillment.

- What would happen if you were to quit your job?
- What would happen if your partner quit his or her job?

Occupations stereotypically associated with high levels of competence, rationality, and assertion were viewed as masculine, whereas occupations stereotypically viewed as feminine were associated with dependency, passivity, nurturance, and interpersonal warmth.

- Describe some masculine and feminine characteristics required for your job.
- Describe some masculine and feminine characteristics required for your partner's job.

Although more women are working today than were before, they are not aspiring to positions as high level as women did 30 years ago.

- Would you describe yourself as aspiring to a higher level position than your parents achieved?
- Would you describe your partner as aspiring to a higher level position than his or her parents achieved?

Role models, especially the maternal model, are closely related to the occupational choices of women and their motivation to pursue these choices.

- Describe how your parents influenced your choice of career.
- From knowing your partner's attitudes, describe what you imagine his or her parents' abilities might have been.

Women preparing for nontraditional, male-dominated fields (e.g., math and science) think men make little differentiation in male and female work roles and other related behaviors or attitudes.

- Do the male colleagues in your workplace differentiate between male and female work roles?
- Do you think your partner will say that male colleagues differentiate between male and female work roles?

(continued)

Exhibit 5.4 *Sex-Role Stereotypes (Continued)*

Sex-role perceptions are affected by parental role behaviors, with maternal employment outside the home resulting in smaller perceived sex-role differences.

- How were you influenced by your mother working or not working outside the home?
- Do you believe your partner's mother worked outside the home?

In research on sex-role stereotypes, men are described by traits called *competency attributes,* such as being independent, objective, competitive, self-confident, and logical, whereas women are seen as lacking these competency traits and possessing traits of *warmth and expressiveness* such as being gentle, tactful, sensitive to the feelings of others, quiet, and tender. Neither men nor women were typically seen as possessing the traits characteristic of the opposite sex.

- Which traits of the opposite sex do you admire most?
- Which traits of the opposite sex do you think your partner will claim to admire most?

Generalized self-esteem measures are as high for women as for men.

- What could you accomplish that would increase your self-esteem?
- What could your partner accomplish that would increase his or her self-esteem?

Note. From *Decisional Dialogues in a Cultural Context: Structured Exercises* (pp. 43–44), by P. B. Pedersen and D. Hernandez, 1997, Thousand Oaks, CA: Sage. Copyright 1997 by Sage. Adapted with permission. Based on materials by Project Born Free, Department of Psychoeducational Studies, University of Minnesota, Minneapolis.

102 THE INTERPERSONAL, INTERCULTURAL, PSYCHOPATHOLOGICAL (IIP) QUESTIONNAIRE

> *Objective:* To examine differences in assigning interpersonal, intercultural, or psychopathological attributions to a client and to understand behaviors that may be considered different from conventional norms.

TIME REQUIRED Several hours

RISK LEVEL Moderate

PARTICIPANTS NEEDED Any number of participants, plus a facilitator for discussion after completing the questionnaire

PROCEDURE Please take the following steps:

1. Distribute the IIP questionnaire in Exhibit 5.5.
2. Ask the students to fill in the information at the top before completing the questionnaire. A pseudonym or symbol may be used instead of the student's name.
3. When students have responded to all items on the rating sheet, post the scores for a group discussion.

DEBRIEFING Counseling and clinical interviewers need to understand how the same situation may be seen differently before and after training in multicultural counseling. This experience seeks to discover patterns in those different responses. Each incident is brief and incomplete, encouraging the rater to project his or her own meanings on the incident. Students should discuss whether they see the presenting problem as primarily a problem of interpersonal communication, a problem of intercultural contact, or a problem of psychopathology. People with less training or education tend to consider the presenting

Note. From *Decisional Dialogues in a Cultural Context: Structured Exercises* (pp. 55–60), by P. B. Pedersen and D. Hernandez, 1997, Thousand Oaks, CA: Sage. Copyright 1997 by Sage. Adapted with permission.

problem as more likely to be intercultural and less likely to be psychopathological. Those with more counselor training or education tend to describe the presenting problem as more likely to be psychopathological and less likely to be intercultural. Some discussion questions are as follows:

1. Can you describe what you mean by *intercultural, interpersonal,* and *psychopathological*?
2. Did students with more training tend to label different behavior as psychopathology? If so, why?
3. Did those with less formal training tend to label different behaviors as intercultural? If so, why?
4. Did you tend to label different behaviors as pathology? If so, why?
5. How can you use what you learned from this experience?

INSIGHT   Culturally different people will view the presenting problems from different perspectives.

Name: Institution: Date:

Number of years as a practicing counselor or psychologist (please circle):

under 1 year   1–3 years   4–6 years   7–10 years   over 10 years

Number of courses taken in counseling or related field (please circle):

1 course   2–5 courses   6–10 courses   over 10 courses

Main area of professional interest:

Specify one (please circle):

Pretest   Posttest

For each incident or situation, indicate the degree to which you feel that the problem is interpersonal, intercultural, or psychopathological in nature. Use the definitions of these terms as you currently understand them. A score of 1 indicates that you consider the adjective to be totally irrelevant to this problem, and 10 indicates that you consider the adjective to be extremely important to this problem.

1. A 65-year-old man lives in a crowded downtown neighborhood yet feels isolated and alone. He feels that people are cold and unfriendly.

    Interpersonal: 1 2 3 4 5 6 7 8 9 10
    Intercultural: 1 2 3 4 5 6 7 8 9 10
    Psychopathological: 1 2 3 4 5 6 7 8 9 10

2. A female college student feels that men are interested only in sex and not in getting to know her as an individual. Although she admits to being very flirtatious, she feels angry and degraded when men respond in a sexual way.

    Interpersonal: 1 2 3 4 5 6 7 8 9 10
    Intercultural: 1 2 3 4 5 6 7 8 9 10
    Psychopathological: 1 2 3 4 5 6 7 8 9 10

3. A caseworker tells a client (male, head of household) that he will need to do some of the work necessary to find him an apartment and a job. The client is angry and resentful, because he feels the caseworker should be doing all these things for him.

    Interpersonal: 1 2 3 4 5 6 7 8 9 10
    Intercultural: 1 2 3 4 5 6 7 8 9 10
    Psychopathological: 1 2 3 4 5 6 7 8 9 10

4. A 28-year-old, unmarried woman is extremely reluctant to make any decision without the permission of her father and his full support.

    Interpersonal: 1 2 3 4 5 6 7 8 9 10
    Intercultural: 1 2 3 4 5 6 7 8 9 10
    Psychopathological: 1 2 3 4 5 6 7 8 9 10

(continued)

5. A 23-year-old woman engages in premarital sex for the first time. She subsequently comes to a counselor suffering from guilt and the fear that her friends and family will view her as promiscuous.

   Interpersonal: 1 2 3 4 5 6 7 8 9 10
   Intercultural: 1 2 3 4 5 6 7 8 9 10
   Psychopathological: 1 2 3 4 5 6 7 8 9 10

6. A Korean woman delivers her baby in a New York Hospital; all aspects of the delivery are normal. The woman soon becomes depressed, as well as feeling angry and resentful toward the hospital staff.

   Interpersonal: 1 2 3 4 5 6 7 8 9 10
   Intercultural: 1 2 3 4 5 6 7 8 9 10
   Psychopathological: 1 2 3 4 5 6 7 8 9 10

7. A person is referred for counseling because he keeps losing jobs because of absenteeism and tardiness.

   Interpersonal: 1 2 3 4 5 6 7 8 9 10
   Intercultural: 1 2 3 4 5 6 7 8 9 10
   Psychopathological: 1 2 3 4 5 6 7 8 9 10

8. A 50-year-old man goes to a counselor for help in choosing a career. As the counselor tries to help the client clarify his feelings and attitudes about different careers, the client becomes very angry and frustrated.

   Interpersonal: 1 2 3 4 5 6 7 8 9 10
   Intercultural: 1 2 3 4 5 6 7 8 9 10
   Psychopathological: 1 2 3 4 5 6 7 8 9 10

9. A person is referred for counseling because he reports having secret conversations with messengers from another planet.

   Interpersonal: 1 2 3 4 5 6 7 8 9 10
   Intercultural: 1 2 3 4 5 6 7 8 9 10
   Psychopathological: 1 2 3 4 5 6 7 8 9 10

10. A 65-year-old woman sees a counselor because she feels that she has a lot of difficulty making friends.

    Interpersonal: 1 2 3 4 5 6 7 8 9 10
    Intercultural: 1 2 3 4 5 6 7 8 9 10
    Psychopathological: 1 2 3 4 5 6 7 8 9 10

11. A man seeks help in trying to understand his teenage son's fixation with rock music. It appears that his son has trouble with absenteeism at school.

    Interpersonal: 1 2 3 4 5 6 7 8 9 10
    Intercultural: 1 2 3 4 5 6 7 8 9 10
    Psychopathological: 1 2 3 4 5 6 7 8 9 10

12. A man approaches a counselor with feelings of depression. He feels that his job is leading nowhere and that his occupational efforts are fruitless.

    Interpersonal: 1 2 3 4 5 6 7 8 9 10
    Intercultural: 1 2 3 4 5 6 7 8 9 10
    Psychopathological: 1 2 3 4 5 6 7 8 9 10

(continued)

13. A 19-year-old sophomore complains to a counselor that she is being sexually harassed by her male professors. She claims that this has occurred throughout her academic life.

Interpersonal:	1 2 3 4 5 6 7 8 9 10
Intercultural:	1 2 3 4 5 6 7 8 9 10
Psychopathological:	1 2 3 4 5 6 7 8 9 10

14. A 32-year-old woman is reluctant to leave her parents' home to live on her own. She feels that to do so would be to lack financial responsibility.

Interpersonal:	1 2 3 4 5 6 7 8 9 10
Intercultural:	1 2 3 4 5 6 7 8 9 10
Psychopathological:	1 2 3 4 5 6 7 8 9 10

15. A 70-year-old man sees a counselor, complaining of chest and neck pains. He has sought medical help but has been diagnosed as medically normal.

Interpersonal:	1 2 3 4 5 6 7 8 9 10
Intercultural:	1 2 3 4 5 6 7 8 9 10
Psychopathological:	1 2 3 4 5 6 7 8 9 10

16. A 31-year-old woman has been seeing a counselor for three sessions; she has remained attentive to the counselor but has said very little about herself. She rarely volunteers any information during the sessions.

Interpersonal:	1 2 3 4 5 6 7 8 9 10
Intercultural:	1 2 3 4 5 6 7 8 9 10
Psychopathological:	1 2 3 4 5 6 7 8 9 10

17. An international student is confused about his feelings. He wishes to stay in the United States and pursue an academic career, yet his sense of nationalism and family unity are pressuring him to return to his native country.

Interpersonal:	1 2 3 4 5 6 7 8 9 10
Intercultural:	1 2 3 4 5 6 7 8 9 10
Psychopathological:	1 2 3 4 5 6 7 8 9 10

18. A 28-year-old woman is referred by her husband because she is constantly using prescription drugs to help her cope with day-to-day existence. The woman is aware of her drug use but denies that it affects her family life.

Interpersonal:	1 2 3 4 5 6 7 8 9 10
Intercultural:	1 2 3 4 5 6 7 8 9 10
Psychopathological:	1 2 3 4 5 6 7 8 9 10

19. A 22-year-old woman approaches a counselor complaining that she cannot focus on relevant issues. She claims that her thinking has suddenly become "diffuse."

Interpersonal:	1 2 3 4 5 6 7 8 9 10
Intercultural:	1 2 3 4 5 6 7 8 9 10
Psychopathological:	1 2 3 4 5 6 7 8 9 10

20. A 20-year-old factory worker is referred to a counselor by his work supervisor. It appears that the man is lazy on the job and that his absenteeism is higher than average.

Interpersonal:	1 2 3 4 5 6 7 8 9 10
Intercultural:	1 2 3 4 5 6 7 8 9 10
Psychopathological:	1 2 3 4 5 6 7 8 9 10

Note. From *Decisional Dialogues in a Cultural Context: Structured Exercises* (pp. 55–60), by P. B. Pedersen and D. Hernandez, 1997, Thousand Oaks, CA: Sage. Copyright 1997 by Sage. Adapted with permission.

103 DEVELOPING CULTURAL LIFE SKILLS

Objective: To identify specific life skills in a multicultural group.

TIME REQUIRED   Several hours

RISK LEVEL   Moderate

PARTICIPANTS NEEDED   Any number of participants, plus a facilitator

PROCEDURE   Please take the following steps:

1. Distribute the listing of life skills and brief descriptions useful for entering a new culture in Exhibit 5.6.
2. After reviewing the list, discuss with students how these skills can be used as a personal audit.

DEBRIEFING   Part of the preparation for entering an unfamiliar culture is doing an audit of those resources a person has available and those resources that he or she needs to secure. This list of skills provides the basis for a careful audit of resources for going into an unfamiliar culture. Some discussion questions might be the following:

1. Which multicultural skills do you already have?
2. Which multicultural skills do you need to develop?
3. How can you best prepare for going into an unfamiliar culture?

Note. From *Decisional Dialogues in a Cultural Context: Structured Exercises* (pp. 87–91), by P. B. Pedersen and D. Hernandez, 1997, Thousand Oaks, CA: Sage. Copyright 1997 by Sage. Adapted with permission.

Exhibit 5.6   *Life Skills: Preparing to Enter an Unfamiliar Culture*

1. *Interviewing:* Participants will simulate both interviewing and being interviewed by people from other cultures, with an opportunity for feedback both from the other person and from a trained facilitator.
2. *Questioning:* Participants will simulate likely situations (asking directions, finding out what happened, or gathering information) that require them to question people from another culture, with an opportunity for feedback.
3. *Comparing:* Participants will learn to identify differences and similarities between themselves and people from another culture through one-to-one discussion groups.
4. *Identifying assumptions:* Participants will listen to a person from another culture describe an incident, idea, or concept and then identify the unstated assumptions that the person is making about that incident, idea, or concept.
5. *Using feedback:* Participants will be trained to appropriately accept feedback from and provide feedback to a person from another culture.
6. *Listening:* Participants should be able to listen closely enough to what the person from another culture is saying that they can repeat back, to that person's satisfaction, the content of what was said and some of the feelings behind that content.
7. *Skill teaching:* Participants from one culture should be able to teach participants from another culture skills necessary to communicate in their own culture.
8. *Organizing facts:* Participants should be able to organize information about another culture into a meaningful pattern of behavior that will help them to understand that other culture.
9. *Describing feelings:* Participants should be able to describe their own feelings and predict what other participants will say they feel about a particular shared group experience.
10. *Fantasizing:* Participants should be able to project themselves into the role of a "problem" between people from two cultures and role-play that fantasy appropriately.
11. *Sensitizing:* Participants should be able to identify aspects of a critical incident that people from another culture might consider offensive and unfair.
12. *Role-playing:* Participants should be able to role-play situations they are likely to experience at some future time involving interaction with people from another culture, both in their own role and in the role of a person from that other culture.
13. *Using help:* Participants should be able to identify aspects of a critical incident that people from another culture might appropriately use to help one another.
14. *Using multimedia:* Participants should be able to demonstrate ways in which pictures, music, or other media might be helpful in understanding another culture.
15. *Contracting:* Participants should be able to identify terms of a "contract," or agreement between themselves and the life skills training program, concerning those skills they wish to learn and their investment in that learning.
16. *Planning:* Participants should be able to present a plan on specific ways they expect to use their learning from the cross-cultural communications course.
17. *Using criteria:* Participants should be able to identify the criteria they use in evaluating the work of people from another culture.
18. *Supporting others:* Participants should be able to demonstrate in simulated critical incidents how they would support people from their own and another culture during an intercultural exchange.
19. *Deferring judgment:* Participants in a creative problem-solving exercise should be able to defer judgment on solutions being presented by people from a variety of cultures while a comprehensive list of alternatives is being compiled.
20. *Reporting:* Participants should be able to report accurately, to the satisfaction of other participants in that intercultural group.
21. *Summarizing:* Participants should be able to summarize accurately the discussion on a particular critical incident among members of their intercultural group.
22. *Problem solving with a system:* Participants should be able to identify and use appropriately the ways in which people from different cultures approach, define, and solve problems.

Note. From *Decisional Dialogues in a Cultural Context: Structured Exercises* (pp. 87–91), by P. B. Pedersen and D. Hernandez, 1997, Thousand Oaks, CA: Sage. Copyright 1997 by Sage. Adapted with permission.

4. What additional competencies not included in this list might be important for visiting another culture?
5. Give examples of how the same skill might function differently in different cultures.

INSIGHT Life skills function differently in each cultural context.

104 INTERNATIONAL STUDENT SURVEY OF STRONG FEELINGS

Objective: To identify topics of strong feeling among international students where counseling might be appropriate.

TIME REQUIRED   An hour to complete the experience and receive counseling

RISK LEVEL   Moderate

PARTICIPANTS   Any number of international students or people unfamiliar with counseling, plus
NEEDED   a counselor

PROCEDURE   Please take the following steps:

1. Distribute the list in Exhibit 5.7 to individual students and ask them to indicate topics about which they might have strong feelings.
2. Distribute the test in Exhibit 5.8, and ask the students to complete it. Review the choices of answer before they begin. Students are to indicate whether they strongly agree, agree, disagree, or strongly disagree with the items, or they can circle the question mark if they do not have strong feelings about that item.
3. Either the student or the facilitator may score the test answer blank according to guidelines.
4. Interpret the patterns of strong feeling for each student to evaluate whether or not these data are useful for counseling. Students may wish to see a summary of their responses to the themes or clusters of items that deal with the same area of concern or topic, and their responses must remain confidential. The facilitator may want to meet with students to discuss their areas of strong feeling. This test is particularly useful to help students who are unfamiliar with counseling but know they need some sort of help.

Note. From *Culture-Centered Counseling Interventions: Striving for Accuracy* (pp. 144–150), by P. B. Pedersen, 1997, Thousand Oaks, CA: Sage. Copyright 1997 by Sage. Adapted with permission.

Exhibit 5.7   *Topics That Provoke Strong Feelings*

1. Meaning of life	6. Self-confidence
2. Adventure and achievement	7. Doubts and assurances
3. Faults of Americans	8. The opposite sex
4. Teachers and classmates	9. Family
5. Academic problems	10. Community

Note. From *Culture-Centered Counseling Interventions: Striving for Accuracy* (pp. 144–150), by P. B. Pedersen, 1997, Thousand Oaks, CA: Sage. Copyright 1997 by Sage. Adapted with permission.

DEBRIEFING
The objective of the International Student Survey of Strong Feelings is to suggest which of the 10 topic areas arouse strong feelings and which do not. Having strong feelings is neither good nor bad, but such feelings may influence adjustment as a student and the achievement of educational objectives. Some discussion questions are as follows:

1. Did the test accurately identify areas of strong feelings?
2. How will identifying strong feelings help the counselor?
3. How will identifying strong feelings help the client if that client is unfamiliar with counseling?
4. Did the student feel uncomfortable revealing areas of strong feelings?
5. How can this test be used to help international students?

INSIGHT
Identifying areas where the international student is experiencing strong positive or negative feelings will help students unfamiliar with counseling to target issues where counseling might be useful.

Exhibit 5.8   *International Student Survey of Strong Feelings*

Instructions

To take this survey, you will need the following materials:

(a) this survey booklet, (b) a special answer sheet for marking responses, and (c) a pen or pencil.

You should be seated away from others (at least every other chair). This will help you to concentrate completely on your own survey. You will finish sooner without distraction. You will start at the beginning and work straight through. If at all possible, finish the survey at one sitting.

Now, go to your answer sheet. Fill in your name, address, date, age, sex, telephone number, college or major, and country of origin.

After you have read the directions, begin with item 1. Mark your answer in the corresponding space on the answer sheet.

If you have any questions, raise your hand. The person giving the survey will answer your questions.

The words *family, home,* and *community* are used throughout the survey. They may refer to either those you have back home or those you have in the United States. However you interpret these three terms, it would be better if you were consistent throughout the survey, using those from either the home country or the United States.

Read This First

Each statement in this section is a concern that some people have. Answer each statement by indicating the extent to which you agree or disagree with those concerns. If you are not sure, mark the answer that is closest to what you believe to be true. The five responses are abbreviated on the answer sheet as follows:

SD = Strongly disagree
D = Disagree
? = Uncertain
A = Agree
SA = Strongly agree

1. I would like to be an artist, musician, or writer.
2. I like exploring the unknown.
3. I do not feel free to discuss my personal problems with anyone.
4. Some teachers act as though a student knows absolutely nothing.
5. I do not take my studies seriously enough.
6. I am afraid of failure or humiliation.
7. I feel I am not living up to my convictions.
8. Some Americans think too much about sex when we are alone together.
9. We need a greater feeling of love in our family.
10. I do not feel that the law treats me the same as it might treat some other people.
11. I enjoy artistic experiences such as art exhibitions, concerts, or plays.
12. I like making or building practical things.
13. We do not study my country enough at the university.
14. Some of my teachers are unfair.
15. I lack confidence when asking a question in class.
16. I often feel sorry for myself.
17. I wish I could really believe in something.
18. I wonder what to look for in a life partner.
19. There were not enough social activities in my home.
20. I feel left out of community affairs.
21. I want to arrive at a meaningful philosophy of life.
22. I like working in an adventuresome occupation.
23. Too few young people go abroad to study.
24. We need recreation at the university we can all enjoy.
25. Americans tend to underestimate the abilities of foreign students.

(continued)

Exhibit 5.8   *International Student Survey of Strong Feelings (Continued)*

26. I become discouraged rather easily.
27. I avoid discussions with Americans about my beliefs.
28. I wonder if I will marry someone who will give me happiness.
29. My family could have been a happier one.
30. I am bored most of my leisure time.
31. I want to help remove social injustice.
32. I like discovering a new idea.
33. Americans are always saying one thing and doing another.
34. Studies demand too much of a person's time.
35. I wish I knew how to study better.
36. I feel that I am not as intelligent as others.
37. There is no one I can go to with a really serious problem.
38. I wonder how I can know what a boy or girl expects before going out on a date.
39. It was hard to discuss my problems with my mother.
40. I hate to ask advice or help from people who might be able to give it to me.
41. I want to work full time to benefit society.
42. I want to own a car.
43. I do not like the gossiping of Americans.
44. Classmates at the university could be more friendly.
45. I worry about examinations.
46. I am afraid of things.
47. Some friends I highly respect are not at all interested in my country.
48. I wonder if I will find the right life partner in marriage.
49. My parents would rather that I didn't go abroad to study.
50. I used to have more friends than I have now.
51. I like having time to read and meditate.
52. I want to have a good job with lots of free time.
53. Americans fail to understand why I spend so much time with my own nationality group.
54. Some of my professors do not understand my difficulties.
55. I am not satisfied with the grades I usually get.
56. My feelings are easily hurt.
57. I sometimes wonder why I came here to study.
58. I wonder if I can find a life partner to marry who has high moral standards.
59. I would like other members of my family to come here.
60. I don't want to become involved in the community.
61. I like being able to help others.
62. I want to enter a high-paying profession.
63. Some Americans act in favor of small cliques and disregard the opinions of the majority of foreign students.
64. Some classmates are inconsiderate of my feelings.
65. I wonder if I have the ability to do university work.
66. I am irritated when things do not go the way I want them to.
67. I worry about little things.
68. I wonder whether or not I could marry someone from some other country.
69. Outside of my family, there is no group where I feel I really belong.
70. People I live with argue too much.
71. I want to be an important person in the community.
72. I have taken things that did not belong to me.
73. Some Americans are unwilling to sacrifice for the good of the nation.
74. I lack the personality and ability to be a leader in a group.
75. I am considering leaving the university.

(continued)

Exhibit 5.8   *International Student Survey of Strong Feelings (Continued)*

76. I lack self-confidence.
77. I am afraid I am losing my cultural values.
78. I don't know what the opposite sex thinks.
79. My parents and I seldom agree on current issues.
80. I feel embarrassed when I have visitors.
81. I want to be able to visit unusual places and interesting people.
82. I am in danger of becoming unemployed.
83. Some Americans try to get along with foreign students by acting like a foreign student themselves and end up looking ridiculous.
84. I lack the ability to participate in sports.
85. I find it hard to concentrate on my studies.
86. I get into moods where I can't seem to cheer up.
87. It is too hard for me to give a reason for my convictions.
88. Outsiders sometimes join our nationality club to get acquainted with our girls.
89. Financial trouble creates difficulty in my home.
90. I buy things I don't need.

Scoring Your Test

Calculate your score for each scale by adding 2 points for strongly agree (SA) or strongly disagree (SD), 1 point for agree (A) or disagree (D) , and 0 points for unknown (?).

Scale	Items	Total score
1. Meaning in life	1, 11, 21, 31, 41, 51, 61, 71, 81	
2. Adventure and achievement	2, 12, 22, 32, 42, 52, 62, 72, 82	
3. Faults of Americans	3, 13, 23, 33, 43, 53, 63, 73, 83	
4. Teachers and classmates	4, 14, 24, 34, 44, 54, 64, 74, 84	
5. Academic problems	5, 15, 25, 35,45, 55, 65, 75, 85	
6. Self-confidence	6, 16, 26, 36, 46, 56, 66, 76, 86	
7. Doubts and assurances	7, 17, 27, 37, 47, 57, 67, 77, 87	
8. The opposite sex	8, 18, 28, 38, 48, 58, 68, 78, 88	
9. Family	9, 19, 29, 39, 49, 59, 69, 79, 89	
10. Community	10, 20, 30, 40, 50, 60, 70, 80, 90	

(continued)

Exhibit 5.8   *International Student Survey of Strong Feelings (Continued)*

Answer Sheet

International Student Survey of Strong Feeling

Name:

Address:

Date:

Age:

Sex:

Telephone number:

College or major:

Country of origin:

1. SD D ? A SA	11. SD D ? A SA	21. SD D ? A SA
2. SD D ? A SA	12. SD D ? A SA	22. SD D ? A SA
3. SD D ? A SA	13. SD D ? A SA	23. SD D ? A SA
4. SD D ? A SA	14. SD D ? A SA	24. SD D ? A SA
5. SD D ? A SA	15. SD D ? A SA	25. SD D ? A SA
6. SD D ? A SA	16. SD D ? A SA	26. SD D ? A SA
7. SD D ? A SA	17. SD D ? A SA	27. SD D ? A SA
8. SD D ? A SA	18. SD D ? A SA	28. SD D ? A SA
9. SD D ? A SA	19. SD D ? A SA	29. SD D ? A SA
10. SD D ? A SA	20. SD D ? A SA	30. SD D ? A SA
31. SD D ? A SA	41. SD D ? A SA	51. SD D ? A SA
32. SD D ? A SA	42. SD D ? A SA	52. SD D ? A SA
33. SD D ? A SA	43. SD D ? A SA	53. SD D ? A SA
34. SD D ? A SA	44. SD D ? A SA	54. SD D ? A SA
35. SD D ? A SA	45. SD D ? A SA	55. SD D ? A SA
36. SD D ? A SA	46. SD D ? A SA	56. SD D ? A SA
37. SD D ? A SA	47. SD D ? A SA	57. SD D ? A SA
38. SD D ? A SA	48. SD D ? A SA	58. SD D ? A SA
39. SD D ? A SA	49. SD D ? A SA	59. SD D ? A SA
40. SD D ? A SA	50. SD D ? A SA	60. SD D ? A SA
61. SD D ? A SA	71. SD D ? A SA	81. SD D ? A SA
62. SD D ? A SA	72. SD D ? A SA	82. SD D ? A SA
63. SD D ? A SA	73. SD D ? A SA	83. SD D ? A SA
64. SD D ? A SA	74. SD D ? A SA	84. SD D ? A SA
65. SD D ? A SA	75. SD D ? A SA	85. SD D ? A SA
66. SD D ? A SA	76. SD D ? A SA	86. SD D ? A SA
67. SD D ? A SA	77. SD D ? A SA	87. SD D ? A SA
68. SD D ? A SA	78. SD D ? A SA	88. SD D ? A SA
69. SD D ? A SA	79. SD D ? A SA	89. SD D ? A SA
70. SD D ? A SA	80. SD D ? A SA	90. SD D ? A SA

Note. From *Culture-Centered Counseling Interventions: Striving for Accuracy* (pp. 144–150), by P. B. Pedersen, 1997, Thousand Oaks, CA: Sage. Copyright 1997 by Sage. Adapted with permission.

105 SHOPPING IN AN UNFAMILIAR CULTURE

Objective: To find out where to buy a list of unusual items in an unfamiliar culture.

TIME REQUIRED   A half day

RISK LEVEL   Moderate

PARTICIPANTS NEEDED   Any number of participants, plus a facilitator

PROCEDURE   Please take the following steps:

1. Develop a shopping list of unusual items that would be difficult to find or difficult to describe without knowing the local language. This experience works best when participants do not know the local language of the shopping area. The list might include local foods, fruits, vegetables, or other items to eat. It may also include potentially embarrassing items such as underwear, condoms, sanitary pads, and so forth or items familiar to the participant's home culture but very scarce in the host culture, such as particular recordings, clothes, pictures, and books.

2. Distribute the shopping list, and tell the participants, divided into two-person dyads, to locate as many items as possible. It is not necessary for the shopper to purchase these items; each group will record the price, the location where it can be purchased, and the name of the person selling the item.

DEBRIEFING   In debriefing the facilitator might ask each team to describe the process of their search for the items on the shopping list and the success they had in finding out where these items are available. Some discussion questions are as follows:

1. What strategy did your group develop to shop successfully?
2. How did you get the cooperation of the host culture merchants?
3. What problems did you encounter, and how did you deal with them?

4. Were there any especially meaningful incidents during your shopping?
5. Did you make any friends in the host culture during this experience?

INSIGHT   It is possible to find one's way around an unfamiliar culture, even though you do not know the local language, if you develop an appropriate strategy.

106 A SIMULATION DESIGNING EXPERIENCE CALLED "MULTIPOLY"

Objective: To describe a complex multicultural event in the categories of a board game.

TIME REQUIRED   A week or so of meetings

RISK LEVEL   High

PARTICIPANTS NEEDED   Any number of participants, plus a facilitator

PROCEDURE   Please take the following steps:

1. Inform students the following: "The process you are about to begin is quite serious and will demand a considerable investment of time and energy but will, we hope, result in a product both stimulating and useful in your group or organization."
2. Divide the students into six groups.
3. Take the rules for a well-known board game and rewrite those rules to fit the conditions of six different ethnic, racial, or cultural roles. The rules for each role will differ from each other in this game as they do in real life. Students will be responsible for drawing up different sets of rules independently and then dividing into groups of six people, one for each role, to coordinate their ideas into one set of rules for that role. Remind students of the need to be sensitive to the different advantages and disadvantages facing each role; to the different aspirations and goals to which each role aspires; to the different acceptable and unacceptable ways of doing things for each role; and to the different style that applies not only to each role group as perceived by themselves, but also as perceived by outsiders. The student may ask, for example:

Note. From *"Multipoly: A Board Game,"* by P. B. Pedersen, 1995, *Simulation and Gaming,* 26(1), pp. 109–112. Copyright 1995 by Sage. Adapted with permission.

- Does each of the six groups have the same ultimate goal? Money? Influence? popularity? power?
- Does each group begin the game with the same resources in terms of money, power, or opportunity?

4. Instruct students to create a new game board with life situations by following these parameters:
   a. Identify policy objectives for each culture being represented.
   b. Identify intercultural situations where the participating cultures are likely to interact, and designate a situation for each space around the edge of the game board.
   c. Identify situations that would create problems for each participating culture, and assign a negative score to the space.
   d. Identify situations that would create opportunities for each participating culture, and assign a positive score to the space.
   e. Assign a net positive or a net negative score and consequence for each participating culture relative to each situation.
   f. Identify additional solutions using decks of instruction cards from which players landing on designated spaces draw a card.
   g. Design each participating culture role to accurately reflect the balance of feasibility and cost–benefit testing of alternative choices interacting with the other cultures in society.
   h. Design the game so that a player in one culture role will finish the game knowing more of that culture's role in society than previously.
   i. Design the game so that a player in one culture role will see the advantages and disadvantages of meeting the needs of other cultures outside the person's own group through cooperation.
   j. Provide opportunities for discussion of how the system could be changed toward a more equitable distribution of opportunities across racial and cultural Multipoly. Change the name of the game to some other more appropriate (and not registered) title—for example, "Multiculturalism"—if necessary.
   k. Fill in the situations for the game board with about seven empty situation boxes on each of the four sides of the game board.
   l. You will also want to indigenize the place names on the game board and develop new decks of cards to fit the situation you are simulating.

5. When the rules of the roles have been completed and the game board finished, take note that when complete, there will be six different sets of rules for the game. Explain the rules and show the game board to each group.

6. Attempt to play the same game together simultaneously, each of the six players being guided by a different set of rules as they encounter the 20 to 30 similar situations on the game board.

DEBRIEFING

The students who designed the game may want to try and play it or, better yet, exchange their game with the game of another team and each team play the game of the other. After having played the game, the students can discuss what they learned about themselves and about other cultures. Some discussion questions are as follows:

1. By taking on the role of someone from another culture, did you learn more about that culture?

2. How did you select the context or situation for the game, and can you evaluate your choice?
3. Were the competing cultures able to find common ground for working together?
4. How does this game help you understand affirmative action policies?
5. What do the terms *win* and *lose* mean in the context of this game?

INSIGHT   The same situation can have very different positive or negative meanings from the viewpoint of different cultures.

107 LIFESTYLES AND OUR SOCIAL VALUES

Objective: To rank order intercultural situations in a small multicultural group in terms of their goodness or social value.

TIME REQUIRED   Several hours

RISK LEVEL   High

PARTICIPANTS NEEDED   Any number of participants, plus a facilitator

PROCEDURE   Please take the following steps:

1. Distribute the grid and brief character sketches in Exhibit 5.9.
2. Ask the students to evaluate the 13 character sketches and where each sketch is in relation to each other from more or less important and in relation to the student's own preferences.
3. Have students write the descriptor of each character in a box in the grid in any random order.
4. Next, have the student rearrange the characters so that each column contains characters that are equal in goodness or badness.
5. Next, have the students again rearrange the characters so that the upper-left-hand corner is reserved for the very best character and the lower right for the very worst.

DEBRIEFING   Facilitators will ask students to reflect on the choices they made and discuss choices made by others in the group. Did students have to deliberate a long time? Which people were most difficult to rank? What does this tell students about their value systems? What ideas do students have about good and bad? Do they have a stable value system, or does it fluctuate according to whim or some other factor? Whom do they

Exhibit 5.9   *The Q-Sort of Different Lifestyles*

1 + +	2 +	3 −	4 − −

The Characters

Assign the following characters a box in the grid above. These descriptions provide "just enough" information about the characters; do not wonder about extenuating circumstances. Make decisions on the basis of the information given. Alternatively, substitute situations from your own setting.

Persistent Student

K, a 14-year-old 7th grader, had hounded his SSP teacher for recommendation for a job. He expressed a deep concern for his needs as related to getting a job. On the day he was taken to his job site, his initial question at the interview was, "Can I have today off?" A youth meeting was being held that afternoon.

Quiet Student

S is very quiet when she is in any kind of trouble. She is very much liked by her peers. Her grades are somewhat low because of poor attendance. She can be very neat and appealing when she wants to.

Encapsulated Teacher

H, like many other teachers, has had limited exposure to cultural values other than his own. However, he has taught children from different cultures for many years and considers himself well qualified and equipped to teach these students in the same way he teaches children from his own culture. He frequently remarks that he minimizes their differences and treats everyone as a human being.

Psychology Teacher

J is a teacher of psychology trained in Minnesota. He has worked in administrative positions, among others with Veterans Administration hospitals, and in neuropsychiatric clinics. He is in his 40s and teaches on the use of projective techniques in psychological treatment.

Responsible Teacher

Mr. M, my high school principal, taught me what the word *responsibility* meant. He was counseling me at the time, and I did not realize it. I rated him after I reached maturity as the best principal and the best teacher I had in my 14 years of schooling.

Inexperienced Teacher

N has no teaching experience. He is very likeable. He was born in a state where two large Indian reservations are located and is teaching Indian culture and writing units.

Taskmaster Teacher

R is a job developer whose responsibility is placing and keeping students at job stations. He always takes the side of the employer at the job station, and he assumes that fault for any failure to succeed in the job lies with the student. He expresses "WASP" work ethic biases with sufficient strength and dogmatism that he does not encourage students to confide in him. Students tend just not to show up.

(continued)

Exhibit 5.9   *The Q-Sort of Different Lifestyles (Continued)*

Rules-Oriented Teacher

I think that teachers who send a student to the office for saying *hell* or *damn* without asking what's wrong or without talking it over with him or her is not really doing their job.

Older Teacher

A taught in the district for 20 years. She graduated from the school she works in. However, she does not interact with or live in the community. She tends toward traditional education and resists innovative change.

Discouraged Student

J is a fair student. He does most of his work. His trouble is that he will stop doing any work when he thinks that he will not succeed.

Smart Student

B is a smart student. She is quiet and shy, but in the right situation she will open up and pour out her problems. The right situation is when she has been around the other person long enough to feel comfortable and trusting of that person.

Aggressive Student

T is a highly aggressive student who is from a broken home, is failing in school, is in trouble with the school officials, and generally causes trouble in the classroom.

Daydreaming Student

F is a student who does not pay close attention, commonly seems to be daydreaming, seldom answers questions verbally, wastes time in class, does not hand in assignments even though they are easy for the other students, and does not seem either happy or satisfied with school.

respect? What do they respect? Would it have made a difference if any of the characters had been of the opposite sex? Some discussion questions are as follows:

1. What race did you assume the characters were? White? Black? Indian?
2. What role does your value system play in your work at the university?
3. Did every student or problem get the same attention?
4. Did you honestly reveal your preference?
5. Does it make any difference?

INSIGHT   We constantly evaluate the people around us from our own cultural perspective.

108 LOCATING POWER NETWORKS IN ORGANIZATIONS

> *Objective:* To identify reciprocated and nonreciprocated affiliation networks in a multicultural group.

TIME REQUIRED   Several hours

RISK LEVEL   High

PARTICIPANTS NEEDED   Any number of participants from the same organization, plus a facilitator

PROCEDURE   Please take the following steps:

1. Compose a list of all members of the group or organization.
2. Distribute the list to all members of the group with instructions to check off the names of members from whom they received help or to whom they gave help in the last week.
3. Ask members to sign their name at the top of their list.
4. Compose a code sheet with the names of participants listed in a vertical column from top to bottom and also listed in the same order at the top of the grid from left to right. An example is given in Exhibit 5.10. This experience is best suited to small working groups of 20 or fewer people.
5. Each student will find his or her name in the column and check the names of those from whom that student has received help from left to right in that row.
6. Create a visual map of these networks by drawing circles for each member around the perimeter of a large sheet of paper and putting one person's name in each circle. The final matrix should indicate both those people selected by each member and whether or not that person was selected back in a reciprocal relationship.
7. Then draw a line between those members who reciprocally identified one another.
8. Present this sociogram to the group for discussion.

Exhibit 5.10 *Grid for Network Analysis*

Name: _____

	A	B	C	D	E	F
A						
B						
C						
D						
E						
F						

Note. From *Intercultural Communication Workbook,* by A. Pedersen, 1990, unpublished manuscript.

DEBRIEFING The debriefing might focus on the following questions:

1. Which students are the "stars" in the group? Which seem to be isolated, and why?
2. Which students seem to have a strong mutual attraction for one another? Which students seem to have a strong mutual rejection of one another?
3. What small groups or cliques do you see in the group? Which students seem to have a strong attraction for members of other gender groups, age groups, cultural groups, or other group?
4. What age groups are represented, and what effect did this have?
5. What other information can be gathered about power networks from this sociogram?

INSIGHT The patterns of who talks with whom symbolize and reflect the power networks in a multicultural group.

109 WRITING AN ETHNOGRAPHY

Objective: To understand and participate in the systematic writing of an ethnography about a particular cultural group.

TIME REQUIRED	Many weeks
RISK LEVEL	High
PARTICIPANTS NEEDED	Any number of participants, plus a facilitator
PROCEDURE	Please take the following steps:

1. Have the students discover the "meanings" of people from another culture. To do that, they need to get inside the culture and to learn its symbols and how its people attach meaning to what is done as well as what is not done.
2. Next, ask students to translate what they have learned to someone outside that culture and communicate the cultural meanings in that culture.
3. Then have students identify universal statements and patterns that apply to all people. The roles of men and women are likely to be different, for example.
4. Next, ask students to identify cross-cultural descriptive statements comparing one culture with another. Comparisons of different cultures provide an example of this level.
5. Have students describe general statements about a particular cultural group that identify that group membership. Each cultural group shares patterns of behavior that indicate identity within that group.
6. Direct the discussion toward general statements about specific cultural groups in particular situations that might not be true in other situations. The group may be direct in some situations and very indirect in others.
7. Ask participants to describe a combination of cultural patterns using the language and perspective of the other culture. What are the "rules" of that culture? How a cultural group does something differently than others is an example.

8. Have students describe stories or incidents that have happened in the culture that demonstrate the importance of their meanings.
9. Instruct those writing an ethnography using the following steps:
   a. Select a cultural group or target population that you find interesting for whatever reason.
   b. Decide what you want to say that might be of interest to others about that particular cultural group.
   c. Make a list of those topics or patterns that are useful in understanding the group, putting each topic on a separate notecard.
   d. Organize the notecards in a logical order, and write your draft by responding to each card in order. This will result in a rough draft of your ethnography.
   e. Organize your rough draft by adding subheadings, moving in logical sequence from one topic to the next.
   f. Share your rough draft with someone who is both articulate and authentic to and about the target culture.
   g. Add an introduction and conclusion.

DEBRIEFING   Writing an ethnography of a group leads to a profound awareness of the cultural meaning system of that group. Every ethnography is incomplete, and the more one learns about a group, the more one realizes how incomplete his or her understanding is. Written ethnographies of many different cultural groups are readily available, and each ethnography approaches the task somewhat differently. Some discussion questions are the following:

1. What is an ethnography?
2. How can an ethnography be a useful educational resource?
3. How would you proceed to write an ethnography?
4. Why is writing an ethnography difficult?
5. What indirect learning occurs as a result of writing an ethnography?

INSIGHT   The discipline of writing about a cultural group and how that culture derives meaning is a useful way of discovering how cultural groups are similar and different at the same time.

110 THE INTERPERSONAL CULTURAL GRID

Objective: To separate expectations from behaviors in analyzing multicultural case examples.

TIME REQUIRED   Several hours

RISK LEVEL   High

PARTICIPANTS NEEDED   Any number of participants, plus a facilitator

PROCEDURE   Please take the following steps:

1. Present the students with the Interpersonal Cultural Grid in Exhibit 5.11 to help them understand the importance of matching culturally learned behaviors with the culture teachers from whom the behaviors were learned.
2. Have students identify one or more significant behaviors and think about the expectation behind the behavior and the culture teachers behind the expectation.
3. Encourage the students to analyze their relationship with their best friend to see if their best friend thinks differently, acts differently, and is in other ways different from themselves in their behaviors. However, since the best friend shares the positive expectations for being a best friend, the differences may actually enrich the relationship.
4. Next, encourage the students to give examples of successful conflict management from their own experience to test the usefulness of the Interpersonal Cultural Grid.

DEBRIEFING   In debriefing the facilitator might want to ask the following questions:

1. If you force the other person to change a behavior against his or her will, what is the likely consequence?

Exhibit 5.11 *Interpersonal Cultural Grid*

Cultural teachers	Where you learned the culturally learned behavior	Why you did the culturally learned behavior	What the culturally learned behavior was
1. Family relations: Relatives Compatriots Ancestors Shared beliefs			
2. Power relationships: Friends Sponsors and mentors Subordinates Supervisors and superiors			
3. Memberships: Organizations Gender and age groups Workplace colleagues			
4. Non-family relationships: Friendships Classmates Neighbors People like me			

2. Are you willing to tolerate different and seemingly negative behavior to preserve shared positive expectations?

3. How can you prevent conflict moving from "cultural" conflict in Cell #2 toward "personal" conflict in Cell #3 and "total" conflict in Cell #4?

4. Why is the conflict likely to escalate if differences in behavior are emphasized before similarities of common-ground shared positive expectations are established?

5. How would you "construct a platform" of shared common ground between two culturally different parties strong enough for both parties to stand and eventually discuss changing their behaviors to accommodate one another?

INSIGHT   Separating culturally learned behaviors from expectations in constructive conflict management helps create win–win outcomes.

■ CHAPTER SIX ■

CONCLUSION: STAYING OUT OF TROUBLE

Experience is probably the best teacher, as the saying goes, but the tuition is often very expensive. Structured multicultural experiences, such as those in this book, provide many opportunities for developing a multicultural awareness. Multicultural awareness, knowledge, and skill are difficult to acquire. There are many important insights about multiculturalism that can be learned, but they cannot be taught directly. The best that a trainer can hope to do is construct and organize a situation in which the learning takes place. Just lecturing, talking to, or telling someone will not likely be heard or understood without a direct experience. The multicultural experiences in this book involve the student as a participant observer in an active rather than a passive role. The experiences themselves are not enough, however. There need to be clearly defined goals and structure to guide the participants toward capturing what they will learn.

Brislin and Yoshida (1994a) identified four basic goals of multicultural training that are useful to consider. First, training helps participants overcome obstacles that interfere with their enjoyment of multicultural experiences. Positive feelings toward the training and the cultures in which they are trained is an important outcome. Second, developing positive and respectful relationships with people from other cultures is important. Indonesians have a saying that if you have a friend, no problem is serious, but if you do not have a friend, every problem is serious. Third, the training will increase productivity so that persons trained can accomplish their tasks more effectively. Fourth, training can help participants manage the stress of adjustment to other cultures more constructively.

The outcome measures of successful multicultural experiences will bring about changes in how people think (cognitive), how people feel (affective), and what people do (behavioral). Brislin, Landis, and Brandt (1983) identified the 10 most important potentially positive outcomes of multicultural training with research documentation as follows:

- a greater understanding of other cultures from their own viewpoint;
- a decrease in negative stereotypes about the host culture;
- a complex rather than simplistic way of thinking about another culture;
- an increase in "world-minded" attitudes about one's own and other cultures;
- greater enjoyment and less anxiety interacting with the host culture;
- a good working relationship with members of the host culture;
- harmonious interpersonal relationships in multicultural work groups;
- adjustment to the stress of living in another culture and better job performance;
- increased comfort and ease in working together as reported by people in the host culture; and
- more effective goal setting and achievement through interpersonal relationships with people from the host culture.

There are also potential problems in the design of multicultural training that can result in negative outcomes if they are not addressed. Gudykunst, Guzley, and Hammer (1996) described some of these potential problems:

- There is an increased demand for multicultural training related to the forces of globalization that can result in training for "quick-fix" solutions and unrealistic expectations for what can be accomplished in brief training experiences. Simplistic multicultural training about how to "stay out of trouble" that disregards deeper issues can turn out "clever racists" who have only learned how to avoid being caught.
- The multicultural experience that lacks theoretical grounding in explicit models or frameworks that explain the interaction and predicted outcomes will be a superficial experience.
- The many different kinds of multicultural training do not always agree on the desired outcomes of training, and this disagreement results in misinformation and confusion about the training process itself.
- Cultural bias is implicit in the multicultural experiences as well as among the participants and leaders of those experiences, requiring that underlying cultural assumptions by all parties be identified.
- The reluctance of the host cultural organization to confront prejudices will inhibit behavioral and attitude changes and can actually reinforce those prejudices if they are not clarified.
- The political climate and organizational culture can impose constraints on the multicultural training experience, resulting in negative outcomes even when all parties want harmony.
- Unless the multicultural training experiences are rewarded and the positive outcomes reinforced in the host culture through systematic follow-up, significant long-term benefits are unlikely to occur.

To enhance positive outcomes and reduce negative problems in multicultural training experiences, presenters need to clearly identify the purpose of the experiences by asking themselves significant questions (Brislin, 1997):

- Can the goals be accomplished better through multicultural experiences than through lectures? Experiences and lectures ideally complement one another in a balance of classroom activity. If the course material is not being understood through lectures, then how can it be better presented through experiences to capture the student's attention? How can the experiences best mobilize the learning through lectures, readings, and other sources of information available to the students? Will the multicultural experience be seen as relevant to the students? If the training experiences relate to students' real-world experiences, they are more likely to be useful.
- How much time will the experience require, including debriefing? Classroom time is valuable and limited, so it must be budgeted carefully. Experiences that require lengthy explanations ahead of time may not be suitable.
- What can possibly go wrong in presenting the multicultural experience? The presenter needs to have thought through a backup plan ahead of time for any potential difficulty. He or she might want to rehearse the experience with a resource person from the target culture before trying it with a class.
- How will others respond to the instructor's using this multicultural experience in the classroom? Thinking through how others outside the training experience, such as parents, colleagues, and supervisors, will react helps anticipate and perhaps prevent future problems.

In addition to the many conceptual problems in presenting multicultural experiences for training, there are many other logistical issues to consider. A. P. Goldstein (2000) presented a delightful but also insightful discussion of the many logistical problems he has encountered in training. He highlighted good teaching techniques:

> Good overheads help, interesting videos help. To-the-point jokes and cartoons help, as do comfortable chairs, fresh coffee and snacks, good lighting, and a room neither too hot nor too cold. But when all is said and done, the ultimate success of any workshop rests primarily on good teaching. (p. 23)

Instructors should prepare more material than they expect to use, rehearse the experience ahead of time and get feedback, arrive at the workshop an hour ahead of time to check the situation and meet the people, give a clear statement of what objectives they hope to accomplish through the experience and move steadily toward completing those objectives, make smooth transitions from one topic to another, reduce downtime and keep the action rolling, maintain a group focus, and engage all members of the experience.

This book attempts to turn multicultural experiences into learning. When the experiences are meaningful, they will be remembered, they will provide a safe context in which to take risks, they will help students anticipate consequences of real-world situations, and they will increase participants' multicultural self-awareness for the culturally learned patterns that control their thoughts and behaviors with or without their permission.

■ REFERENCES ■

Brislin, R. W. (1997). Introducing active exercises in the college classroom for intercultural and cross-cultural courses. In K. Cushner & R. W. Brislin (Eds.), *Improving intercultural interactions: Vol. 2. Modules for cross-cultural training programs* (pp. 91–108). Thousand Oaks, CA: Sage.

Brislin, R. W. (2000). *Understanding culture's influence on behavior* (2nd ed.). Fort Worth, TX: Harcourt.

Brislin, R. W., Cushner, K., Cherrie, C., & Yong, M. (1986). *Intercultural interactions: A practical guide.* Thousand Oaks, CA: Sage.

Brislin, R. W., Landis, D., & Brandt, M. (1983). Conceptualizations of intercultural behavior and training. In D. Landis & R. W. Brislin (Eds.), *Handbook of intercultural training: Vol. 1. Issues in theory and design* (pp. 1–34). Elmsford, NY: Pergamon Press.

Brislin, R. W., & Yoshida, T. (1994a). The content of cross-cultural training: An introduction. In R. W. Brislin & T. Yoshida (Eds.), *Improving intercultural interactions* (pp. 1–14). Thousand Oaks, CA: Sage.

Brislin, R. W., & Yoshida, T. (Eds.). (1994b). *Improving intercultural interactions.* Thousand Oaks, CA: Sage.

Crookall, D., & Arai, K. (Eds.). (1995). *Simulation and gaming across disciplines and cultures.* Thousand Oaks, CA: Sage.

Cushner, K., & Brislin, R. W. (1996). *Intercultural interactions: A practical guide* (2nd ed.). Thousand Oaks, CA: Sage.

Cushner, K., & Brislin, R. W. (1997). *Improving intercultural interactions: Vol. 2. Modules for cross-cultural training programs.* Thousand Oaks, CA: Sage.

Fowler, S. M., & Mumford, M. G. (1999). *Intercultural sourcebook: Cross-cultural training methods* (Vol. 2). Yarmouth, ME: Intercultural Press.

Gertz, B. (1969). How to become a more sophisticated saboteur in groups. In C. R. Mill (Ed.), *Selections from human relations training news* (pp. 87–88). Washington, DC: NTL Institute.

Goldstein, A. P. (2000). *The workshop: An irreverent guide.* Sebastopol, CA: National Training Associates.

Goldstein, S. (2000). *Cross-cultural explorations: Activities in culture and psychology.* Boston: Allyn & Bacon.

Gudykunst, W. B., Guzley, R. M., & Hammer, M. R. (1996). Designing intercultural training. In D. Landis & R. Bhagat (Eds.), *Handbook of intercultural training* (2nd ed., pp. 61–80). Thousand Oaks, CA: Sage.

Haney, W. V. (1979). *Uncritical Inference Test.* San Francisco: International Society for General Semantics.

Hofstede, G. J. (2001). *Culture's consequences: Comparing values, behaviors, institutions, and organizations across nations* (2nd ed.). Thousand Oaks, CA: Sage.

Hofstede, G. J., Pedersen, P. B., & Hofstede, G. (2002). *Exploring culture: Exercises, stories, and synthetic cultures.* Yarmouth, ME: Intercultural Press.

Kagan, S. S. (1999). *Leadership games: Experiential learning for organizational development.* Thousand Oaks, CA: Sage.

Kohls, L. R. (1996). *Survival kit for overseas living: For Americans planning to live and work abroad.* Yarmouth, ME: Intercultural Press.

Kowner, R. (2002). Japanese communication in intercultural encounters: The barrier of status related behavior. *International Journal of Intercultural Relations, 26,* 339–361.

Luft, J. (1969). The Johari window. In C. R. Mill (Ed.), *Selections from human relations training news* (pp. 74–76). Washington, DC: NTL Institute.

Marsella, A. J. (1998). Toward a "global-community psychology": Meeting the needs of a changing world. *American Psychologist, 53*(12), 1282–1291.

Moran, R. T., Mestenhauser, J. A., & Pedersen, P. B. (1974, Summer). Dress rehearsal for a cross-cultural experience. *International Educational and Cultural Exchange, X*(1).

Pedersen, A. (1990). *Intercultural communication workbook.* Unpublished manuscript.

Pedersen, P. B. (1994). International students and international student advisors. In R. W. Brislin & T. Yoshida (Eds.), *Improving intercultural interactions* (pp. 148–167). Thousand Oaks, CA: Sage.

Pedersen, P. B. (1995a). *The five stages of culture shock: Critical incidents around the world.* Westport, CT: Greenwood/Praeger.

Pedersen, P. B. (1995b). Multipoly: A board game. *Simulation and Gaming, 26*(1), 109–112.

Pedersen, P. B. (1997a). *Culture-centered counseling interventions: Striving for accuracy.* Thousand Oaks, CA: Sage.

Pedersen, P. B. (1997b). Doing the right thing: A question of ethics. In K. Cushner & R. W. Brislin (Eds.), *Improving intercultural interactions: Vol. 2. Modules for cross-cultural training programs* (pp. 149–164). Thousand Oaks, CA: Sage.

Pedersen, P. B. (1999). *Multiculturalism as a fourth force.* Philadelphia: Brunner/Mazel.

Pedersen, P. B. (2000a). *A handbook for developing multicultural awareness* (3rd ed.). Alexandria, VA: American Counseling Association.

Pedersen, P. B. (2000b). *Hidden messages in culture-centered counseling: A triad training model.* Thousand Oaks, CA: Sage.

Pedersen, P. B. (2000c). One in the eye is worth two in the ear. *Simulation and Gaming, 31*(1), 103–106.

Pedersen, P. B., & Hernandez, D. (1997). *Decisional dialogues in a cultural context: Structured exercises.* Thousand Oaks, CA: Sage.

Pedersen, P. B., & Ivey A. E. (1993). *Culture-centered counseling and interviewing skills.* Westport, CT: Greenwood/Praeger.

Pedersen, P. B., Ivey A. E., Ivey M. B., & Kuo, Y. Y. (2001). *Instructor's manual for intentional group counseling: A microskills approach.* Belmont, CA: Brooks/Cole.

Pedersen, P. B., & Lee, K. S. (2000). Happy hell or lonely heaven: The brain drain problem. *Asian Journal of Counseling, 7*(2), 61–84.

Porter, J. W., & Haller, A. O. (1962). *Michigan international student problem inventory.* East Lansing: Michigan State University.

Shweder, R. A. (1990). Cultural psychology—What is it? In J. W. Stigler, R. A. Shweder, & G. Herdt (Eds.), *Cultural psychology: Essays on comparative human development* (pp. 73–112). Cambridge, MA: Cambridge University Press.

Singelis, T. (1998). *Teaching about culture, ethnicity, and diversity.* Thousand Oaks, CA: Sage.

Singelis, T., & Pedersen, P. B. (1997). Conflict and mediation across cultures. In K. Cushner & R. W. Brislin (Eds.), *Improving intercultural interactions: Vol. 2. Modules for cross-cultural training programs* (pp. 185–187). Thousand Oaks, CA: Sage.

Sue, D. W., Arredondo, P., & McDavis, R. J. (1992). Multicultural counseling competencies and standards: A call to the profession. *Journal of Counseling and Development, 70,* 477–486.

Sue, D. W., Bernier, Y., Durran, A., Feinberg, L., Pedersen, P. B., Smith, E. J., & Vasquez-Nuttal, E. (1982). Position paper: Cross-cultural counseling competencies. *Counseling Psychologist, 19*(2), 10, 45–52.

Tyson, L. E., & Pedersen, P. B. (2000). *Critical incidents in school counseling.* Alexandria, VA: American Counseling Association.

Ward, C., & Rana-Deuba, A. (2000). Home and host culture influences on sojourner adjustment. *International Journal of Intercultural Relations, 24,* 291–306.

Weeks, W. H., Pedersen, P. B., & Brislin, R. W. (1977). *A manual of structured experiences for cross-cultural learning.* Yarmouth, ME: Intercultural Press.

Wilson, J., & Omar, M. (1978). *F.S.I.: A guide to self-taught skills in cross-cultural communication* (U.S. State Department staff training memo).

■ INDEX ■

Action Project, 226–227
Adapting to the Culture of a University, 259–263
Aging, 28–29
Airline travel, 166–171
Alter Ego exercise, 183–184
American and Contrast-American Values, 198–202
American Auction, 205–206
American perspective, 198–202
Analyzing a Transcript, 244–245
Applications of Critical Incidents, 242–243
Assertiveness, 133–134
Assessment, psychological, 274–278
   international students, 282–287
Attitudes and beliefs
   about individual uniqueness, 131–132
   American and contrast-American values, 198–202
   assessment of international student's, 282–287
   awareness of stereotyped thinking, 113–116
   challenging culturally learned assumptions, 79–80
   conflict management in high- and low-context cultures, 105–106
   cultural behavior self-assessment, 15–16
   cultural considerations in psychological assessment, 274–278
   cultural identity self-assessment, 38–39, 56–57, 240–241
   cultural perspectives on education, 90–91
   cultural perspectives on privacy, 96–98
   culturally defined truth, 74–75
   culturally learned perceptions, 17–18, 42–43, 58–59, 290–292
   culture-based value conflicts, 117–118
   debate on cultural issues, 88–89
   fact vs. inference, 76–78
   predicting responses of a culturally different person, 119–120
   private property concepts, 139–140
   separating expectations from behavior, 135–138, 300–301
   sex-role stereotypes, 266–273
   structured exchange between visitor and host culture counterpart, 252–258
   student self-assessment of multicultural competence, 101–104
   toward money, 205–206
Auction exercises, 107–108, 205–206
Audiotape analysis, 176–178, 207–208

Being "Abnormal," 131–132
Biases
   awareness of culturally learned patterns, 64–65
   projection of culturally-mediated interpretation, 19–20
   student self-assessment, 15–16
   See also Stereotypes

Capturing Cultural Bias, 15–16
Capturing Cultural Metaphors and Similes, 70–71
Checkers and Chess, 34–35
Classroom Debate, 88–89
Coalitions and Trust Formation, 40–41

Cognitive functioning
  awareness of culturally learned patterns, 64–65
  awareness of stereotyped thinking, 113–116
  challenging culturally learned assumptions, 79–80
  culturally learned ethical thinking, 126–128, 196–197
  culturally learned evaluative thinking, 50–51
  decision-making criteria, 68–69
  fact vs. inference, 76–78
  influence of culturally defined roles, 66–67
  listening to internal voice, 145–146
  simultaneous holding of contrasting perspectives, 111–112
  unspoken feelings or thoughts, 183–184, 224–225, 244–245
Collectivist cultures, *xii*
  communication style, 94
  educational methods, 90–91
Communication
  collectivist vs. individualist orientation, 94
  cues to cultural context, 207–208
  cultural perspective taking, 147–148
  cultural significance of certain words, 95
  emotional statements, 176–178
  identifying subscripts, 244–245
  importance of cultural patterns in, 21–22, 48–49
  intercultural barriers, 166–171, 203–204
  in military culture, 92–93, 179–182
  nonverbal description of culture, 60–61
  projection of culturally-mediated interpretation, 19–20
  sharing cultural background information, 27
  symbolic representation of culture, 62–63, 70–71
  synthetic culture interactions, 193
  unspoken feelings or thoughts, 183–184, 224–225
Community resource people, 119–120
  interviewing, 68–69, 109–110
Confidentiality, 7
  cultural perspectives on privacy, 96–98
Conflict management
  communication in military culture, 92–93
  compromise and cooperation, 228–231
  cross-cultural, 30–31
  cultural differences in, 121–122

examining critical incidents, 209–210
finding common ground, 129–130
in high- and low-context cultures, 105–106
separating expectations from behavior in, 300–301
synthetic culture exercise, 193–194
videotape analysis, 176–178
Counseling relationship
  cultural considerations in assessment, 274–278
  cultural value systems in, 151–152
  unspoken feelings or thoughts, 153–155, 183–184, 244–245
Critical Incidents in Airline Travel, 166–171
Critical Incidents in Multicultural Ethics, 196–197
Critical Incidents in Tourist Groups, 221–223
Critical Incidents Involving Ethnic Minorities, 209–217
Critical Incidents With International Students, 218–220
Cross-Cultural Tradeoff, 252–258
Cultural Bingo, 27
Cultural Impact Storytelling, 50–51
Cultural Perspective Taking, 147–148
Cultural psychology
  awareness of intragroup cultural diversity, 3
  goals of, 4
  individual development, 5
  multicultural perspective, 4
  universalist and relativist views, 4
Cultural Value Systems in a Counseling Relationship, 151–152
Cultural Value Systems With Conflicting Points of View, 117–118
Culturally Learned Parent Roles for Immigrants and Refugees, 232–234
Culture, concept of, 3
Culture-Centered Genogram, 156–157
Culture-Centered Interview Guide, 246–251
Culture Shock Ratings and Symptom Checklist, 52–53
Current events
  cultural perspectives, 143–144
  role-playing controversial cultural issues, 141–143

Debate on cultural issues, 88–89
Debriefing, *xvi*
  homework assignments, 239

objectives, 8
one-hour experiences, 81
Decreasing Cultural Barriers, 203–204
Describing Cultural Identity, 56–57
*Describing the Feelings of a Resource
   Person*, 119–120
Developing Cultural Life Skills, 279–281
Development, individual
   aging effects, 28–29
   cultural context, 5
   culturally learned perceptions, 17–18
Dialogue Within Ourselves, 66–67
Dissonance reduction, 5
Double-Loop Thinking, 111–112
Drawing Symbols of Your Culture, 60–61
Dual relationships, 8

Educational methods and systems
   adapting to university culture, 259–263
   cultural perspectives on, 90–91
   developing teaching materials from per-
      sonal experience, 242–243
Elderly people, 28–29
Ethical thinking, 126–128, 196–197
Ethnography, 298–299
*Evaluating a Workshop With a Pretest and a
   Posttest*, 174–175
Evaluation of multicultural experience
   instructor interpretations, 11
   objectives, 8–9, 12
   pretesting and posttesting for, 174–175
   superficial interpretation, 8
   See also Debriefing

Family, 156–157
   culturally learned parent roles for immi-
      grants and refugees, 232–234
Fantasy Walk in the Woods, 42–43
Fighting Fair, 121–122
Finding Common Ground in an Argument,
   30–31
*Finding Common Ground in Sports and
   Athletics*, 235–236
*Finding Common Ground With Your Best
   Friend*, 129–130
Food, 172–173
Four Contrasting Ethical Orientations,
   126–128
Free Drawing Test, 64–65

Game theory, 124–125
Gender stereotypes, 266–273

Genogram analysis, 156–157
Geography, 13–14
*Getting Feedback From Other Group
   Members*, 149–150
Gift Giving, 32–33
Gift Giving Across Cultures, 139–140
Group behavior
   awareness of in-group cultural differences, 3
   compromise and cooperation, 124–125,
      228–231
   culturally defined hidden agendas, 46–47
   ethnographic analysis, 298–299
   group sculpturing exercise, 147–148
   individual dominance, 133–134
   individual priorities and, 107–108
   leader–follower relationships in, 25–26
   multicultural group process dynamics,
      72–73
   perceptions of individual uniqueness,
      131–132
   power structure, 296–297
   recognizing contribution of culturally dif-
      ferent member, 32–33
   recognizing multicultural dynamics, 36–37
   responses to outsider attempting to find
      common ground, 187–195
   self-perception *vs.* perceptions of others,
      99–100, 149–150
   separating expectations from behavior,
      135–138
   social activism, 226–227
   values identification, 107–108
   vulnerabilities of multicultural groups,
      54–55

*Happy Hell or Lonely Heaven: The Brain
   Drain Problem*, 84–87
Hearing the Devils and the Angels, 224–225
Hearing the Sounds of a Cultural Context,
   207–208
Hidden Agenda, 46–47
High- and Low-Context Cultures in Conflict,
   105–106
Hofstede, G. J., *xii*
Homework assignments, 239
How to Sabotage Multicultural Groups,
   54–55

Immigrant experience, 232–234
Individualist cultures, *xii*
   communication style, 94
   educational methods, 90–91

Inference–Observation Test, 76–78
Information-gathering strategies, 264–265
Insight, *xvi*
Instructor role and responsibilities, 7–8, 81,
    304–305
    interpretation, 11
*Intercultural Communication Skills
    for Help Providers in the Military,*
    179–182
*International Student Survey of Strong
    Feelings,* 282–287
International students, 162
    adapting to university culture, 259–263
    indications for counseling, 282–287
    problem areas for, 163–165, 218–220
    reentry decision, 84–87
Interpersonal Cultural Grid, 300–301
*Interpersonal Intercultural Psychopatho-
    logical Questionnaire,* 274–278
Interpersonal relations
    compromise and cooperation, 124–125
    conflict management across cultures,
        30–31
    counseling relationship, 151–152
    cross-cultural contact, 5
    culturally defined ways of disagreeing,
        121–122
    culturally learned values, 293–295
    examining critical incidents, 209–217
    finding common ground, 129–130, 172–
        173, 235–236
    goals of multicultural studies, 303
    importance of trust in cross-cultural
        coalitions, 40–41
    leader–follower relationships, 25–26
    power networks, 296–297
    private property concepts and, 139–140
    recognizing culturally learned rules, 34–35
    separating expectations from behavior,
        300–301
    sharing cultural background information,
        27
    stereotyped thinking and, 44–45
    structured exchange between visitor and
        host culture counterpart, 252–258
Interpreting a Projective Picture, 58–59
Interpreting Policy in a Cultural Context,
    48–49
Interviewing Local Resource People,
    109–110
Inventing a Multicultural Retrospective,
    36–37

Johari Window, The, 99–100

Laboratory experiences, 159
Learning to Grow Old, 28–29
Life skills, 279–281
Lifestyles and Our Social Values, 293–295
Listening to the Voices, 145–146
Locating Power Networks in Organizations,
    296–297
Lump Sum: A Budget Simulation, 228–231

Making History Live, 123
Melting pot metaphor, 4
Michigan International Problem Inventory,
    163–165
Military culture, 92–93, 179–182
Minority experiences, 209–217
Money, 205–206, 228–231
Multicultural Group Process Recall, 72–73
Multicultural studies
    classroom experiences, *xv–xvi*
    cultural specificity, 5
    didactic approach, 5
    diversity and similarity awareness among
        primary school students, 82–83
    evolution of, 4
    experiential approach, 5
    identifying unanswered questions, 237
    importance of, *xii–xiii*, 4
    learning about another culture by
        observation, 264–265
    objectives, 5, 10, 303–304
    opportunities for, *xi*
    potential problems in, 304
    preparation for multicultural experiences,
        7, 81, 304–305
    pretesting and posttesting to evaluate,
        174–175
    student discomfort with, *xii*
    student self-assessment of multicultural
        competence, 101–104
    teaching challenges, *xi–xii*, 305
    teaching resources, 9–10
    use of structured classroom experiences in,
        5–9, 303
Multipoly, 290–292

Native Americans, 145–146
No Questions Asked, 264–265
Nominal Group Process, 133–134
Nonverbal description, 60–61

One-hour experiences, 81
Orientation for a Cross-Cultural Experience, 160–162
Outside Experts, 21–22

Partners: A Sex-Role Training Experience, 266–273
Perception Versus Reality, 17–18
Personal Cultural History, 240–241
Plural Versus Singular Cultural Perspective, 94
Policy formulation and interpretation, 48–49
Potluck Dinner, 172–173
Power relations, 296–297
Predicting the Decisions of a Resource Person, 68–69
Preparation for multicultural experience, 7, 81, 304–305
Primary school experiences, 82–83
Prisoners' Dilemma, 124–125
Private property concepts, 139–140
Psychological assessment, 274–278
  international students, 282–287
Public and Private Self, 96–98

Race/ethnicity, awareness of intragroup diversity, 3
Refugee experience, 232–234
Rehearsal Demonstration Model, 183–184
Retrospective review, 36–37
Risk level of classroom intercultural experiences, *xvi*
  warm-up experiences, 11
Role-Playing a Hypothetical Problem in a Group, 141–142
Role-Playing a Newspaper Incident, 143–144
Role-Playing a Transcript, 185–186
Role-Playing Cultural Stories, 23–24
Role-playing experiences
  cross-cultural experience, 160–162
  examining controversial cultural issues in, 141–142
  experiences of international students, 84–87
  game simulation design, 290–292
  group responses to outsider attempting to find common ground, 187–195
  historical figures from different cultural backgrounds, 123
  recognizing cultural stories, 23–24
  synthetic cultures, 135–138
  use of multicultural interviews, 185–186

Scripts for Trigger Videotapes, 176–178
Seeing Ourselves as Others See Us, 44–45
Self-Assessment of Multicultural Awareness, Knowledge, and Skill, 101–104
Self-concept
  cultural identity, 38–39, 56–57, 240–241
  cultural patterns in self-talk, 66–67, 153–155
  diversity and similarity awareness among primary school students, 82–83
  family factors, 156–157
  perception of individual uniqueness within group, 3
  perception of others vs., 99–100, 149–150
Separating Expectations From Behavior in 10 Synthetic Cultures, 135–138
Sex-role stereotypes, 266–273
Shopping in an Unfamiliar Culture, 288–289
Simulation Designing Experience Called "Multipoly," 290–292
Social activism, 226–227
Spiritual activity, 145–146
Sports, 235–236
Stereotypes
  awareness of, 113–116
  interpersonal relations affected by, 44–45
  risk of misinterpreting multicultural experience, 8
  sex role, 266–273
Stereotypes of Different Groups, 113–116
Stopping a classroom exercise, 8
Student discomfort
  in multicultural studies, *xii*
  preventing, 6–7
Student knowledge and understanding
  adapting to university culture, 259–263
  cultural life skills, 279–281
  self-assessment of multicultural competence, 101–104
  self-perception, 99–100, 149–150
  of world geography, 13–14
Symbolic representation of culture, 62–63, 70–71
  money as, 205–206
Synthetic Culture Training Laboratory, 187–195
Synthetic cultures, 135–138
  group responses to outsider attempting to find common ground, 187–195

Talking About Multiculturalism in Primary Grades, 82–83

Test of Reasonable Opposites, 79–80
Testing the Underlying "Truth," 74–75
Threatening situations, 8
Tolerance of ambiguity, 5
Tourist experience, 221–223
Triad Training Model, 153–155
Trust, 40–41
    prisoners' dilemma, 124–125
Truth, 74–75
Two Cultural Perspectives of Education,
    90–91
Two-hour experiences, 159
Two Levels of Communication in Military
    Culture, 92–93

Unanswered Questions and Knowledge
    Gaps, 237

Values Auction, 107–108
Videotape analysis, 176–178

Warm-up experiences, 11–12
Weekend workshops, 159
Western and Non-Western Perspectives,
    38–39
What Other People Say, Feel, and Mean, 19
World Picture Test, 13
Writing an Ethnography, 298–299

■ ABOUT THE AUTHOR ■

Paul B. Pedersen is a visiting professor in the Department of Psychology at the University of Hawaii, Honolulu. He has taught at the University of Minnesota, Syracuse University, and the University of Alabama at Birmingham, and for six years he taught at universities in Taiwan, Malaysia, and Indonesia. He has authored, coauthored, or edited 40 books, 99 articles, and 72 chapters on aspects of multicultural counseling. He is a fellow in Divisions 9 (Society for the Psychological Study of Social Issues), 17 (Society of Counseling Psychology), 45 (Society for the Psychological Study of Ethnic Minority Issues), and 52 (International Psychology) of the American Psychological Association. For more information about Dr. Pedersen's background, please see http:// soeweb.syr.edu/chs/pedersen/index.html.